FOREWORD

Mental health and total well-being go hand in hand. Given that mental disorders account for 15 percent of the total disease burden in the developed world, the protection and promotion of mental health seems just as important as other work promoting our physical, environmental, or spiritual health.

Each of these four components relies on the others. Lose just one, and the whole house may fall. This is why keeping people mentally well recently has been gaining such international attention, particularly as external pressure on individuals and communities continues to rise.

The Ministry of Health is proud to co-host this third World Conference on the Promotion of Mental Health and Prevention of Mental and Behavioral Disorders here in Auckland. It is organized by the Mental Health Foundation of New Zealand, The Carter Center in the United States, the World Federation for Mental Health and The Clifford Beers Foundation of the United Kingdom, with the co-sponsorship of the World Health Organization.

It aims to build on what already has been achieved at the inaugural World Conference in Atlanta and the second conference in London. Robust academic debate is the prime focus, but of equal importance are the international connections we both create and reforge outside the main event, in both the plenaries and the various social events.

Health professionals are increasingly part of a global community, in both work opportunities and in sharing ideas, so the contacts you make here this week will go a long way towards strengthening that sense of community. It is so much easier to send a query to a colleague overseas when you already know the person behind the e-mail address.

And while I encourage New Zealand delegates to make the most of this opportunity, I must also draw attention to what our overseas guests might learn from us, in particular our efforts within the New Zealand health sector to foster innovation and quality improvement.

Hon. Annette King
Minister of Health
New Zealand

FROM RESEARCH
TO EFFECTIVE PRACTICE

to

Promote Mental Health and Prevent Mental and Behavioral Disorders

Proceedings of the
Third World Conference on the
Promotion of Mental Health and Prevention of
Mental and Behavioral Disorders

Auckland, New Zealand
September 15-17, 2004

Editor
Elena Berger, DPhil

Associate Editor
Irene Saunders Goldstein

The conference oversight committee represented the World Federation for Mental Health, The Clifford Beers Foundation, the Mental Health Foundation of New Zealand, in collaboration with The Carter Center. Its members were:

Beverly Benson Long, MS, MPH (Chair), World Federation for Mental Health
Thomas Bornemann, EdD, The Carter Center
L. Patt Franciosi, PhD, World Federation for Mental Health
Clemens M. H. Hosman, PhD, The Clifford Beers Foundation
Sheppard G. Kellam, MD, World Federation for Mental Health
Michael Murray, Chartered FIPD, MSc, The Clifford Beers Foundation
Alison Taylor, PhD, MSc, The Mental Health Foundation of New Zealand

The development of this document was made possible by Work Order HHSP23300400461P, Requisition Reference 04M000163, Center for Mental Health Services (CMHS), Substance Abuse and Mental Health Services Administration (SAMHSA), U.S. Department of Health and Human Services (DHHS). The views expressed herein are those of the authors/speakers and do not reflect the official position of CMHS/SAMHSA/DHHS.

Suggested citation: Berger, E., Ed. (2005). *From Research to Effective Practice.* Proceedings of the Third World Conference on the Promotion of Mental Health and Prevention of Mental and Behavioral Disorders, September 15-17, 2004. Rockville, MD: U.S. Department of Health and Human Services, Substance Abuse and Mental Health Services Administration, Center for Mental Health Services.

ISBN 0-9763865-1-8

Front cover photos courtesy of Tourism Auckland, New Zealand.
Abstracts reprinted with permission of The Clifford Beers Foundation.

PREFACE

This conference is the third in a biennial series that began at The Carter Center in December 2000 and continued in London in September 2002. We established at the beginning of the process a series of themes that we thought would be important and enduring over time. Those themes include identifying evidence-based programs and practices around the world and creating a venue in which to share those evidence-based approaches. We wanted to provide an opportunity to highlight the enormous research advances in promotion and prevention. We appreciated that this is a relatively young field in terms of recognition. The evidence is growing daily, and we wanted to create a supportive environment in which the research could be reviewed at regular intervals.

We wanted to discuss methods of effective advocacy that eventually could lead to influencing policy and ensuring that prevention and promotion assumed an appropriate role inside government and other systems of mental health care throughout the world. We wanted to promote international exchange and cooperation, and we hope that out of this latest conference many of you built relationships that you did not have before—perhaps research relationships or consultation relationships or others. Participants certainly have done so at the previous meetings, and we hope it continues to happen.

We wanted to promote the improvement of training around the world where prevention and promotion are incorporated into larger mental health training. We recognized the importance of training for people who work on the front line—in all kinds of programs that promote mental health, or implement preventive interventions as research is moved into wider practice. Workers in the field need support as they support their clients, and they need information about the latest advances. Training programs to increase their expertise require material appropriate to their local circumstances, the level of their work, and the priorities of their own health systems. These are matters that we included in the purview of the conference alongside research, program development, advocacy, and the dissemination of knowledge.

A secondary, but no less important, goal of these meetings was to begin to develop an international consortium of organizations interested in the program topics. We are gradually making progress in this direction, and we know that the Auckland conference will be followed by further steps in collaboration.

The series will continue with the Fourth International Conference on the Promotion of Mental Health and Prevention of Mental and Behavioral Disorders in Oslo on October 11-13, 2006, when the NGO Voksne for Barn will be the local host organization. We look forward to another successful meeting in Norway, where we hope to see again many colleagues who joined us in New Zealand.

Thomas H. Bornemann, EdD
Chair, Conference Program Committee
Director, The Carter Center Mental Health Program

SPECIAL THANKS

The conference organizers gratefully acknowledge the following financial supporters:

In New Zealand

Ministry of Health
Northern District Health Board Support Agency and Northern Regional District Health
    Boards
SPARC (Sport and Recreation New Zealand)
Ministry of Youth Development
Royal Society of New Zealand
Mental Health Commission
Hapai Te Haoura Tapui (Regional Maori Public Health Provider)
ACC (Accident Compensation Corporation)

International Supporters

Australia
 Federal Department of Health and Ageing

United States
 Department of Health and Human Services
    National Institutes of Health/National Institute for Mental Health
    Substance Abuse and Mental Health Services Administration/Center for Mental Health
        Services

and also

The Carter Center Mental Health Program
INTERCAMHS (International Alliance for Child and Adolescent Mental Health and
    Schools)
Vermont Conferences on the Primary Prevention of Psychopathology, Inc.

ACKNOWLEDGEMENTS

The organizers of the Third Biennial World Conference on the Promotion of Mental Health and Prevention of Mental Disorders wish to express their appreciation to Sir Paul Reeves, former Governor-General and former Anglican Archbishop of New Zealand, for serving as patron of the conference and speaking at its opening session.

The conference organizers also warmly thank Mrs. Rosalynn Carter, former First Lady of the United States, for serving as patron of the conference series. Mrs. Carter, a leading advocate for mental health causes, showed her support by participating in two program sessions and also by attending many other sessions and activities throughout the meeting.

Special thanks are owed to the Ministry of Health in New Zealand for its commitment to the enterprise. The Minister of Health, the Honorable Annette King, was abroad at the time of the conference, but she sent a videotaped welcoming speech for the opening session and provided a message for the printed program. The Associate Minister of Health, the Honorable Ruth Dyson, MP, spoke at the opening session. Karen Poutasi, Director General of Health in the Ministry, chaired the international Policy Forum the evening before the official opening of the conference and hosted a dinner for distinguished guests. Janice Wilson, Deputy Director General, Ministry of Health, spoke at the Policy Forum and participated in events throughout the conference. The Ministry also provided generous financial sponsorship.

An international Program Planning Committee, chaired by Thomas Bornemann, director of the Mental Health Program at The Carter Center (Atlanta, Georgia, USA), developed the conference sessions. The dedicated work of this group over a long period is gratefully acknowledged. Members of the committee included:

Katherine Acuff (United States)

John Copeland (United Kingdom)

Preston Garrison (United States)

Helen Herrman (Australia)

Clemens Hosman (The Netherlands)

Beverly Long (United States)

Peter McGeorge (New Zealand)

Michael Murray (United Kingdom)

Alison Taylor (New Zealand)

Debbi Tohill (New Zealand)

Mark Weist (United States)

The Program Planning Committee benefited greatly from the efficiency and experience of Katherine Acuff, who acted as its coordinator and undertook a heavy workload as consultant to The Carter Center. After the long preparatory process, she continued to deal ably with unanticipated program issues at the conference itself. Lynne Randolph at The Carter Center also provided considerable support for program matters.

The Mental Health Foundation of New Zealand served as local host, and the Organizing Committee in charge of local arrangements was chaired by Alison Taylor, then the Foundation's chief executive. The committee's members included:

Sue Baker, Mental Health Foundation

Vicki Burnett, consumer representative

Deb Christensen, Auckland Regional Consumer Network

Mali Erick, Pacific Islands representative

Cheryl Hamilton, International Union for Health Promotion and Education

Mike Loveman, SF (Supporting Families)

Tim McCreanor, Auckland University

Shayne Nahu, Ministry of Health

Ray Nairn, University of Auckland

Iritana Rudolph, Hapai Te Hauora Tapui

Pale Sauni, Auckland College of Education

Tui Taurua, Hapai Te Hauora Tapui

Debbi Tohill, Mental Health Foundation

Jan Tonkin, The Conference Company

Takutai Wikiriwhi, Ngati Whatua

Warm thanks are due to all committee members for their successful efforts to ensure that the meeting ran smoothly and had a distinctive New Zealand voice. The conference was notable for its friendly atmosphere and for the many thoughtful touches in the program that conveyed local customs and hospitality. Visitors from abroad were impressed by the welcome they received.

Alison Taylor provided strong leadership for the New Zealand arrangements. In addition to thanking her for her dedication to the project, the organizers wish to recognize the special contribution made by Debbi Tohill, at that time Human Resources and Administration Manager of the Mental Health Foundation of New Zealand. Ms. Tohill took charge of many administrative matters before and after the conference, competently handled a crucial stage of the planning process during Dr. Taylor's maternity leave, finalized the accounts after the meeting, and was unflappable throughout. Sue Baker, the foundation's marketing and fundraising manager, organized excellent local publicity.

At the World Federation for Mental Health, secretary general and chief executive officer Preston J. Garrison participated in the planning process from its earliest stages through the final accounting. He provided invaluable advice on many matters.

The abstracts are published by kind permission of The Clifford Beers Foundation. Executive Director Michael Murray supervised the organization of the abstracts and the design and preparation of the conference program book, with the competent assistance of Colin Reed.

In the United States the organizers wish to acknowledge the interest and support of officials in two components of the Department of Health and Human Services. At the National Institute for Mental Health in the National Institutes of Health, thanks are due to Karen Babich, director of the Office of Global Mental Health. At the Center for Mental Health Services in the Substance Abuse and Mental Health Services Administration, Nancy J. Davis, public health advisor, has shown longstanding interest in the conference series. Also at the Center for Mental Health Services, Paul J. Brounstein participated in planning arrangements for the meeting and later supervised the preparation of the proceedings.

Elena Berger and Irene Saunders Goldstein prepared the conference material for publication. Jean Brown was responsible for the final layout. Betty Standiford, Deborah Maguire, and LaJuana Acklin provided technical help. An anonymous donor and the Sheppard Pratt Health System, Baltimore, USA, provided support for the editor's office.

CONTENTS

Presentation Abstracts

Pre-Conference Events

INTRODUCTION:

CONFERENCE AIMS AND THEMES

INTRODUCTION: CONFERENCE AIMS AND THEMES

As background for the presentations and discussions in symposia and plenary sessions, the main themes and foci of the conference appeared in the conference syllabus and are reproduced here. Similar material appeared in the London conference program and published proceedings. As indicated below, a range of questions guided the content of presentations and discussions. This Auckland conference was designed to build upon the organization and aims developed at both the Inaugural World Conference held in Atlanta in 2000 and the Second World Conference held in 2002 in London.

Participants at the Auckland conference were asked to evaluate progress made since the London meeting, develop new and/or updated strategies and action plans, and broaden support for evidence-based prevention and promotion in mental health across cultures, social class, and gender. Another important aim was to encourage partnerships among representatives of the broad spectrum of disciplines and stakeholders who attended the conference.

The conference organizers wanted to increase understanding of the relevance of mental health promotion and the prevention of mental and behavioral disorders, and of the importance of its evidence base. They aimed to encourage further motivation of persons in the field as well as development of practical knowledge, models, and instruments to support effective promotion and prevention in national and local communities. In addition, the conference sought to facilitate collaborative contacts among various stakeholders within countries and international collaboration across countries and regions. It aimed to strengthen the nascent international coalition for effective prevention and promotion (the Global Consortium for the Advancement of Promotion and Prevention in Mental Health, GCAPP). The organizers invited all participants and participating organizations to generate specific proposals for action to move this field forward in future years on a global basis.

Focus on Promotion and Prevention

The series of biennial conferences encourages the development of promotion of mental health and prevention of mental and behavioral disorders worldwide. Both concepts can have multiple meanings.

Promotion of mental health, as targeted in these conferences, refers to all actions aimed specifically to enhance and strengthen positive mental health. Derived from the Ottawa Charter on health promotion, mental health promotion strategies emphasize the need to promote people's mental health by developing personal skills and resilience, by creating supportive environments, and by empowering people and communities. Mental health promotion aims to protect, support, and sustain emotional and social well-being by promoting factors that enhance and protect mental health, while showing respect for culture, equality, social justice, and personal dignity. It includes also a focus on social and economic factors and actions to defend human rights.

The concept of prevention can cover a wide range of strategies and objectives, from primary prevention to secondary and tertiary prevention, including rehabilitation. Along this broad spectrum, differences among prevention, treatment, and care are not always clear.

The biennial conferences focus especially on primary prevention and early intervention before the onset of a diagnosable mental disorder. This perspective is endorsed by the World Health Organization in its *World Health Report 2001*, in which that organization differentiates among promotion/prevention, treatment, and rehabilitation.

Primary prevention can be divided into universal, selective, and indicated prevention. ***Universal prevention*** refers to interventions that target the general public or whole population groups that have not been identified on the basis of increased risk. ***Selective preventive interventions*** target individuals or groups whose risk of developing mental or behavioral disorders is significantly higher than average based on the presence of biological, psychological, or social risk factors or the absence of protective factors. ***Indicated prevention*** targets high-risk individuals who are identified as having either minimal but detectable signs or symptoms foreshadowing a mental disorder, or biological markers that indicate a predisposition for mental or behavioral disorders, but who do not meet the diagnostic criteria for such a disorder.

Not all people at risk actually develop a diagnosable disorder. A diagnosable disorder currently is present in none of the individuals or groups described using the term primary prevention, and universal, selected, and indicated prevention can be considered subdivisions of primary prevention.

Secondary prevention can include indicated prevention, but it focuses mainly on early identification and early interventions in people who already have a diagnosable disorder. This strategy addresses the large number of people in society with a mental or behavioral disorder but who do not receive treatment. Neither secondary prevention of existing disorders nor rehabilitation (tertiary prevention) are addressed specifically in the biennial conferences; these subjects receive significant attention in numerous other conferences on mental health care. An important strategy to promote positive mental health in the community could focus, of course, on persons who might have a psychiatric or neurological disease.

Although this conference differentiates between **prevention** and **promotion**, in both theory and practice, these fields are narrowly related and partly overlap. Many prevention programs use a positive orientation and target the strengthening of personal skills and supportive environments. On the other hand, health promotion activities to reduce discrimination and violence, to empower local communities, and to enhance mental health promotion in school or work environments, for example, can contribute significantly to the prevention of such problems as substance abuse, depression, anxiety, and burn-out.

Themes and Questions

The structure of this conference was based on two dimensions: the lifespan and the principal steps in developing and implementing effective promotion and prevention. Symposia presentations clustered around the following four periods of the lifespan:

1. Pre-school, with attention to a mentally healthy start to life
2. School-aged children and adolescents
3. Adults, with attention to issues related to stress in the workplace
4. Older people, with attention to such issues as active participation

In addition, a number of presentations addressed issues common across various domains of the lifespan, for example, prevention of depression, the media and mental health promotion, and terrorism, trauma, and mental health.

Each set of symposia considered a different aspect of the trajectory of activities that should lead to evidence-based mental health effects in the targeted populations:

- Research on promotion and prevention worldwide
- Evidence-based programs, policies, and principles
- International exchange and cultural variation
- Advocacy, policy making, and organization
- Development of training and expertise

A keynote presentation preceded each set of symposia to set the scene for the ensuing presentations and discussions.

Overview of Themes with Discussion Questions

Theme 1: Research on promotion and prevention worldwide

This theme addressed the issue of developing insight into the onset of mental health problems and the development of positive mental health. Related topics included epidemiological, etiological, and practice-based knowledge; participants were encouraged to reflect on their meaning and use in effective prevention and promotion. Discussion questions included:

- What methods and strategies are available to develop knowledge that can be used to identify mental health needs and malleable risks and protective factors, and to develop effective prevention and promotion programs and activities?
- What are the main mental and behavioral problems, priorities, and challenges for prevention and promotion in each of the lifespan domains? What is their social and economic impact?
- How are the various problems (mental, physical, and social) related to each other? What does this mean for prevention and promotion policy?
- What do we know about malleable risk, protection, and mental health–promoting factors? Is the evidence for their impact on mental health strong enough to select them as a focus for preventive interventions and mental health promotion?
- How can scientists work together effectively with practitioners, consumers, community leaders, and policy makers to identify mental health priorities in their communities and countries?
- How can we integrate a cultural dimension into the analysis of mental health problems?
- What can we do to strengthen the research base of prevention and promotion worldwide and to encourage the involvement of multiple disciplines?

Theme 2: Evidence-based programs, policies, and principles

Improving mental health and reducing mental and behavioral disorders in the population at risk or in the population as a whole cannot be achieved without the support of multiple national partners, both governmental and nongovernmental. A national policy for health promotion and prevention can facilitate the development and implementation of effective programs, the involvement of many stakeholders across countries, and the efficient use of scarce resources. Discussion questions included:

- What models of effective national policies and infrastructure for prevention and health promotion are available? Which models work in developing countries and which in developed countries? How can we stimulate and support countries that to date have not developed such a national policy?
- How can we facilitate the involvement of national policy makers and politicians, and how can we influence national policies? What kinds of information do policy makers need? What are effective strategies for advocacy? How can we overcome barriers?
- Should a separate policy be developed for mental health promotion and prevention, or can such a policy be an integral part of a national public health policy or national health promotion policy?
- What effective models are available for integrating mental health promotion into health promotion programs, public health policies, or other public-sector arenas, such as education, employment, justice, and human rights? What models are available for integrating prevention into mental health care and primary health care?
- How can local communities benefit most effectively from supporting national policies?

Theme 3: International exchange and cultural variation

Effective prevention and promotion efforts that improve mental health in the community and reduce the occurrence of mental and behavioral disorders in the population are possible only when core stakeholders develop effective partnerships. Discussion questions included:

- How can we encourage the international exchange of programs?
- Who are important stakeholders for mental health promotion and prevention of mental and behavioral disorders in each of the domains along the lifespan?
- How can we develop effective and sustainable partnerships between and among various categories of stakeholders? What are examples of successful partnerships? What are conditions for success? What pitfalls exist and how can we cope with them?
- What roles do the various stakeholders play in the development, evaluation, dissemination, and implementation of effective programs and policies?
- How can we cope effectively with variation in interest between stakeholders, given that the primary interest of some stakeholders is not in mental health? How can we cope with differences in value systems and cultural orientation?

Theme 4: Advocacy, policy making, and organization

Significant progress has been made over the last two decades in the development of effective programs and policies. Although available knowledge is not easily accessible by all, during the past few years a number of initiatives have been undertaken to enhance dissemination and implementation processes. Nevertheless, the complexity of developing programs and policies that demonstrate an evidence-based impact on targeted populations according to their objectives often is not fully appreciated. Increased insight into the principles of effective program design, dissemination, and implementation is needed, especially because effective programs and best practices now are transferable across communities, countries, and regions. Discussion questions included:

- Why is evidence-based prevention and promotion important? What do we mean by *evidence-based* and *best practices*? What criteria should be used to select evidence-based programs and policies?
- What effective evidence-based programs are currently in use in areas around the world to promote mental health and prevent mental and behavioral disorders? What are their short- and long-term outcomes? What interventions and strategies do/do *not* work?
- What methods can be used to develop valid knowledge on short- and long-term outcomes and on the cost-effectiveness of promotion and prevention?
- What are the advantages and pitfalls of exchanging effective programs and policies across communities, countries, regions, and cultures? What is necessary to make this type of exchange possible and meaningful? Under what conditions can international databases of effective programs support national and local practices?
- What can be done to improve systematically the efficacy, effectiveness, and cost-effectiveness of preventive interventions and mental health promotion? What are the ingredients and the cultural or contextual conditions needed to improve these interventions? What can we learn from past failures?
- How can we enhance the large-scale implementation of programs and strategies that work?

Theme 5: Development of training and expertise

To integrate promotion and prevention strategies successfully in such settings as communities, schools, primary health care, workplaces, and the media, it is necessary to develop a competent workforce to develop, implement, and evaluate promotion and prevention programs. The development of a competent workforce is a precondition for effective prevention and promotion policy and practice. Discussion questions included:

- Who within the workforce should have a role in promotion and prevention (for example, stakeholder groups, disciplines, nonprofessionals, and community leaders)?
- Is it necessary to develop a core group of promotion and prevention experts?
- How can we educate and train such a workforce? What competencies are required? What effective training programs are available? What further opportunities are available to develop the competence of those who are involved in such work?

- Who should and can take responsibility for developing such a workforce and providing training facilities?
- How can we encourage a "learning community" that generates new knowledge and expertise?
- What are the options for developing an effective workforce in low-income and developing countries?
- What opportunities exist for international collaboration in the provision of training programs?

References

World Health Organization. (1986). *Ottawa Charter for Health Promotion*. Copenhagen: World Health Organization. Outcome document of the 1st International Conference on Health Promotion, Ottawa, Canada, November 17-21, 1986.

World Health Organization. (2001). *World Health Report 2001. Mental health: New understanding, new hope*. Geneva: World Health Organization.

POLICY FORUM

POLICY FORUM: TRANSLATING PROMOTION AND PREVENTION IN MENTAL HEALTH INTO POLICY

Karen Poutasi, MB ChB, DPH, MBA, FAFPHM
Chair, Policy Forum
Director-General of Health
New Zealand Ministry of Health

As I was thinking about the title of the forum, I realized that it represents the middle ground for the Third Biennial Conference. The conference covers evidence to practice, and in the middle is policy. Tonight we're focusing on policy, and over the next three days of the conference, you will address how to take policy into action. I think I'm entitled to say, as director-general of health, that policy is only so good as it sees life in action.

It is my pleasure to chair this policy forum. Picking up on the World Health Organization's theme of "health for all" and on the theme of "no health without mental health," in New Zealand recently we have talked a lot about how we get in front of ill health. We've got a large change process going on putting greater emphasis on primary health care.

Of course mental health is a key component of that process, so tonight I would like to think about getting in front of mental ill health. How do you do that? You do that through health promotion, to promote mental wellness as well as mental health prevention, which is prevention of mental disorders. All of that sits well in front of treatment services.

Of course those treatment services are important, and I would say that for mental health, just as I would say that for health services in general. The ambulance at the bottom of the cliff is tremendously important, but even more important, I would say—and it's an *and*, not a *but*—is the fence at the top of the cliff and having an environment that keeps people away from the fence at the top of the cliff in any event. The environment is the health-promoting environment, mental health promotion; the fence is prevention of mental disorders; and the ambulance at the bottom is treatment services. Tonight we're talking about how we translate promotion and prevention in mental health into policy.

It's now my pleasure to introduce our panelists. Each member of the panel will have five minutes to expand on the theme of the forum, and then we'll have dialogue between the audience and the panelists.

Charles G. Curie, MS, ACSW
Administrator
Substance Abuse and Mental Health Administration
Department of Health and Human Services
United States

Mr. Curie was nominated by President George W. Bush and confirmed by the United States Senate in October 2001 as administrator of the Substance Abuse and Mental Health Services Administration (SAMHSA). As SAMHSA administrator, Mr. Curie reports to Health and Human Services Secretary Tommy Thompson and leads a $3.2 billion agency responsible for improving the accountability and effectiveness of the nation's substance abuse prevention, addictions treatment, and mental health services.

New Zealand, I can say with certainty, has been leading the way on the concept of recovery and translating recovery into policy.

That's clearly what we have been striving to do at SAMHSA. We've tried to take the charge that Secretary Thompson gave me to determine the direction that SAMHSA should be going to make an impact on the lives of people with serious mental illness, as well as addictive disorders.

One of the first steps we have taken is to look at what advocates have been saying for years, at what consumers themselves have been saying for years, as well as family members. If we listen to how they articulate what they need to address their illness, consistently we hear, over and over again, not programmatic terms, not terms around particular kinds of treatment—which is basically what our life is about in the field of mental health or public policy. We think in terms of treatment and we think in terms of programs. People with mental illnesses think in terms of their lives.

From the very first time I ran an aftercare group twenty-five years ago upon entering the field, asking the question of people with serious mental illness coming out of mental hospitals, "What do you need?", consistently you heard objectives such as "job," "home"—a safe place to live—"connectedness to family and friends"—meaningful relationships where you can affirm others and others can affirm you. I say it another way, "a date on the weekends"—having a relationship with that someone special.

The vision that we are articulating at SAMHSA is to make the ultimate outcome in the lives of the people we serve as concrete as possible: "a life in the community for everyone." Once you begin to articulate that ultimate outcome, all the other outcomes you use to measure your effectiveness—in terms of the programs, your funding, the policies you are developing—need to flow out of that outcome.

We now have seven domains that we are using to measure the effects of our programs, and they reflect recovery. The biggest challenge we have is operationalizing recovery. It's always a pleasure to be with Mrs. Carter. Mrs. Carter made a profound comment about the major difference between the President's mental health commission report we submitted last year and President Carter's mental health commission report: "Today we see recovery as possible." Trying to operationalize that is the biggest challenge.

We realize our vision through accomplishing a mission. Our mission is to build resilience and to facilitate recovery. Our traditional mission statement was to assure access to quality assessment, treatment, and prevention services—still a core part of our mission—but we felt it was important to reframe our mission to include the end game of how to attain that vision of outcomes in people's lives.

We have gone about this through having a mental health commission issuing several concrete recommendations and then developing these domains and outcome measures. We're looking at such things as alleviation of symptoms, educational and vocational goals, whether people have a stable housing situation, whether they're connected to family and friends and community, whether they are following through with their recovery plan. If we're measuring this, then we're going to know if we're on the right track.

In conclusion, we need to be working at how we intervene early, using the knowledge we have. We recognize that if we have an earlier intervention, if we have proactive assessment in appropriate settings, we can prevent mental illnesses from becoming disabling. We know about a window of opportunity in adolescence when some of the mental illnesses, such as bipolar disorder, begin to manifest themselves. Many times that contributes to the substance abuse problems we see. If the mental health issue goes undiagnosed, it could contribute greatly to the substance abuse problems—and then the disease, if it's not assessed early enough, can become debilitating.

Karen, I appreciated your remarks on primary care integration. We also know that mental health is essential to all health. But we've had a system of care—if you want to call it *system*—in the United States where mental health has been in a silo, in its own area different from primary and physical health care. In the future we need to bring that together, to have mental health screening be part of a physical, part of children's assessment in terms of how they're doing developmentally, and also part of adult screening.

We have begun to use *recovery,* to talk about *consumer- and family-driven services*—which advocates have asked for, which the data tells us makes much sense. Some of the things we're doing to actualize that from a policy standpoint are outlined in the mental health commission report and in what I just articulated regarding how we're doing it.

One last thing I'll mention is the SAMHSA Matrix. The Matrix is our guide to operationalize recovery. On the horizontal axis are eleven priority areas. The pressure that all mental health authorities have is that there are many needs and a lack of resources. Instead of living by a philosophy of "a thousand flowers blooming," these are solid "redwoods" in which to invest our dollars—what the data and the field are telling us we need to do to strengthen our system. On the vertical axis are the cross-cutting principles to make sure we're doing things right. We update the Matrix on an annual basis. It guides our policy development, our budget development. It's a communication tool. By looking at it, you can relate to it. It has become part of the fabric of how SAMHSA works. (The SAMHSA Matrix is reproduced on page 165.)

I'm glad my colleague Tom Insel is here from the National Institute of Mental Health, because NIMH is a clear partner. Another thing we need to do is to realize—policy in action—a science-to-services agenda and to address the gap of fifteen to twenty years between a scientific finding and common practice. There are ways we are working to shorten that time as well as part of our process.

Helen Herrman, MD
Professor and Director of Psychiatry
St. Vincent's Mental Health Service and the University of Melbourne
Melbourne, Australia
World Health Organization, Collaborating Centre for Research and Training in Mental Health

Dr. Herrman is director of academic programs at the Australian International Health Institute and professor in public health and psychiatry at the University of Melbourne; until recently she was professor and director of psychiatry at St. Vincent's Mental Health Service, Melbourne, and the University of Melbourne. She directs a World Health Organization Collaborating Centre for research and training in mental health. For a year in 2001-2002, she was acting regional advisor in mental health for the WHO's Western Pacific Region.

I was asked to look at the role of international organizations in our endeavor here, but I have some initial remarks about mental health as part of health. As you remarked, Karen, I've come from the world of public health into mental health, which perhaps helps me to understand the particular value of the role of mental health professionals. A number of us in this room are mental health professionals. A number come from public health. A number come from education or from consumer organizations and family groups and many other realms.   But the mental health professionals have a role to make sure that they endorse, rather than stand across, the work of promotion and prevention.

The example of heart health is a very important one. Thirty years ago cardiologists were very worried that the work of health promoters in exercise and diet would mean that cardiac care units were underfunded. In fact we all know that they've moved on together and have produced some major reductions in deaths and morbidity from heart disease over the past thirty years in many parts of the world.

With both mental health and heart health, there is a great divide over social groups. It's those who are disadvantaged, as we all know and will be discussing in the coming days, who have the worst mental health and higher rates of mental disorder, just as with heart health.

So what's the role of any of us here, as well as the role of organizations internationally? As I understand it, the role of international organizations is to encourage work in countries through international action and collaboration. There are a number of ways to think about this. Working with colleagues in WHO, including Dr. Bornemann, Dr. Saxena, and others, has helped me to understand this. WHO is one among a number of organizations—the professional organizations, the World Federation for Mental Health, the World Psychiatric Association, the scientific organizations, and the nongovernmental organizations of various types.

In what ways can they all help? The first and most important way, perhaps, is to add credibility. We can say that mental health is important, but it makes an enormous difference if there is an opportunity to gather our forces internationally and to bring this information to bear on the Australian government or the government of the United States, or Malaysia or Thailand or somewhere else in this region or elsewhere.

A colleague from another country in this region asked me just last week, "How do I convey to the voters in our country, who aspire to having more wealth and a better car and a better house, and think this will make them happy—how do I make them understand that promoting mental health is important?"

I think part of the answer is, "What does mental health do for us? It's an important component of equity that we improve mental health. It improves community safety if people are mentally healthy. It reduces violence and is associated with less substance abuse."

And how can this be conveyed across cultures? Mental health is expressed in many ways across cultures, and that needs to be considered in each country. The mental health professional can endorse and support that, and work with many other sectors in the community to put the structures in place to convert scientific evidence into policy and practice—and then to monitor the effect.

The next contribution, after adding credibility, is how do we generate more evidence and disseminate evidence? In lower- and middle-income countries, where there is perhaps at least as much if not more need for promotion of mental health and prevention as well as treatment services, we often have the least evidence. How do we translate the existing evidence into the lower-income countries? And how do we gather the experience?

Margaret Barry's work on this topic has made a great impact on me. How do we gather the experience of what people are doing already when they don't have the resources to publish or evaluate? In service of that, how do international organizations work to assist middle- and lower-income countries to implement effective programs, and, furthermore, how *not* to implement ineffective programs? Clemens Hosman has pointed this out to us as well. Many of the organizations represented here will discuss this over the next few days.

Another way to contribute is to produce national guidelines and provide guidance to best practice. In a way it's saying the same thing again. But if we can say to governments that there are internationally sanctioned, endorsed ways to promote mental health—acknowledging the work done by Mrs. Carter and The Carter Center, with the World Federation, WHO, WPA, and others—that does us great service.

Fostering collaboration between countries is another and, perhaps, final way that this can be done. The collective action of all organizations with direct and indirect responsibility for promoting mental health across countries cannot fail to impress our national governments.

Thomas R. Insel, MD
Director
National Institute of Mental Health
National Institutes of Health
United States

Dr. Insel is director of the National Institute of Mental Health, the component of the National Institutes of Health charged with generating the knowledge needed to understand, treat, and prevent mental disorders. With a budget of more than $1.3 billion, NIMH leads the nation's research on disorders that affect an estimated 44 million Americans, including one in five children.

Let me provide just a slightly different perspective. Charlie Curie talked about the importance of being sensitive to consumers and to their need for recovery as a goal—and it's an extraordinarily important message for us to hear. Helen Herrman talked about the importance of culture and understanding the international perspective, and also the importance of collaborating across different perspectives in order to be able to provide the very best service.

I'm going to provide a slightly different twist to this, which is to take over from where Charlie stopped. He was talking about the importance of what we often describe as the science-to-service cycle, making sure that our services are informed by the right science, and, in turn, that the science is informed by the real need in the community and in families.

We like to think that the essence of that is providing evidence-based care. Other people have talked about the need to make sure that there's an evidence base for the care that is delivered and, most of all, to make sure that those treatments and those interventions that we know are helpful actually get taken up and used in the places where they're most needed.

That is so much a part of what we're about, when we talk about the need for moving science to service. We don't do a very good job of that, as most of you know.

But there's another piece to it that we don't like to talk about as much—that is, there are an awful lot of problems that we all face for which there isn't really an evidence base yet. I'd like to think that we had the evidence base that we needed for all the things that we are responsible for and for the kinds of problems that families and consumers bring to us. But in fact, we're not there.

My agency is very focused on how we can begin to get that evidence. In the case of talking about promotion of mental health and prevention of disability, we really are talking mostly, in this case, about, how do we understand the nature of risk? Certainly if we were talking about the same sort of perspective on hypertension, the question there is, how do we identify who is at risk and how can we begin to help them to develop healthy lifestyles so that they don't develop severe hypertension and all its consequences?

We're not quite where we need to be in the case of mental illness. We don't have the "cholesterol" measure that we need. We don't have the interventions we need. We think we know something about the lifestyle changes, but sometimes we're wrong. And we have a long way to go to provide that evidence base. That's where the research comes in. I'd like to think that with $1.3 billion we could do that each year. But it's a long haul.

The good news is that we have the tools now that we didn't have in the past. We are making a lot of progress in particular areas, specifically in genomics with neuroimaging to look at the brain in the sorts of studies that can be done now in large populations to understand more about the epidemiology of some of these illnesses. But we still have a way to go, even to catch up with the kinds of perspectives and types of tools that are available for cancer, heart disease, and for most other medical disorders. I agree with the previous speakers that it's best for us to keep mental illnesses in the context of medical illnesses and to be thinking of them in much the same way.

We have a huge challenge in front of us. But it's an exciting opportunity that we have here, to take these various perspectives together and think about—to go back to Charlie's initial comment—how can we make sure we deliver the best we can for the people on the front lines, the families who are really struggling with many of these very severe chronic illnesses?

David Morris, PhD
Director, Social Inclusion Programme
National Institute for Mental Health
United Kingdom

Dr. Morris directs the Social Inclusion Programme at the National Institute for Mental Health in England, part of the Department of Health and the Modernization Agency. He has worked in conjunction with the Social Exclusion Unit at the Office of the Deputy Prime Minister on its mental health program, which culminated in the national report "Mental Health and Social Inclusion" published in June 2004. He now has lead responsibility for the report's implementation.

I want to offer you some low-key, local observations from a personal perspective. I'm not qualified to give an international perspective on this issue at all. My views are derived at the simplest level from two sets of experience.

First, I've worked in mental health in the U.K. at the national and regional levels, working for the late National Health Service Executive, which was the organization with responsibility for trying to get local health communities to act on policy imperatives. This was done through supporting organizational development on the one hand and performance management on the other—carrot and stick.

Second, concurrently with this, I set up, in alliance with others, various programs to try to shift the content of policy to reflect the values of social inclusion and community engagement, both things that are associated with a mental health promotion/prevention agenda.

This last role felt at times like a Trojan horse production job, building vehicles—usually from recycled materials, the sorts of things that many other people have expressed in many different ways often—in which to introduce ideas into the corridors of power. But that, I think, is what makes a difference.

The opportunity to face in both directions at the same time, working upward to ministers and downward to services, was an intrinsic part of working at the regional level in the U.K. Although it came to an end with the abolition of the regions as part of the government's agenda to shift the balance of power downward, it was a salutary experience. It taught me a lot, because it felt that to be working with the developmental side of the business, at the same time as doing such things as ensuring that local processes for investigating homicides and suicides were sufficient and effective, was quite a challenge, and it taught me a lot about the factors that influence policy making.

A few observations based on that rather protracted biography:

Never underestimate the capacity of the service-user (consumer) movement or, anyway, the persuasive voice of the service user. The minister with responsibility for social inclusion is Lord Rooker, the key government minister from the Office of the Deputy Prime Minister who, jointly with our Department of Health minister, introduced and launched the Social Exclusion Unit's report. His view of things was very much shaped by the personal conversations and experiences in which he engaged as part of this role, as well as more formal briefings. The capacity of the user movement should not be underestimated in any way. There's a long way to go, but clearly, without a sustained focus on the user movement and the empowerment of service users, we wouldn't be where we are today.

But equally, don't overestimate what service users can do to influence the policy agenda on mental health promotion if isolated from communities. Community-level interventions—the things that contribute to the mental health of communities—historically have had less appeal to politicians than the issues associated with a high public profile of mental health problems, notably perceived public risk.

Paradoxically, perhaps, in the U.K., policy on managing risk in a post-institutional environment has been accompanied, since about 1995, by political interest in the *moral right to proper services and, more importantly, to mainstream life*. Our ministers are currently engaged in the social inclusion agenda as a moral right. This is an important aspect of the way policy is made. Policies need to be delivering services that are supportive and sound, as well as safe, as our work on the social inclusion agenda demonstrates. This can lead to policy production on the very things that mental health promotion actually is about: community renewal and engagement, social regeneration, employment, self-esteem, access to local amenities, and interventions to reduce the negative impact of environmental factors on people's mental health and their communities. These are mental health promotion outcomes from mental health service inputs.

Another thing: *Money matters*, at least to a degree. The ability to demonstrate the likely cost savings of effective prevention can generate policy. In reality it doesn't seem to do so that much, probably because we have underinvested in our health economics—or not, until recently anyway, done enough to connect our understanding of the financial burden of mental ill health to a financial analysis of how best to offset that burden through investment in mental health promotion. Irrespective of international work in this regard, there is little evidence that, at the local level within commissioning agencies, this kind of cost-benefit analysis happens. We would want to move to a world in which we could calculate the financial savings to be made to mental health services by proper investment in, for example, employment support, training leisure services staff at libraries and swimming pools in relation to their contribution to offsetting the day-to-day barriers to inclusion experienced by disabled people, including those with mental health issues. But we are a fair distance from this at present, and the moral argument remains an important source of momentum.

Advocacy in respect of mental health promotion may succeed in driving policy, but that is no guarantee of policy being implemented. Health organizations are stretched financially. We have spent an additional £300 million since 2000 on mental health services, supporting the development of a new range of community-based mental health teams, but cost pressures inevitably remain.

A key political driver to change is *"joined-up" government action*. This term enjoys particular favor. There seems to be a real commitment to replace "silo" thinking and organization with cross-sectoral working.

Another related lever is a renewed commitment to focusing on mental health as a *public health issue*.

To sum up, there is an appreciable moral dimension in current policy making, which should resonate with the values of advocates in this field. Advocacy needs to be based on the appropriate political hooks; a focus on seeing government "joining up" is one of these and increasingly the public health agenda is another. Arriving at mental health promotion from the inside, from services, is, in my view, a valued strategy to achieve mental health promotion goals.

Finally, sustaining a mental health promotion perspective demands action with wider communities. Advocacy from expert lay people is not enough. Alliances with other communities of nonusers and noncarers (noncaregivers) are likely to be the key condition for sustainability.

Janice Wilson, MB ChB, FRANZCP
Deputy Director-General of Mental Health
New Zealand Ministry of Health

Dr. Wilson was appointed to the position of deputy director-general of mental health, Ministry of Health, from July 1, 2000. She joined the Department of Health in 1993 as director of mental health and also was appointed to the position of chief psychiatric advisor in 1993. A psychiatrist and fellow of the Royal Australasian and New Zealand College of Psychiatrists, Dr. Wilson held the honorary position of president of that organization from 1997 to 1999.

I talk tonight from the perspective of a bureaucrat, someone who works in central government and who often is tasked with having to assist government in forming policy. It seems to me, in my experience in working in central government for the last ten or eleven years, that three things are helpful in trying to get the ideas about mental health promotion into policy.

One issue is evidence. It's not just reading about it. It's evidence that is well articulated in such a way that it actually captures the interest of the government of the day, captures their imaginations, and convinces them. But it's also evidence that does not just interest government, but evidence that interests all the stakeholders who are here today and who are involved in the journey of mental health—mental health consumers, family members, providers of services, community, and the rest of health and the rest of government, as Mr. Morris has pointed out.

A second issue is leadership. Leadership is everywhere, not just leadership from government. It's not just leadership from me or people in my position. It's leadership by all the stakeholders. But the key question within the mental health perspective is, where does the strength of that leadership come from? Is it from public health? Are we addressing mental health promotion from a public health perspective? Is it a public health issue as well as a mental health issue?

A third issue is convincing everyone of the intersectoral nature. Mr. Morris has outlined that particularly well—the holistic approach, the whole-of-government approach. This is a bigger-than-health issue. This is everyone's issue.

My question is, what else is needed besides evidence to make things happen? Suppose, in the next three days at this conference, we find a body of evidence that is conclusive and I want to take that to the minister of health in a middle-income country to say, "Here is the evidence. Please go ahead and use it." Do I need something else with the evidence to persuade the minister to use it?

Dr. Insel. The flat-out answer is, we don't know. If we knew, we wouldn't have to ask the question. It would happen. Clearly a large barrier exists between knowing that something works and to actually have it implemented.

I would turn it around and ask, what are we facing or doing that inhibits change and that could be removed? There are so many. The economics of health care absolutely inhibits the kinds of changes that we'll be talking about. I think you're right. If we knew that doing X would have those kinds of effects in terms of prevention and promotion, unless we can change the economics of why, it really won't happen.

Let me take your question one step further and suggest that in this discussion, it becomes most challenging when you get down to the details of a certain problem. The devil is in the details here. One issue mentioned was early intervention for young mothers without support. There is an evidence base.

While the conversation was going on, I thought about how we deal with trauma. That's a beautiful model for looking at preventive intervention. We know a small percentage of people who have had a highly traumatic experience will develop post-traumatic stress disorder (PTSD); it will happen within a certain timeframe. We should be able to intervene to prevent that. In fact, most of what we've done, until recently, may have made the situation worse, rather than better, because we haven't stuck with good science. We've done something like debriefing, which seems like an intuitively good idea, but in fact probably increases the risk of PTSD, not decreases it. We need to make sure that we've got the science before we go to the point of implementation.

Dr. Herrman. A number of complex reasons in any one community may relate to understanding the evidence. But there's also the simple underpinning idea that there isn't a consensus on the value of mental health. We need a clear recognition, across public health and public life and mental health, that there is more to mental health than the obverse of mental illness. Some people do not believe we can treat mental illness; many people believe that prevention of mental illness is farfetched; and most people have very little conviction about the social determinants of mental health. The social shaping of our genetic expression is a scientifically exciting field, but one that really hasn't translated itself into public and professional understanding. My sense is that we need the evidence, but in order to generate it and then to use it, we have a lot of work to do in this room to take it further.

Dr. Morris. I agree with everything that's been said, but we should be realistic about its application. Evidence is, of course, very important, but we all know of areas of health where the evidence is copper bottomed, and still things aren't done in line with the evidence. The application of evidence is frequently mediated by local political processes and other priorities, it seems to me, if we're honest. I think this is the case in mental health.

There's another angle on this. In recovery and mental illness, we've got a very long history, in countries like New Zealand and the United States and the U.K., of defining what needs to be done through the subjective experience of people who have had mental health problems. This is highly respectable; we'd be nowhere without it. But when you work across government and non-governmental organizations you often find that these agencies call for significant elaboration of this as a valid base of evidence.

In the U.K., one of the areas we've been pursuing is the arts and culture. Some key agencies in the world beyond mental health start from the position of saying, how can we show—through, for example, a reliable study of sufficient size—that participation in arts activities are beneficial?

When you go to service user groups and say, "How do you feel about participating in an RCT on this," they say, "What is wrong here? We've all been telling you for years how we benefit from arts activities!"

We need to be quite canny about how we use the arguments for the evidence base in our discussions with the various cultural and political organizations with which we have to deal.

Q Clemens Hosman, professor of mental health promotion and prevention of mental disorders, The Netherlands. I am involved in developing a coalition of international organizations for mental health promotion and prevention of mental disorders. I would like to return to the issue of implementation. Several organizations around the world now are trying to describe the status quo in terms of what we have in programs for which there is at least some reasonable evidence that it works. Of course, the evidence needs to be strengthened; replication studies need to be done.

Also SAMHSA is developing a huge database on effective programs, as are the World Health Organization and the European Union. Suppose we now have a range of databases describing programs that reasonably work. It puzzles me how to get them implemented. Who in your view is responsible for the process of implementation on the local level? How can we develop a trained workforce with expertise in health promotion, mental health promotion, prevention, to do this work?

In my country we have learned a lot, and I'm very grateful, especially to the United States, for all the research over the last twenty years. We are making use of a lot of that research. We now are trying to build a research base, but we have done the job the other way around. We started in the 1970s to build an implementation practice that was not evidence-based. Now we are trying to add the science base. In the Netherlands now, for example, in every community mental health center, every addiction clinic, every public health service, is a health prevention and promotion intervention team, with people who have been trained by universities to do that work.

I'm not saying that this is *the* model, but it is *a* model. Thinking more globally, who should do this work, and how do we get this expertise? Should we expect that mental health professionals, therapists, are capable by virtue of having taken a course in implementation to do that work? Or do we need trained experts in health promotion or prevention to be the organizers, to be the persons who are triggering and convincing community-based organizations to do this work?

Mr. Curie. It is critical to take advantage of the movement in physical health right now in prevention and promotion. We are seeing the same challenges in that arena that we have been facing in mental health: resource issues. Most of our dollars are going into treatment of people who are already ill and trying to save the people who are drowning in the river instead of preventing them from getting in the river—knowing we have to do both.

When we talk about integrating primary health care and mental health, we need to keep in mind prevention and promotion. The more we can assure that mental health promotion, mental illness prevention, and substance abuse prevention become part of the prevention agenda for public health, the more we can begin to set the stage for the financing. That's a major aspect in the United States; we're looking at Medicaid and Medicare. Secretary Thompson feels strongly about shifts in resources to incentives to pay for prevention and promotion services. If the government, along with the private sector, can begin to institutionalize that type of thought and do it, as we're moving the prevention agenda ahead on the physical health side, I think that can help us tremendously.

At the community level, we are engaged in our Strategic Prevention Framework. You need to put up money for incentives. That has to be a critical part of the formula—asking communities to come together and identify risk factors that contribute to substance abuse, mental illness disability, and those protective factors that need to be in place to promote good mental health, and begin to emphasize a science-based approach that can actually measure over time in terms of gauging outcomes.

Several levels need to be addressed. I think we should take advantage of the overall health movement right now in prevention and not just try to do it ourselves, to take advantage of integration, not just for treatment, but also for prevention and promotion.

Q Steve Druitt, Mental Illness Education ACT, Australia. Regarding Mr. Morris's comment, is there a best model for making joined-up action or intersectoral action happen and to get people involved?

Dr. Wilson. The whole-of-government initiative that I referred to is not led by health, but by our Ministry of Social Development. Maybe the answer is to have a social services agency take the lead to avoid stigma. This agency umbrellas social development, even when it's health social development. Maybe that is one way to get other agencies to buy in, because it's slightly more neutral.

Over the last three or four years, our government has done a lot of work to get agencies to work together. The chief executives meet together to talk about these issues and how to find solutions to them across government.

Q Jennie Parham, Auseinet, Australia. I am manager of a project that supports implementation of promotion and prevention at the national level. What responsibility do you think mental health has in working with and driving mental health promotion? What strategies would be effective in encouraging psychiatrists to pay attention to the issues of mental health promotion and prevention?

Dr. Wilson. I was trying to be provocative to some extent. I think public health needs to take the lead, but the mental health sector has a lot of knowledge. In particular you've heard of the role of mental health consumers. I would say all stakeholders have a role, so we have a working partnership. The view we take in the ministry is that it is partnership leadership.

How do you change psychiatrists is your question. We are trying to change the whole mental health culture, and the way people think about mental health is much more holistic and not just about mental illness. That's a hard job, and we could spend all evening talking about that. That's what the strategy is about and the road we are embarked on.

WELCOME SESSION

Welcome to New Zealand

Sir Paul Reeves
Patron of the Mental Health Foundation of New Zealand
Auckland, New Zealand
Former Governor-General and Anglican Archbishop of New Zealand

To everyone attending this conference, welcome. Welcome to Auckland and welcome to Aotearoa New Zealand. You will have sensed that we are a country of many peoples, many traditions, many cultures, and many faiths. The truth is, we are still shaking down to the reality of who we are. It is a very good time to be a New Zealander.

At the heart of this country is a treaty between Maori and the Crown, and that compact is a powerful force in our national life and governance. It's no accident that the first plenary this morning focuses on indigenous health perspectives.

Health—be it physical, mental, or spiritual—is influenced by specific environments and contexts, so I hope you will learn something about us. There is more to this country than fine modern hotels. Just leave open the possibility that another view from another place tucked away in the South Pacific can enrich your own assumptions and your understandings.

Maori know Auckland as Tamakimakaurau, Tamaki of a hundred lovers. This fertile peninsula has been contested and fought over for centuries. Once Auckland was called the Queen City, but now apparently we are the City of Sails. This refers, of course, to our love of sailing and the beautiful Waitemata Harbor and the Hauraki Gulf, where last year we lost the America's Cup. I have to tell you, too, that Auckland also is the City of Sales—many garage sales, liquidation sales, mortgagee sales, and little-known fire sales. We are a great city!

If I had a mental health or behavioral disorder, I would hope that you would become a better practitioner for having been at this conference, and that you will understand and treat me better. Your theme, From Research to Effective Practice, is a real challenge. As we say, the proof of the pudding is in the eating.

Good luck with your conference and, once again, welcome to everybody!

Welcome Video

Hon. Annette King
Minister of Health
New Zealand

I am delighted to have this opportunity to welcome you all here. With such an obviously diverse and experienced group of mental health professionals in attendance, my only regret is that I am unable to take part in your discussions personally.

May I take this opportunity to welcome my Cabinet colleague and Associate Minister of Health Ruth Dyson, and Sir Paul Reeves, our former Governor General, who is patron of both this conference and the Mental Health Foundation.

I'm also particularly delighted to be sharing the podium—at least in spirit—with a quite remarkable American, former First Lady Rosalynn Carter. As you know, The Carter Center's Mental Health Program has done much to improve the quality of life for people who experience mental illnesses by reducing stigma and discrimination. These are issues close to our hearts in New Zealand, so it is a very special welcome we extend to Mrs. Carter today.

Here I must pause to acknowledge the organizers of this conference, those who have worked so long and hard to bring you all together.

Thanks to the Mental Health Foundation of New Zealand, which is hosting the event in partnership with a number of organizations: the World Federation for Mental Health, The Clifford Beers Foundation from Great Britain, and The Carter Center from the U.S. The World Health Organization is a co-sponsor.

While I'm sure this conference will raise some interesting challenges for you all to consider, I would like to mention one of my own particular concerns, the sometimes unrecognized link between mental health and our own total well-being.

As we know, mental illnesses are actually a lot like physical illnesses. They happen for a scientifically verifiable reason—not as a result of character flaws, or possession by demons, or any one of the raft of reasons commonly put forward by the uninformed.

As a society, we are coming to understand that we can treat mental illness, just like we can treat physical illnesses. There should be no personal stigma attached.

This government has taken a lead in attempting to change the perceptions of our society on these issues, but I'm here to tell you that no government can have all the answers. This is a change that society as a whole must embrace if it is to be successful.

With that in mind, we launched our first Like Minds, Like Mine advertising campaign in 2000. The objective was to raise awareness of the commonality of mental illness and the impact of exclusion and discrimination.

The second phase of the campaign, launched last year, asked people to think about how their own behavior may be discriminatory by showing the benefits of understanding, inclusion, and support. This was under the heading "You Can Make a Difference."

And finally, the campaign's most recent message—"Know Me Before You Judge Me"—goes further by challenging people to think about their own personal beliefs and attitudes, and changing their own behavior. It aims to replace the predictable and stereotypical image of people who experience mental illness with a new and positive suggestion that now all people who experience mental illness are no different from the rest of us. We all have hopes, fears, and aspirations.

I look forward to the feedback from this conference on how other nations are endeavoring to promote both evidence-based prevention programs and promotion of mental health within their own societies.

Welcome from the Prime Minister

Hon. Ruth Dyson
Associate Minister of Health
New Zealand

Good morning and welcome. Prime Minister Helen Clark regrets that she is unable to be here to open this Third International Conference on Mental Health Promotion and the Prevention of Mental and Behavioral Disorders, and she has asked me to read to you a short message on her behalf:

> It is a privilege to host such an important national conference in the field of mental health. Our government is committed to improving mental health services, and a great deal of progress has been made already, thanks to the appropriate leadership in the field

by the Ministry of Health in response to the government's directions, and thanks to the positive response, hard work, and dedication of those in the sector.

In New Zealand we have spearheaded a strategic approach focusing on mental health promotion and prevention, and you will no doubt hear about our activities in more detail during the conference.

A prestigious list of speakers from New Zealand and abroad will share their knowledge and expertise with you over the next few days. I am sure their presentations will generate much fruitful discussion and lead to further innovations in the mental health field. It is a real pleasure to welcome you all, and I hope you will also have the opportunity to enjoy some of New Zealand's scenery and experiences while you're here.

I also would like to extend a warm welcome to everyone here today, particularly our distinguished guests and speakers who have traveled a long way to be here.

I want to make special mention of the honorary conference chair, Rosalynn Carter, from The Carter Center in the United States. The former First Lady is an inspiration to many, and it is a great honor to have you here. I believe the Inaugural World Conference on Mental Health Promotion and Prevention of Mental and Behavioral Disorders was held at The Carter Center, so it is a fitting connection to have you in our country for the third conference.

Other acknowledgements are in order, to patron Paul Reeves; Materoa Mar, chair of the Mental Health Foundation; and the organizers, who have worked so hard to make the vision of this conference a reality.

As you have all heard, my parliamentary colleague, Health Minister Annette King, is unable to be with us today. She is in Shanghai, China, on other health business, but thanks to the wonders of technology at least we got to see a glimpse of her before she jetted off! I know Annette has talked a little about the *Like Minds, Like Mine* campaign, the need to be aware of mental illness in our society, and how our own attitudes and behaviors can affect people who experience mental illness.

We live in an increasingly complex, stressful, and fast-moving world, and a number of factors in various parts of our lives can affect our mental wellness. We are increasingly seeing the need for a holistic approach to mental health that looks at the total wellness of people.

Oranga Ngakau

Following the launch of the *Like Minds, Like Mine* campaign, in February 2004 Annette launched *Oranga Ngakau,* a resource produced by the Mental Health Commission for people who access mental health services. The booklet is designed to inform them of how things work, who might treat them, how to get in and out of services, and what types of services they might use. It gives advice on how to take an active role in your recovery, what to do to give the treatment a better chance of working, and what to do if you disagree with your diagnosis.

But the most significant aspect of the *Oranga Ngakau* publication is that it was written by service users. I sincerely hope—and I know Annette expressed the same wish when she launched the booklet—that it makes the recovery journey easier for them.

Mental Health Promotion Strategy

Building on Strengths is the title of our Mental Health Promotion Strategy here in New Zealand. It aims to educate the health sector on mental health promotion, outline actions for the

Ministry of Health to take in this area, and provide guidance to the sector on what it can do to better promote positive mental health.

Building on Strengths is based on a model that "recognizes that all people have potential and capacity to grow, change, and adapt." Everyone has abilities and strengths that can be fostered and developed in the right environment. *Building on Strengths* emphasizes our innate qualities—the resourcefulness and resilience that exist in everyone—rather than dwelling on what is "wrong," such as illness or deficit.

We recognize that we need to consider all aspects of people's lives to be able to create environments that contribute to positive mental health and well-being. In addition to strengthening individuals and developing their resilience and personal skills, we also need to create environments that support positive mental health.

Our communities need to be able to act for themselves in a way that best promotes positive mental health for their people.

Primary Health Organizations

Mental health promotion and prevention is part of a continuum and should be considered across all parts of the health sector.

We are currently developing the capacity of the primary health care sector to address the needs of those persons with mild to moderate mental health problems through our Primary Health Organizations (PHOs), which are really taking off all over the country.

I know of several PHOs that are providing exciting new mental health services, using a range of professionals such as mental health nurses, psychologists, counselors, and others.

Working Together

But we also know that important factors outside the realm of health, such as education, meaningful employment, and suitable housing, have an impact on the total wellness of a person. This highlights the importance of the health sector working closely with other government agencies, local government, and local communities to promote positive mental health.

The Ministry of Health's *Second National Mental Health Plan*, which is currently going through a consultation process with the sector, recognizes that people with a mental illness often need support in various aspects of their lives. One of the objectives of the draft plan is to look at the wider influences on people's mental health—such as housing—and to work with other agencies to identify and address areas where people with mental illness may be falling between the gaps. The plan, when it is released, will take a long-term approach by building on the first National Mental Health Plan's goal of improving access to mental health services over the next eight years.

Cultural Difference

Respecting cultural difference and being aware of different cultural perspectives is also an important part of effective mental health promotion and prevention. *He Korowai Oranga: The Maori Health Strategy* emphasizes the importance of whanau health and well-being. Whanau means family and can refer to the wide diversity of families represented within Maori communities. Whanau is recognized as the foundation of Maori society and plays a central role in the well-being of Maori individually and collectively.

From Research to Effective Practice

Mrs. Carter has introduced the two reports that we are launching at this conference, one on promotion and the other on prevention. These reports are possible only because of dedicated work by our colleagues. Many people in this room have contributed to these reports. I wish to thank these contributors for the generous support of their time and expertise.

The primary targets for these publications are governments, particularly governments of low- and middle-income countries. But I must add that the targets are not only ministries of health, but rather governments in their entirety. Our message is not only for ministries of health, but also for ministries of education, child care, labor and employment, justice, social welfare, environment, urban planning, immigration, emergency and disaster assistance, and, eventually, ministries of finance, which must be motivated to provide more resources for these activities. I hope that participants at this conference not only will receive this message themselves, but also will help transmit this message to the target governmental and nongovernmental organizations that should be active in this area. We look forward to your contributions and activity in this endeavor. We hope that we will be able to convince those organizations that positive mental health adds value to life and investment towards this objective is highly worthwhile.

OPENING SESSION

Planning the Program

Thomas H. Bornemann, EdD
Chair, Conference Program Committee
Director
The Carter Center Mental Health Program
Atlanta, Georgia, United States

We at The Carter Center Mental Health Program feel a special connection with this conference series. The first conference was held at The Carter Center in Atlanta on December 5-8, 2000, after several years of planning in collaboration with the organizers, the World Federation for Mental Health and The Clifford Beers Foundation. We were excited to host the event, pleased that it had the co-sponsorship of the World Health Organization, and very gratified when the WHO Director-General at that time, Dr. Gro Harlem Brundtland, came to give the closing plenary address.

That first conference generated a lot of momentum. It was apparent that there was considerable international interest in promotion and prevention. As work proceeded on the second conference, the importance of growing an international network for promotion and prevention gathered even more attention. The organizers began to think not only about the future of the conference series, but about establishing a consortium that would bring together interested organizations for other cooperative activities.

And now today we've reached the third conference, and a level of planning, program content, government interest, and audience enthusiasm that we could not have imagined when we were preparing for the first one nearly four years ago. The promotion and prevention movement has grown tremendously in that short time.

I have had the distinct privilege of chairing the conference program committee for this meeting and of working in close collaboration with a number of international colleagues who have made this event happen. I'll start with the Mental Health Foundation of New Zealand. I cannot say enough about both the quality and the quantity of work that they have produced under enormous pressure. They really have been the glue that has held us all together, and they deserve a huge round of applause. I particularly want to acknowledge the individuals involved: chief executive Alison Taylor and her colleague Debbi Tohill, who have been inspirationally involved in all of this for those of us not in New Zealand. From the World Federation for Mental Health, we have president Patt Franciosi, CEO Preston Garrison, Elena Berger, and Beverly Long, whom I will get to in a moment. From The Clifford Beers Foundation we have Michael Murray, who is largely responsible, along with the New Zealand Foundation folks, for the program book you have on abstracts and other materials. That was an enormous task. We have Clemens Hosman, from the universities at Nijmegen and Maastricht in The Netherlands, who has been behind all of this in terms of understanding the science of this field, and we owe him a debt of gratitude as well. I would like to acknowledge Kate Acuff, a senior health policy consultant to the Mental Health Program of The Carter Center, who has been responsible for a lot of the background work for the conference and who has been an invaluable aide to all of us in its development, and I also want to recognize my own staff back in Atlanta who unfortunately were not able to join us here.

At this point, I would like to take the liberty of the chair to give special recognition to a person who has been a stalwart in the field of promotion and prevention, Beverly Long. She has been a part of this committee and has kept us on task throughout a very tough year and a half. More importantly, her courage and steadfastness in this area have served as background for nongovernmental organizations such as WHO taking us seriously. The field owes Beverly Long a debt of gratitude.

Also, the Ministry of Health of New Zealand has been marvelous to work with. The program planning committee is very grateful for the interest of the Minister of Health, The Honorable Annette King, the Associate Minister of Health, The Honorable Ruth Dyson, and the Ministry's Director General of Health, Dr. Karen Poutasi. Dr. Janice Wilson, Deputy Director General in the Ministry, has been especially supportive in every way.

I want to tell you about one event that is very special to all of us on the planning committee. We had an addition to the planning group that we did not anticipate in the beginning. His name is Sam. He's now four months old. Alison Taylor, chief executive of the Mental Health Foundation, had a baby in the middle of all this. If you can imagine trying to organize this international conference and have a baby at the same time! So we all welcome Sam as a part of our planning process, and we will miss his cooing on our international conference calls at eight o'clock in the morning New Zealand time. Sam added an extra dimension to our thoughts about promoting good mental health and reminded us all as we considered the program about the importance of a healthy, happy start in life.

The Future of Promotion and Prevention

Beverly Benson Long, MS, MPH
Chair, Global Consortium for the Advancement of
**   Promotion and Prevention in Mental Health**
Past President
World Federation for Mental Health
Atlanta, Georgia, United States

In thinking about this meeting and my remarks this morning, I am reminded of the first President's Commission on Mental Health convened in 1977, more than a quarter-century ago, at the very beginning of the U.S. presidency of Jimmy Carter. Mrs. Rosalynn Carter and President Carter had been strong leaders and advocates for mental health since the early 1970s, when Jimmy Carter was governor of Georgia. When he came to the White House, the new President convened the first President's Commission on Mental Health. Mrs. Carter was named chair of the commission, and it was my pleasure to serve as a member. Mrs. Carter continues her role as the world's standard bearer for all aspects of mental health. She demonstrates her support for prevention as an integral part of improving mental health around the globe through all of her activities and by her presence and contributions to these biennial conferences. We are delighted in every way to have you with us. Thank you, Mrs. Carter.

I am not sure whether it was coincidental, but not long after the Carter Commission issued its final report in 1978, the mental health consumer movement in the U.S. and elsewhere became an important part of the mental health scene. With us today are a few of the pioneers who first stepped forth to face the discrimination among the general public toward people who experience mental illnesses—consumers, they sometimes are called. Much of the progress made since then we owe to those few who have contributed so much to better understanding and to improving the lives of persons affected by mental health problems. We salute you and thank you for what you have done to advance the cause of mental health throughout the world.

The final report of the Carter Commission (1978) stated: "At present our efforts to prevent mental illness or to promote mental health are unstructured, unfocused, and uncoordinated. They command few dollars, limited personnel, and little interest at levels where resources are sufficient to achieve results" (p. 53).

That was twenty-six years ago. What has changed since then?

Not much, if we look only at government allocation of resources to mental health. As late as the mid-1990s in the U.S., only about 1 percent of the total allocation of overall health resources, both human and financial, went to mental health. More discouraging to those of us who focus on prevention as an integral component of the mental health continuum, *not more than 1 to 2 percent of that 1 percent goes to prevention and promotion.* These are U.S. figures, but from discussions with others, and according to the World Health Organization, I understand that the situation is not any better in most places in the world. It is important to remember that the fundamental barrier to the advancement of mental health does not reside within the mental health field. The barrier is the allocation of inadequate resources—both human and financial—for overall health.

Since 1978, however, progress has been made in mental health science and technology, in treatment, in structured advocacy, and, to some small degree, in the public's perception of mental illness and the interdependence of mental and physical health. Treatment in some developed countries, including the U.S., has improved. But in the U.S., at least, treatment typically takes place in a patient-doctor context and has not become part of a public health–supported approach that focuses on prevention, treatment, and rehabilitation/recovery. And in under-developed and developing countries, a focus on mental health, along with general health, is seriously lacking.

The goal of GCAPP is to win recognition that a global mental health/public health system includes prevention and promotion side-by-side with treatment and care. Again, we are painfully aware that mental health historically has been overlooked as a determinant of health. Only very recently have the disability and the cost to society of mental and behavioral disorders been "discovered" and gradually become recognized. But understanding is emerging about the interwoven connections and interactions between mental and physical health within a social context. These recent developments offer a special opportunity to build collaborative efforts among the experts in multiple related fields to reduce the incidence and, at the same time, the prevalence of these life-damaging mental/physical disorders.

Recognizing that reducing the number of new cases of mental and behavioral disorders is both humane and increasingly necessary, in light of rising prevalence and its associated health costs, and understanding that no one field in isolation can solve the problem, our goal, then, is to provide a focus and a forum to bring together the relevant sciences and disciplines for the purpose of developing a collaborative effort. This series of conferences is designed to benchmark the status of the field and to help identify needed actions to accomplish our overall goals.

The first conference, held at the Carter Center in 2000, was built around five linked and interactive themes or components that make up the matrix of prevention and promotion in population-based mental health. These components include research, dissemination of good programs, advocacy, policy, and training. At the 2002 London conference, life development stages were added to broaden the matrix. The interrelationship of the themes set the context in which to develop a public health systems approach. Recommendations were made at the London conference to develop work groups for each theme and to provide information that will enhance the building of prevention and promotion at each developmental life stage.

The most well-defined need that has emerged from the conferences is the need for ongoing interaction and collaboration among the five components. We must build pathways and bridges, and open doors, between these components (or, as some say, "silos"). We need to connect the dots and to promote a genuine systems approach if progress is to be realized.

We all are advocates, as individuals. We would not be here if we did not believe, in our hearts and our minds, that mental health in its full potential is a goal to be advanced. Mental health is central to overall health and good quality of life for all people. But as an organized advocacy group, we must recognize—and act on the realization—that we must empower those who are policy makers, those who determine where the human and financial resources are distributed, if we are to see real progress.

Let us remember that twenty-six years ago it was reported that "our efforts to prevent mental illness or to promote mental health are unstructured, unfocused, and uncoordinated. They command few dollars, limited personnel, and little interest at levels where resources are sufficient to achieve results."

Things are changing. Right now we need to continue working very hard and very smart, so that in 2010 we can report that "our efforts to prevent mental illness and promote mental health are well structured, well focused, and well coordinated. They are realistically funded, have well trained and appropriate personnel, and priority interest at levels where resources are sufficient to achieve results."

Margaret Mead, who was president of the World Federation for Mental Health in 1956-57, said it all. She said, "Never forget that a small group of thoughtful, committed citizens can change the world. Indeed, that is the only thing that ever has."

Note: The quotation from Margaret Mead is used courtesy of the Institute for Intercultural Studies, Inc., New York.

Reference

Report to the President from The President's Commission on Mental Health. (1978). Vol. 1. Washington, D.C.: U.S. Government Printing Office.

How We Started

Michael Murray, Chartered FIDP, MSc
Chief Executive Officer
The Clifford Beers Foundation
United Kingdom

On behalf of the organizers, I'd like to welcome you to the conference. I hope that this conference will add to your enjoyment of your visit to New Zealand. I want first to thank Alison Taylor and Debbi Tohill and all the people in the Mental Health Foundation for making this conference possible. It's been a tremendous job. When I walked into the room this morning, I was surprised that there were so many people here. It made me think about the time I said to Alison, "We should have charged more."

Let me tell you about the history of the conference and what we're trying to achieve. It is a vision that a small group of people have been working to achieve for the last several years.

First, however, it is important to acknowledge the work that other people have done over the years. Prevention and promotion isn't something new. For example, some ninety years ago Clifford Beers and the mental hygiene movement held an international conference. We also know that over the last twenty to thirty years, effective programs have been developed and perfected. Such work has brought the movement into prominence, and prevention and promotion now are on the political as well as the social, economic, and health agendas.

As a small group, we have some part to play in this process. What is the part we now think we need to play?

This series of conferences began in 2000. The conferences emerged from two strands of action that had taken place earlier. The first strand was the work done by the World Federation for Mental Health and its prevention section. They did tremendous work over many years, generating interest in prevention and promotion. The second strand was that of The Clifford Beers Foundation, which organized a number of international conferences during the 1990s. These conferences were attended mainly by participants from Europe, but when we attracted people from around the world, we realized that working in isolation really wasn't a sensible thing for The Clifford Beers Foundation to do.

In 1997 I sat down with the then president of the World Federation, and we discussed the possibility of combining our efforts to have a biennial world conference. We were joined quickly by The Carter Center, and, with the support of the World Health Organization, we arranged to hold these world conferences. That was the first time a consortium came together, albeit on an informal basis.

We wanted to organize a series of world conferences, but not just for the sake of having conferences. We needed a catalyst to bring together the many people who were working in different countries and different disciplines to form a broader group, in order to tap into their expertise and knowledge and to work to improve prevention and promotion. That small consortium held the first world conference at The Carter Center in Atlanta in 2000.

Many good outcomes resulted from that conference, but one of the major appeals, which helped shape the future, was a plea to develop an even broader consortium of governmental and nongovernmental agencies. We all realized we faced a huge and complex problem in achieving this, and, unless we combined our resources, we knew we would not make much progress. That was the idea, and we started to move forward to a formal consortium.

There was a long list of issues that we felt needed to be addressed, and perhaps we can mention some. First, a lot of good work in the area of best practices and model programs has been carried out, but only a limited range of effective programs actually has been implemented. More investment in research and program development is needed, particularly throughout the developing world, where many of the programs we know to be effective are not implemented; even in the more developed nations, many such programs often are not widely known.

Second, the very scarce resources we possess often are not managed as effectively as they could be. For example, it is important to disseminate programs more effectively, to be more attentive to needs of persons from different cultures, and to talk with people from different parts of the world in a language all can understand. This was a major factor as to why we chose to come to New Zealand. New Zealand leads the world in many aspects of cultural awareness and collaborative working.

How is the consortium attempting to address these and other important issues? As Bev Long mentioned, we wanted to put together a framework. Five interactive and linked themes were chosen on how best to carry out effective prevention and health promotion research. First, how can we work together to find a method to make sure, wherever possible, that the research we carry out is effective? Second, how can we help people to take effective programs and implement them in their own countries? The third area we wanted to look at was international exchange of research about programs and implementation. How do we motivate people from different countries to work together? The fourth link was to encourage advocacy, to try to build coalitions, and to try to help organizations develop in response to these challenges. Last but not least, none of these activities would be possible unless we were able to help in the training of organizations and the people working in different fields who are actively engaged in prevention and promotion.

That was the path we have walked along for the last six or seven years. Have we been successful? When we look around this room, we can say, "Yes, we have." This is the largest number of people that have attended any of our conferences, even though we are in a small country, and, for many of us, it has been a long way to travel. This room is full, and that's a sign of success.

I want to talk for a moment about the formal consortium itself, because establishing such a body could be a difficult task. How do we get people to work together? How do we get people to say that the "consortium is more important than we are"?

We have held a number of meetings to establish the consortium. Following the Atlanta meeting, we had a gathering of some of the major international organizations working in the area of promotion and prevention. The first such meeting took place in Rockville in April 2003, and, after considerable discussion and debate, a second organizational meeting was held earlier this year at The Carter Center. Just this week we gathered again to try to put the final touches to a discussion paper, and we have agreed that by April 2005 the Global Consortium for the Advancement of Promotion and Prevention in Mental Health will be a living entity so we can move forward together.

What does that mean for the delegates here? As members of the consortium we are very confident that we have not yet got everything right, so we hope that during this conference, you will give us your ideas and suggestions. In every break-out session a chairperson will ask you for your input about anything you want to share with us for consideration. We really would like to have your ideas, your suggestions, and your criticism, because this consortium will work only if people unite together.

I invite you to join with us and to take a very active part in these proceedings, to tell us exactly what you think, and to enjoy the conference to its full extent.

Is an Ounce of Mental Health Promotion Worth a Pound of Cure?

Rob Moodie, MBBS, MPH
Victorian Health Promotion Foundation
Melbourne, Australia

Irene Verins, BA(Hons)
Victorian Health Promotion Foundation
Melbourne, Australia

Introduction

This paper first presents some of the arguments for why societies and governments should invest in mental health promotion. It presents some of the recent approaches, ideas, and experiences in mental health promotion from Victoria, Australia, and then presents some of the big challenges that lie before us. It finishes with a plea that promoting our own mental health is a must for those involved in mental health promotion.

Why Invest in Mental Health Promotion?

A major study in Australian schools has shown that up to 30 percent of depressive symptoms in high school students can be attributed to harassment or bullying at school (Bond et al., 2001). This is an exceptional finding, which needs further work to validate it, but if it is true, should we limit our role to trying to identify and then treat those who might be harassed, or should we also change the culture within schools to reduce bullying to an absolute minimum? Should we also be trying to change the culture of bullying that occurs more broadly, in workplaces, in schools, and in homes?

In other words do we just keep the ambulance at the bottom of the cliff, or should we aim to build and strengthen the fence at the top of the cliff?

From a recent VicHealth study we found that the major preventable risk factor for women's ill health between the ages of fifteen and forty-five years is intimate partner violence (VicHealth, 2004a). We also found that the violence manifests itself in anxiety; depression; alcohol, tobacco, and drug abuse; and suicide.

If this is the case should we ignore it, treat it as an inevitable part of the human condition, treat the (mainly) women with anti-depressants and tranquillizers, or should we also prevent the violence, mitigate its ramifications when it happens, and start a major push to deal with the causes—and promote men's mental health?

Mental health is an indivisible part of public health, contributes to the functions of society, and has an effect on overall productivity. Mental health contributes to human, social, and economic capital (Moodie & Jenkins, 2004).

We increasingly are learning about the contribution of mental health to physical health. A review has demonstrated that depression, social isolation, and lack of social support are as significant risk factors for coronary heart disease as conventional risk factors such as smoking, high cholesterol, and hypertension (Bunker et al., 2003).

As with physical health, poor mental health unequally affects those who are socially and economically disadvantaged, while also contributing directly to poverty (Fryers, Meltzer, & Jenkins, 2003).

Some Experiences from Australia in Mental Health Promotion

Development of national action plans for promotion, prevention, and early intervention for Mental Health 1999 and 2000 has led mental health promotion work in Australia. The 2000 plan is a comprehensive approach that includes the theoretical and conceptual framework for action covering fifteen priority groups. It provides a framework for a coordinated national approach to the promotion of mental health, and prevention and early intervention for mental health problems (DOHA, 2000).

The national action plans represent the establishment of an important partnership among public health, health promotion, and mental health. The consequence of this relationship has been emerging integration across the silos of policy, research, and practice. The work is built on an understanding that the key determinants of good mental health actually lie outside the health sector; thus we need to engage a wide variety of partners. Effective partnership has developed through an understanding of how other sectors work and how we can develop synergies across different groups (e.g., arts, mental illness services, sports, business and industry, philanthropy, local government, and education) (VicHealth, 2004a).

Understanding and emphasizing the inherent common sense of mental health promotion has been a key to action. For example, in many areas we have good evidence of casual factors but little evidence of effectiveness of interventions, but this has not prevented action that will provide more evidence and create a very useful pool of experience (see the Auseinet, beyondblue and VicHealth websites). We have tried to establish a common language and have used common frameworks, one of which is presented in Table 1.

Our work at VicHealth has been based on a recognition of all those organizations that can, and do, promote mental health, such as education, sport, and recreation; arts and popular culture; local and state/provincial governments; health promotion and public health; the health care industry; justice; labor and industry; and the media.

Similarly we need to include and recognize those in our community who can, and do, promote mental health, such as teachers; parents, uncles, aunts, grandmothers, grandfathers; sports coaches; mental health consumer advocates; choir leaders, drama teachers, youth leaders; employers; entrepreneurs, social entrepreneurs, and for profits; police and judicial officers; and nurses, social workers, and doctors.

In many cases these groups and individuals may not know that they do promote mental health, or that they could. Some do not know that they actively demote mental health—for example, the sports coach who focuses only on the best players and ignores and marginalizes the rest, or the teachers who bully students, or the employer who actively exploits division and conflict in an organization as a means of maintaining control.

Table 1. Framework for the Promotion of Mental Health and Well-Being

Key Determinants of Mental Health and Well-Being		
Social inclusion	**Freedom from discrimination and violence**	**Access to economic resources**
• Supportive relationships • Involvement in group activities • Civic engagement	• Valuing of diversity • Physical security • Self-determination and control of one's life	• Work • Education • Housing • Money

Population Groups and Action Areas	
Population groups	**Health promotion action**
• Childen • Young people • Women and men • Older people • Indigenous communities • Culturally diverse communities • Rural communities	• Research, monitoring, and evaluation • Direct participation programs • Organizational development (including workforce development) • Community strengthening • Communication and marketing • Advocacy • Legislative and policy reform

Settings for Action						
Housing	Community	Education	Workplace	Sport and Recreation	Health	Academic
Transport	Corporate	Public	Arts		Justice	Government

Intermediate Outcomes			
Individual	**Organizational**	**Community**	**Societal**
Projects and programs that increase sustained: • Involvement in group activities • Access to supportive relationships • Self-esteem and self-efficacy • Access to education and employment • Self-determination and control • Mental health literacy	Organizations that are: • Inclusive • Responsive • Safe, supportive, and sustainable • Working in partnerships across sectors • Implementing evidence-based approaches to their work	Environments that are: • Safe, supportive, sustainable, and inclusive • Enhanced community cohesion • Enhanced civic engagement • Increased awareness of mental health and well-being issues	• Integrated, sustained, supportive policy and programs • Strong legislative platform • Resource allocation

Long-Term Benefits			
• Increased sense of belonging • Improved physical health • Less stress, anxiety, and depression • Less substance misuse • Enhanced skill levels • Mental health literacy	Integrated inter-sectoral resources and activities	• Community valuing of diversity; actively disowning discrimination • Less violence and crime • Improved productivity	• Reduced social and health inequalities • Improved quality of life and life expectancy

Source: VicHealth website, www.vichealth.vic.gov.au, September 29, 2004 (reformatted).

Investments in Social Inclusion, Diversity, and Economic Participation

Sports and Active Recreation

For many years we have been involved in the replacement of tobacco sponsorship in sport, given that legislation requires VicHealth to spend 30 percent of our grant (currently approximately AU$8 million per annum) through sporting and active recreation bodies.

More recently VicHealth has changed direction to focus on increasing levels of participation in sport and active recreation, by improving the capacity of clubs and associations to welcome, encourage, and maintain active participants, coaches, managers, and volunteers. Thus we use social inclusion both as a method to increase levels of participation (which is what the sports groups want) and as an outcome in itself.

Racism is an unfortunately common feature in sport in Australia. State and federal governments have been working with sporting organizations to develop:
- Codes of conduct to indicate behaviors deemed unacceptable to sport and the penalties that will be applied if these behaviors exist
- Resource materials to assist sporting organizations to manage racism within their clubs
- A widespread communication and marketing campaign—"If racism wins, sport loses"— designed to increase awareness of the damage caused by racism within the sporting environment (VOMA, 2004)

Arts

The Women's Circus, started in 1991 as a project of the Footscray Community Arts Centre in Melbourne, is an initiative to empower women through the development of circus skills. It welcomes all women, but gives priority to women who have been victims of physical and sexual abuse, women over age forty, and women from diverse cultural and linguistic backgrounds (Women's Circus, 2004).

Somebody's Daughter Theatre Company was started in a women's prison in 1980. The company works in art, drama, and music with women, and now young people, who have been excluded from the cultural and social life of the community (Somebody's Daughter, 2004).

Vocal Nosh is a program to teach singing and develop local community choirs, based on the notion of eating and singing together. It is founded on principles of creative participation, cooperation and celebration, respect and inclusiveness. It now is expanding through teaching leaders skills to scale up the program across the state of Victoria (Community Music Victoria, 2004).

Urban Planning

The Planning Institute of Australia has been providing professional development and training for its members, underpinned by the understanding that good (mental) health can be planned into a community, as can poor mental health. This project includes focus on the physical design and layout of new and old communities, traffic management, provision of public transport, walking and bicycle paths, the re-siting of shopping precincts, and community amenities (Planning Institute of Australia, 2004).

But by the mid-twentieth century, following the near universal experience of urbanization in the 1950s, other health risks emerged. In developed countries such as Canada, Australia, the United States, and New Zealand, vulnerability to injury, alcohol and drug misuse, cancer, kidney disease, obesity, suicide, depression, and diabetes have become the modern indigenous health hazards (Cunningham & Condon, 1996). Compared to nonindigenous members of the population, life expectancy is significantly lower for indigenous peoples, and the incidence of most diseases is higher, sometimes by rates of two or three times (e.g., for diabetes, mental disorders, and some cancers) (for further discussion, see Kunitz, 1994).

Health Determinants

Leaving aside early colonists' views about "constitutional inferiority," explanations for current indigenous health status can be grouped broadly into four main causes: genetic predisposition, socio-economic disadvantage, resource alienation, and political oppression (Durie, 2003, August 23, 408–409).

Possible genetic predispositions have been investigated in alcohol disorders, schizophrenia, and bipolar disorders, though they generally are regarded as less significant than socio-economic disadvantage, which is often central to the contemporary indigenous experience. Poor housing, low educational achievement, unemployment, and inadequate incomes are known to correlate with a range of health problems and facilitate lifestyles that predispose to disease and injury (National Health Committee, 1998).

But socio-economic factors by themselves do not explain health disparities between indigenous peoples and nonindigenous populations. For example, when Maori and non-Maori at the same levels of deprivation are compared, Maori health status still remains lower than non-Maori. Maori patients are more likely to be admitted to a psychiatric inpatient unit (63 percent for Maori, 33 percent for European); Pacific inpatient episodes are 35 percent above the national average, while Maori have a rate that is 22 percent above average (Gaines et al., 2004). While there has been some call for health policies that are race and color free, the reality is that ethnicity, race, and color are very much part of the epidemiological pattern and should not be regarded simply as proxies for deprivation.

Among other possible explanations for increased rates of indigenous mental health problems, alienation from natural resources along with environmental degradation have been identified as a cause of poor health in several countries. But it is not only alienation of physical resources that is important. Intellectual and cultural resources also are relevant to mental health to the extent that deculturation contributes to poor mental health and a positive personal identity (Duran & Duran, 1995).

Several writers also have drawn a link between colonization and poor health (Cohen, 1999). They argue that loss of sovereignty along with dispossession (of lands, waterways, customary lores) created a climate of material and spiritual deprivation with increased susceptibility to disease and injury.

All four positions can be justified and conceptualized as a causal continuum. At one end are "short distance" factors, such as the impacts of abnormal molecular and cellular processes, while at the other end are "long distance" factors, including governmental policies and the political standing of indigenous peoples. Values, lifestyle, standards of living, and culture, so important to mental health, lie midway.

Maori Models of Health Promotion

Given the range of causative factors, mental health promotion requires a broad approach that covers a wide spectrum of interventions. To bring together the several components and to visualize the scope, a Maori model for mental health promotion has been developed in New Zealand (Durie, 1999). It uses the imagery of Te Pae Mahutonga, a constellation of stars popularly referred to as the Southern Cross (*Crux Australis*) that is visible high in the southern skies and acts as a marker of the magnetic South Pole (Hyde, 2003). Te Pae Mahutonga has long been used as a navigational aid and is closely associated with the discovery of Aotearoa.

Because it is an indigenous icon, Te Pae Mahutonga also can be used as a symbolic chart for mapping the dimensions of mental health promotion (New Zealand Ministry of Health, 2002) and the promotion of health for indigenous children and young people (Durie, 2003a). The four central stars can be used to represent four key foundations of health: cultural identity and access to the Maori world (Mauriora), environmental protection (Waiora), well-being and healthy lifestyles (Toiora), and full participation in wider society (Whaiora). The two pointers symbolize two key capacities that are needed to make progress: effective leadership (Nga Manukura) and autonomy (Mana Whakahaere).

Mauriora: Cultural Identity and Access to the Maori World

The first foundation concerns cultural identity and access to the indigenous world. Good health depends on many factors, but among indigenous peoples cultural identity is considered to be a critical prerequisite; deculturation has been associated with poor health, whereas acculturation has been linked to good health (Isajiw, 1990). In modern urbanized societies indigenous peoples often have limited access to their own worlds. The alienation from their physical resources is common enough so that ongoing links with tribal land have very often been severed. But many indigenous languages also have been threatened or even lost altogether, and access to cultural institutions such as tribal meeting houses often has been restricted by geographical dislocation and cultural estrangement.

A task of health promotion, therefore, is to facilitate access by indigenous people to the indigenous world: access to language and knowledge, culture and cultural institutions, sites of heritage, and indigenous networks—especially family and community.

Waiora: Environmental Protection

The second health foundation, Waiora, is linked more specifically to the natural world and includes a spiritual element that connects human wellness with cosmic, terrestrial, and water environments. A central element of indigeneity is the close association between people and their accustomed environments—land, waterways, the air, beaches, harbors and the sea, and native flora and fauna. Good health is compromised where there is atmospheric pollution, contaminated water supplies, smog, random mining activities, or commercial developments that exploit the land they cover, or where access to traditional sites is barred.

Toiora: Healthy Lifestyles

A third foundation for mental health concerns personal well-being and healthy lifestyles. Indigenous peoples have their own perspectives on health and well-being. A frequently discussed Maori health perspective is known as Te Whare Tapa Wha, a construct that compares good health to the four sides of a house and prescribes a balance between spirituality (taha wairua), intellect and emotions (taha hinengaro), the human body (taha tinana), and human relationships (taha whanau).

Major threats to health come from unbalanced lifestyles: products of contemporary living and modern societies, such as the use of alcohol and drugs, unsafe roadways, tobacco use, disregard for the safety of others, unprotected sex, sedentary habits, social isolation, estrangement from family and friends, and risk-taking. Many indigenous peoples, young and old, are trapped in risk-laden lifestyles and have little chance of ever being able to realize their full potential.

Whaiora: Participation in Society

A fourth foundation for health, Whaiora, is about indigenous participation in wider society measured against material circumstances, social equity, cultural affirmation, justice, and effective representation. Full participation is dependent on the terms under which people participate in society and the confidence with which they can access quality personal services, sport and recreation, meaningful employment, or political voice.

Disparities between indigenous and nonindigenous populations are well documented and confirm gaps on almost every social indicator (Te Puni Kokiri, 2000). Health promotional goals need to consider ways in which indigenous participation in society can be increased, especially in relationship to the economy, education, health services, modern technologies, incomes, and decision-making.

Nga Manukura: Leadership

A common indigenous experience has been for public agencies and health professionals to assume positions of leadership on behalf of indigenous peoples. Not only did that approach foster both dependency and assimilation, it also undermined indigenous leadership, now generally regarded as an essential component of mental health promotion. Indigenous leadership should reflect a combination of skills and a range of influences, and includes tribal leadership, community leaders, sectoral leaders (such as health professionals or teachers), elected representatives, and academic leaders. An indigenous workforce is critical for indigenous mental health promotion.

Nonindigenous health professionals have important roles to play, but they should not suppress the leadership that already exists in indigenous communities. While tribal and community leaders may not have technical and professional skills, they do possess an intimate knowledge of their people and have the advantage of being able to communicate in a vernacular that makes sense.

Mana Whakahaere: Autonomy

Colonization often supplanted indigenous forms of governance and management, creating instead dependency and marginalization. It is clear from the Draft Declaration of the Rights of Indigenous Peoples, however, that dependency is not compatible with human dignity or good health. Campaigns by indigenous peoples for greater autonomy have resulted in tension and sometimes open conflict with states. Although disputes remain about property rights, control of resources, representation, and the manner in which goods and services are made available to indigenous peoples, a number of pathways are able to give expression to the spirit of self-governance. Some of these pathways, such as tribal development programs, assume a high level of indigenous control and leadership. Similarly, even though they operate within the framework of a state contract, a number of nontribal community organizations have their own systems of governance and management.

But key to autonomy are the constraints of capability and authority. In many countries, including New Zealand, indigenous workforce development has been afforded some priority, though not without creating controversy, especially when affirmative action programs have been introduced or indigenous world views have been woven into the curriculum or indigenous values have been applied to clinical interventions and key performance indicators.

Implications

Te Pae Mahutonga is one way of bringing together the threads of mental health promotion. It is not so much a model for best practice as a schema to identify the parameters of practice and to signpost the strategic directions that might be pursued by states, the health and education sectors, and indigenous peoples themselves. Most importantly, indigenous health issues cannot be seriously addressed unless they are part of a wider discussion that includes cultural identity, the natural environment, constitutional arrangements, socio-economic realities, and indigenous leadership.

Inevitably this broad approach raises challenges for the state, the professions, and, of course, for mental health practitioners, policy makers, and planners. A particular issue concerns the way indigeneity is recognized. While most governments are willing to recognize cultural diversity as a modern reality, not all are willing to accept indigenous peoples as populations with unique rights based not solely on cultural distinctiveness, but also on a long-standing relationship with the territory, predating colonization. Even when treaties have been signed to that effect, there has been debate about their enforceability in modern times.

Some political leaders also are inclined to view health spending entirely according to individual health need and dispute population-based funding as a rational basis for addressing health problems, especially when ethnicity or race is the basis. But while the principle of equality as between individuals can be defended as a democratic principle, it is only one principle that underpins a modern democracy. Health policies based entirely on individual need run the risk of missing the contexts within which people live their lives and that are integral to good mental health. Equality as between populations also must be factored into health policies, and in that respect indigenous peoples have well-established claims for recognition as distinctive populations.

The Interface

There is, of course, a vital role for indigenous practitioners of mental health promotion and health education. Their contribution to indigenous health and more broadly to indigenous development will stem mainly from being at the interface between two worlds: the indigenous world and the globalized world (Durie, 2003b). Living at the interface and inhabiting two spheres could be a source of confusion. But it also can be a site of potential. Wise leadership requires careful management of the interface, so that the benefits of modern technologies and science can be transferred to indigenous people in ways that strengthen indigenous world views and contribute to good health.

From Research to Effective Practice

For too many indigenous people the interface between the indigenous world and society at large has become a giant chasm within which human potential has been drowned. Indigenous workers have a special role to play in negotiating the interface. By virtue of their backgrounds and their professional training, they have access to two bodies of knowledge. They are in a position to bridge the gap between the world where indigenous values dominate and the world dominated by science, technology, and global imperialism.

Conclusion

I want to make only five points.

The first is that indigenous peoples have not been shielded from mental ill health and a host of accompanying behavioral disorders. Conclusive and extensive evidence exists that, for a variety of reasons, they are overrepresented in hospital admissions, prison incarceration, school failure, unemployment, and alienation from key societal and community pathways.

Second, there is an association between mental health and the world views that indigenous peoples hold dear. The indicators of "good" mental health are not universal, and indigenous peoples place particular emphasis on the quality of relationships with family, tribe, community, the land, sites of heritage, and traditional knowledge. Health risks appear to be greater where those world views have been fractured. But evidence also exists that culture does not necessarily confer immunity. A range of mental health problems occur in people who are strong in their own culture and language. Sometimes the carriers and guardians of culture may be under more stress and pressure than others and consequently assume greater risk.

Third, socio-economic factors are important contributors to poor mental health among indigenous peoples. Measured against almost all socio-economic indicators, Maori, for example, fare less well than other New Zealanders. Educational outcomes are worse; standards of health are lower; unemployment is higher; and incomes are correspondingly poorer. It is now well documented that there is a strong correlation between the prevalence and incidence of mental disorders and socio-economic deprivation.

Fourth, socio-economic disadvantage is not sufficient to explain the indigenous position. Even where there is equality of living standards, indigenous people suffer worse health and a greater range of mental disorders. Indigeneity appears to be a risk factor in its own right, but the precise relevance of that factor is uncertain. While genetics may play a part, the evidence is not overwhelming to support a genetic basis for the disparities. Possibly genetic factors might play a contributing role in some disorders, such as diabetes, alcohol disorders, and possibly affective disorders, but generally genetic predisposition cannot be seen as the most important determinant. Other possibilities also must be considered, including deculturation, societal prejudice, and the multiple impacts of a life lived at the interface between two worlds, without being firmly committed to either.

The fifth point, and it is amply illustrated in indigenous models of health promotion such as Te Pae Mahutonga, is that the prevention of mental and behavioral disorders, and the promotion of positive mental health require approaches that are consistent with indigenous perspectives, values, and world views, and also with best practice and evidence-based policies. The promotion of good health will be ineffective if it is based on an assumption that all people subscribe to the same views of health and aspire to similar goals. Insofar as most indigenous peoples live at the interface between two worlds, health promotion should be delivered in a way that aligns with the dual realities within which indigenous populations live in modern times.

References

Cohen, A. (1999). *The mental health of indigenous peoples: An international overview*. Geneva: World Health Organization.

Cunningham, J., & Condon, J. R. (1996). Premature mortality in aboriginal adults in the Northern Territory, 1979-1991. *Medical Journal of Australia, 165*(6), 309-312.

Deloria, V. (1994). *God is red*. Colorado: Fulcrum Publishing.

Duran, E., & Duran, B. (1995). *Native American post-colonial psychology*. Albany: State University of New York.

Durie, M. (1999). Te Pae Mahutonga: A model for Maori health promotion. *Health Promotion Forum of New Zealand, 49*, 2-5.

Durie, M. (2003a). Te Pae Mahutonga: Mental health promotion for young Maori. In M. Durie, *Nga Kahui Pou: Launching Maori futures* (pp. 141-156). Wellington: Huia Publishers.

Durie, M. (2003b). Indigeneity: Challenges for indigenous doctors. In M. Durie, *Nga Kahui Pou: Launching Maori futures* (pp. 269-288). Wellington: Huia Publishers.

Durie, M. (2003, August 23). Providing health services to indigenous peoples (editorial), *British Medical Journal, 7412*, 408-409.

Gaines, P., Bower, A., Buckingham, B., Eagar, K., Burgess, P., Green, J., & Mellsop, G. (2004). *Mental health classification outcomes study: Brief report*. Auckland: Health Research Council.

Hyde, V. (2003). *Night skies above New Zealand*. Auckland: New Holland Publishers.

Isajiw, W. W. (1990). Ethnic-identity retention. In Breton, R., Isajiw, W. W., Kalbach, W. E., & Reitz, J. G. (Eds.), *Ethnic identity and equality* (pp. 34-91). Toronto: University of Toronto Press.

Kunitz, S. J. (1994). *Disease and social diversity: The European impact on the health of non-Europeans*. New York: Oxford University Press.

National Health Committee. (1998). *The social, cultural and economic determinants of health in New Zealand: Action to improve health*. Wellington: National Health Committee.

New Zealand Ministry of Health. (2002). *Building on strengths: A new approach to promoting mental health in New Zealand/Aotearoa*. Wellington: New Zealand Ministry of Health.

Te Puni Kokiri. (2000). *Progress towards closing social and economic gaps between Maori and non-Maori*. Wellington: Ministry of Maori Development.

United Nations, Committee on Indigenous Health. (2002). *The Geneva Declaration on the Health and Survival of Indigenous Peoples*. New York: United Nations Permanent Forum on Indigenous Issues.

United Nations, Working Group on Indigenous Populations. (1993). *Draft Declaration on the Rights of Indigenous Peoples: Report of the Eleventh Session of the United Nations Working Group on Indigenous Populations*. Geneva: United Nations.

Waldram, James, Herring, D. Ann, & Young, T. Kue. (1995). *Aboriginal health in Canada: Historical, cultural, and epidemiological perspectives*. Toronto: University of Toronto Press.

Indigenous Issues, Lower-Income Countries, and Mental Health Promotion

Leslie Swartz, PhD, MSc
Child, Youth and Family Development
Human Sciences Council
and
Department of Psychology
University of Stellenbosch
South Africa

The fact that international issues were placed so firmly on the agenda of this meeting gives me great hope that there is now, as there was not always before, a growing realization and practical commitment to looking globally at mental health issues, to considering carefully the applicability of research that is based in one type of context to the world as a whole, and to the enormous task not only of promoting mental health and preventing mental disorder worldwide, but also of systematically and soberly evaluating what we know and what we don't know.

The task that faces us is a daunting one. By now it is well established that we have an enormous gap between research evidence in mental health in wealthier countries and what is available in poorer countries. Vikram Patel and Athula Sumathipala (2001) elegantly showed just how big is the gap between "developed" and "developing" countries in terms of mental health research evidence, and other contributions since then have reinforced this view. For example, one area in which I am especially interested is that of early intervention with caregivers and infants. Mark Tomlinson and I (Tomlinson & Swartz, 2003a) showed that the research gap in this field was similar to the general picture in mental health. More than 90 percent of infants are born in poorer countries, but more than 90 percent of what we know about infant mental health comes from wealthier countries, with Australia and New Zealand, in fact, over-represented in the literature. If we look a little more broadly than mental health, as we should, the picture remains more or less the same. For example, Isaakidis and colleagues (Isaakidis, Swingler, Pienaar, Volmink, & Ioannidis, 2002) show that although there has been some improvement in recent years, if one balances disease burden against evidence from randomized controlled trials (RCT) in sub-Saharan Africa, we still have a long way to go in terms of finding out what works and what does not.

Within this context we must not underestimate the importance of recent contributions of mental health researchers in a number of developing countries, who have shown that it is possible to generate evidence in these contexts for mental health interventions that meet the stringent design criteria for research evidence internationally (Sumathipala, Hewege, Hanwella, & Mann, 2000; Chatterjee, Patel, Chatterjee, & Weiss, 2003; Araya, Rojas, Fritsch, Acuna, & Lewis, 2001). It is not my purpose here, though, to present a comprehensive review of mental health research in developing countries. I just want to flag the fact that the Global Forum for Health Research, with the support of the World Health Organization (WHO), currently is busy with a project to map mental health research in developing countries, and the results will be ready for dissemination in about a year's time. The underlying aim of this mapping exercise is to provide an informed basis for addressing the 90-10 gap in mental health research and to contribute to a process, which has already started, of ensuring that we come to know more about mental health issues where the risk factors are enormous and the burden probably the highest.

Here I'd like to discuss in personal terms some of the challenges that face us in wrestling with the complicated question of the "indigenous" in mental health promotion and prevention research. These challenges are multiple—ideological, methodological, theoretical, and practical. And, of course, all these levels are interlinked. Let me start by relating two stories.

The first story comes from Tom Csordas, the American anthropologist who has done wonderful work to develop our understanding of embodiment and who has done extensive fieldwork among the Navajo.

> *NASA and the Old Man*. When NASA was preparing for the Apollo project, they did some astronaut training on the Navajo Indian reservation. One day a Navajo elder and his son were herding sheep and came across the space crew. The old man, who only spoke Navajo, asked a question, which his son translated: "What are the guys in the big suits doing?" A member of the crew said they were practicing for their trip to the moon. The old man got really excited and asked if he could send a message to the moon with the astronauts. Recognizing a promotional opportunity, the NASA people found a tape recorder. After the old man recorded his message, they asked the son to translate. He refused. So they brought the tape to the reservation, where tribal leaders listened and laughed, but refused to translate the elder's message to the moon. Finally, NASA called in an official government translator. He reported that the moon message said, "Watch out for these guys; they've come to steal your land." (Csordas, 2004, 1)

The second story comes from our own work with very poor mothers and infants in an informal settlement near Cape Town. In designing our intervention for these mothers and babies we were very concerned that our intervention, designed as it was by white people and based on research done in wealthier countries, should not be culturally inappropriate to a South African context. We were particularly anxious to ensure that what we produced was in a culturally acceptable idiom that linked with, and did not impose on, indigenous meanings of childbirth, reproduction, and mental health. In order to make our work as culturally acceptable as possible, we worked very closely over a long period of time with mothers from the community, and preliminary findings currently under analysis by Mireille Landman seem to suggest that we have had some success in this regard. In interviews with mothers in the community who have received our intervention, Mireille has found not one response where the mothers describe the intervention as contextually or culturally inappropriate. I will return to this issue later, but the story I want to tell comes from our painstaking work to try to develop cultural congruence for our project.

In order to explore the issue of cultural congruence, we spent considerable time discussing with mothers from the community both the cultural appropriateness of aspects of care giving we regarded as important, based on our clinical experience and on our reading of the literature. We interrogated as fully as we could our own assumptions, for example, that engaging in proto-conversation and turn-taking with infants was good for them developmentally. In addition, we were very concerned about the idiom in which we presented the intervention and the questions we needed to ask about childcare.

An interesting example of this concerned the question of whether caregivers play with their infants. Mothers with whom we worked on designing our protocol and translating it into Xhosa (the language spoken in the community) were incredulous that we would even think that it was possible to "play" with an infant. At first, we were nonplussed by this—could it be the case that mothers in our community do not engage in the play and the give and take with their infants that we regard as so important developmentally? It emerged in further discussion, however, that there is a specific Xhosa word for what we would call "play." That Xhosa word, *ukudlala*, refers to playing a game. The word *ukutheketisa*, by contrast, refers specifically to the mixture of

From Research to Effective Practice

vocalisation, tickling and jiggling, and general back-and-forth that we would regard as playing with a baby. There is more to the word *ukutheketisa*, however; literally translated, it means "teasing" of the baby. Though the term is not used in any way that is derogatory or demeaning to the infant, connotations to this Xhosa term may well tell us something about slightly differing assumptions about the meaning of infancy in that context as opposed to the assumptions we ourselves hold.

My aim in telling this story, however, is not to show the importance of carefully interrogating local meanings and connotations, though this, of course, is very important. Instead I want to describe what happened on one of the afternoons on which we were having our most intensive discussions with our informants about meaning and culturally appropriate messages for mental health promotion and prevention work in this community. As the afternoon of our discussions wore on, the mothers from the community grew more and more restless and inattentive. Initially we attributed this to what we suspected was our culturally inappropriate style of running the meeting, but the reason for the restlessness was far more mundane. Late afternoons on South African television are soap opera time. One of the most glitzy, one of the most stereotypically North American, one of the most nauseatingly consumerist of these soaps is *The Bold and the Beautiful*. *Bold*, as it is commonly known in Khayelitsha (as opposed to *Days,* for *Days of our Lives*), is enormously popular in the community and is regarded by many who live there as the most popular television program in that community. The mothers with whom we were working so carefully on issues of how most appropriately to engage with this community could not wait to get home to their television sets to watch *The Bold and the Beautiful,* which, we can safely assume, was not designed carefully to be culturally appropriate to viewers in an informal settlement on the southern tip of Africa.

If we look at both these stories—Tom Csordas' story about NASA and the Navajo, and my story about informal settlements and soap operas in South Africa—we can see immediately that any notion that we may have about "indigenous" issues existing apart from broader politics and broader social and cultural influences is bound to be false. The point I am making here is by no means new. But something I don' t understand fully is the continuing allure of abstracted, essentialist, and romanticized ideas of "culture" and "indigenous people," ideas that I believe to be at best useless and at worst dangerous for work that focuses on mental health promotion and the prevention of mental disorder. It' s easy to give crude examples of this. For example, Mark Tomlinson and I (2003b) have discussed how some contributors to a book designed to increase understanding of indigenous approaches to childrearing had not even visited the communities about whose childrearing practices they claimed to have knowledge. But more important than these crude examples (and there are many of them) is the continuing trend for literature to be produced that claims either of two things:

1. That little or no literature exists on the benefits of indigenous approaches to mental health, or
2. That the existing literature on indigenous approaches to mental health is prejudiced against such approaches and is derogatory towards them.

There are, of course, important exceptions to these two related strains in the literature (see, for example, Yen & Wilbraham, 2003a, 2003b), but the strains remain very dominant (Swartz, 1998, 2002). Within this tradition, researchers tend to proceed in the following way:

1. Set up a "straw man" of either neglect or denigration of indigenous approaches to mental health, and then:

2. Point to one of the following:
    a. The widespread use of indigenous healers in many communities, and/or
    b. Few anecdotal accounts of indigenous healing processes, and/or
    c. Views of some practitioners on the promotive, preventive, or curative value of their work

    to argue that

3. Indigenous healing approaches are beneficial.

As a way of changing outmoded views about "superstition," this type of argument was enormously important in previous years (from about the 1970s on) to open our thinking about these issues, and many organizations, including the WHO, have moved far on from there. But I think it is important to understand why this type of literature continues, apparently unabated.

I have argued previously that one of the reasons for this continuing literature—literature that ignores the proliferation of accounts that are sympathetic to indigenous healing approaches—is ideological. Nobody, including myself, wishes to be seen to be racist or politically insensitive to systems of knowledge and behavior that are valued by a great many people. Rather than engage with substantive questions, such as whether indigenous systems of healing work or don' t work, and to risk being branded culturally or politically insensitive, outsiders simply declare the merits of indigenous healing approaches. Insiders, too, may have an interest in maintaining this state of affairs. Historically, so much denigration of indigenous healing has taken place that the assertion of its merits becomes an important part of identity politics.

To continue on this theme of widespread approval for "indigenous" approaches to healing in the absence of sufficient engagement with the question of evidence, I can give another example. One of the greatest challenges to a newly democratic South Africa, the meeting of which challenge our state president, to his great credit, has made a cornerstone of his second term of office, is that of delivery on policies. We have wonderful social and health policies in South Africa, but we have been struggling with providing what the policies say we should be delivering, especially to the poorest and most vulnerable citizens. One way in which politicians have managed to sidestep the issue of nondelivery has been to point out that the apartheid regime encouraged dependency and lack of self-reliance. Our new democracy, it is claimed, is respectful of the strengths and traditions of South African communities—so far, so good. But it is a small step from this point for politicians then to argue that the state does not and should not provide what it says it should in the way of social and health services, because the state does not want to interfere with, denigrate, and cut across indigenous approaches to personal and social development. In this political logic, nondelivery on services mutates into respect and support for indigenous coping mechanisms that communities have developed for themselves.

This type of political argument could just be dismissed as yet another example in another country of how politicians duck and dive, but in South Africa it has an especially profound implication in the context of HIV/AIDS, a central issue for health in general, and mental health in particular, as I will discuss briefly later. South Africa has some excellent policies on HIV/AIDS, and a great deal of good is being done about the epidemic in our country. But as the world knows, our state president and our health minister have not always given us the leadership we deserve on this key issue for the future of our country, our continent and, indeed, the world. I want to mention one aspect of this issue that is relevant to the present discussion. In the long and painful debate about the provision of antiretroviral therapy (ART) in South Africa, our minister of health, Dr. Manto Tshabalala-Msimang, has been advocating the importance of indigenous foods, such as the African potato, as important in the care of people with HIV/AIDS. In January 2005, a scientific report appeared in the journal *AIDS* that assessed the potential impact of two indigenous African herbal remedies on the progression of HIV in the context of ART, one of the remedies being *Hypoxis hemerocallidea* (African potato) (Mills, Foster, Heeswijk, Phillips, Wilson, Leonard, Kosuge, & Kanfer, 2005). The authors point to the need for

> the extreme caution that should be taken in introducing herbal drugs into the routine care of HIV patients in any setting including the developing world, and underscore the need for appropriately designed pharmacokinetic studies to unveil the true drug interaction potential of herbal drugs with antiretroviral agents. Failure to do this may result in bidirectional drug interactions, which may put patients at risk of treatment failure, viral resistance or drug toxicity. (Mills et al., 2005, 96)

The minister has not, in the face of this scientific evidence, raised any cautions about use of the African potato. She has, however, without citing good scientific evidence, claimed that there is scientific proof that lemon, olive oil, and garlic can work wonders for people with AIDS symptoms (Tshabalala-Msimang, 2005). At the opening of the recent national AIDS conference in Durban, South Africa, the minister reiterated her faith in indigenous methods of treatment, and argued that South Africans should not accept solutions to the AIDS epidemic that are imposed from outside the country.

I do not want to deny the crucial importance of nutrition for HIV care, and I am not qualified to comment on whether certain herbs and foods are good for people with HIV, but the key issue here is that the minister of health has been using (implicitly or explicitly) broader political issues, including identity politics and the important political need for the reassertion of value to historically denigrated indigenous knowledge systems, to defend the nonprovision of ART in South Africa.

I could go on about the overtly ideological issues surrounding the question of what we know and don't know about indigenous approaches to mental health promotion and prevention efforts, but I want to turn now to three more technical problems that we face. The first I call the evidence problem, the second the comorbidity problem, and the third the definition problem. I'll deal with each of them in turn.

The Evidence Problem

Research on mental health and mental health practice has benefited enormously recently from the increasing rigor applied to how we decide what works and what doesn't work. The Cochrane initiative and the proliferation of literature on evidence-based mental health have been extremely important. But the move toward a focus on evidence as quite narrowly and stringently defined poses special challenges to those working in poorly resourced settings. I don't want to rehearse here the many general objections that exist to evidence-based mental health (Williams & Garner, 2002). I also don't want to deny the huge strides that have been made in developing RCTs in developing countries. We now know that good RCTs, for example, can be conducted in developing countries, and the importance of this fact cannot be overestimated. But we also know that a world of difference exists between efficacy and effectiveness of interventions

(Swartz, Tomlinson & Landman, 2004), and I would argue that this difference is much greater in poorer countries than elsewhere.

Consider, for example, the question of whether voluntary counseling and testing for HIV can have mental health promotion and prevention benefits. This is an important question, especially because in Africa such a huge proportion of health resources have to go into HIV since the epidemic is so widespread and destructive. As Melvyn Freeman (2000) has argued cogently, we need to use all opportunities we can in resource-poor contexts to promote mental health, and HIV counseling represents a key opportunity. Researchers have conducted some very good studies on voluntary counseling and testing (VCT) in sub-Saharan Africa, and VCT has been shown to have a range of benefits. But when we look closely at these studies, we can see limitations to their applicability. In reviewing these studies, Poul Rohleder and I (2005) have shown that each of them evaluates VCT either as administered by a specially trained professional or in the context of the extra infrastructure of an RCT. When we examined what happens in the real world of VCT as it is administered by lay community workers, recruited precisely because of their links with the community and their familiarity with indigenous issues, we saw a very different picture from what happens in studies that collect evidence for the efficacy of VCT. These community workers were inserted into a stressed health system staffed by overworked nurses who perforce focused almost entirely on bureaucratic issues, such as getting through patient loads and on task orientation (van der Walt & Swartz, 2002). In addition, counselors must work in a system in which staff are not always mindful of the potential emotional effects of what they do. As one counselor put it:

> I remember, one of the doctor [...] she see that client, and then she told, "with this shingles, you think you are this 80% or 20% of HIV people." And then the client didn't reply back. "I think you are this 80%. You have HIV. So, go to room 7, and then they are going to tell you, you have your, if, they finish draw your blood." And then she come to me and knock on the door, and I say, "Okay, have a seat." When she start sit, she cry, I can' t do nothing. "What' s going on? Why you crying?" About half an hour, just give that chance to cry here, and then after that I ask, "Do you know that you tested?" - "I' m HIV." - "Did the doctor draw your blood?" - "No." - "So, why?" - "No, the doctor said." And the doctor is more that a counselor, is a doctor. The doctor can' t lie. Really can' t lie, but the <u>way</u> she put the things! They <u>way</u> she saying! Because on, on that space there' s no need, you can' t say. But is a doctor. As a result what <u>I</u> did. I just think: No. She gave me a hard time now! Because this person <u>already</u> crying, <u>already</u> broken heart already! So, the first time must go straight to the doctor, "Look, if you are going to say like this, I think you supposed to counsel, and do everything! And you must do everything to that person! Otherwise you give that broken people to me! Who' s going to pick up all that?" (Rohleder & Swartz, 2005)

Clearly, the gap between the ideal world of counseling and health promotion and the real world of health care is enormous. Furthermore, the resources that are necessary to produce the conditions under which an intervention can be isolated and evaluated are commonly far in excess of those available in the health care system and in society as a whole. Studies commonly are funded by external monies and cost far more than wide-scale implementability would allow. We have, for example, compelling preliminary evidence that early interventions conducted by community members and in an idiom that, if not totally determined by indigenous beliefs then influenced by them (Tomlinson & Swartz, 2002), may be helpful to caregivers and infants

From Research to Effective Practice

- Occupational disruption. This occurs when usual occupations are disrupted through changes in society and the environment.
- Occupational dysfunction. Usually associated with illness or injury and may well be a temporary situation if adequate remedial resources (such as health care) are available.
- Occupational alienation. Separation and estrangement from the mainstream of society and networks of community (for example, the refugee experience).
- Occupational imbalance. Restricted engagement in occupations that meet unique physical, social, mental, or rest needs (for example, work overload). (adapted from Watson, 2004b, 56; see also Whiteford, Townsend, & Hocking, 2000)

The value of an occupational analysis for those of us interested in indigenous issues and mental health is that the analysis holds the promise of making the links that we need to make between our rather abstract ideas about worldview and the concrete reality of people's day-to-day lives. We can ask very simple questions, for example:

1. What does person X do all day? (A useful way of answering this question is to look at activities over a specific period of time—two weeks, say—and to plot them).
2. To what extent do these activities match what the person would like to be doing?
3. What are the barriers that lead to the gap (if there is one) between B (what the person wishes to do) and A (what the person does do)? These barriers may be located at a number of intersecting levels, including the personal, the social, and the environmental.

Because occupation is not only about what people do, but also about what people are and what they become, about how they make meaning in their lives through what they do, an occupational analysis should help show us how systems of meaning, indigenous or otherwise, realize themselves through people's everyday lives. We then can begin to design work to examine the links between occupation and the meanings ascribed to it and generated from it and mental health outcomes. This approach is rather new and untested, but early studies suggest that an occupational approach provides a systematic understanding of people's lives (see the contributions to Watson and Swartz, [2004]). As a mental health professional, I always have tended to focus on rather abstract concepts, such as "mental health," "culture," or "the indigenous." I believe that an occupational approach can help us locate these rather abstract ideas in actual practices.

Concluding Comment

By way of brief conclusion, I suggest that, as a scientific community, we need to be more fearless and systematic in our interrogation of terms such as "indigenous." We need to think carefully about the enormous challenges we face in developing methodologies for generating implementable evidence in low-resource contexts. We need to think about what are our appropriate units of analysis. And we need, simply, to think more carefully and systematically about what people in vastly differing contexts do all day. We need to ground all our theories in material reality.

In making these suggestions, and in this talk as a whole, I am well aware that I am raising far more questions than I am answering—and the questions are directed as much to myself and to my own practices as they are to anyone else' s. But I hope I have succeeded today in raising questions that help lead to further questions and to some action.

References

Araya, R., Rojas, G., Fritsch, R., Acuna, J., & Lewis, G. (2001). Common mental disorders in Santiago, Chile: Prevalence and socio-demographic correlates. *British Journal of Psychiatry, 178*, 228-233.

Becker, J. T., Lopez, O. L., Dew, M. A., & Aizenstein, H. J. (2004). Prevalence of cognitive disorders differs as a function of age in HIV virus infection. *AIDS, 18 Suppl. 1*, S11-S18.

Brew, B. J. (2004). Evidence for a change in AIDS dementia complex in the era of highly active antiretroviral therapy and the possibility of new forms of AIDS dementia complex. *AIDS, 18 Suppl. 1*, S75-S78.

Chatterjee, S., Patel, V., Chatterjee, A., & Weiss, H. A. (2003). Evaluation of a community-based rehabilitation model for chronic schizophrenia in rural India. *British Journal of Psychiatry, 182*, 57-62.

Cooper, P. J., Landman, M., Tomlinson, M., Molteno, C., Swartz, L., & Murray, L. (2002). Impact of a mother-infant intervention in an indigent peri-urban South African context: Pilot study. *British Journal of Psychiatry, 180*, 76-81.

Csordas, T. J. (2004). Healing and the human condition: Scenes from the present moment in Navajoland. *Culture, Medicine and Psychiatry, 28,* 1-14.

Desjarlais, R., Eisenberg, L., Good, B., & Kleinman, A. (1995). *World mental health: Problems and priorities in low-income countries*. New York: Oxford University Press.

Freeman, M. (2000). Using all opportunities for improving mental health: Examples from South Africa. *Bulletin of the World Health Organization, 78*, 508-510.

Freeman, M. (2004). HIV/AIDS in developing countries: Heading towards a mental health and consequent social disaster? *South African Journal of Psychology, 34*(1), 139-159.

Isaakidis, P., Swingler, G. H., Pienaar, E., Volmink, J., & Ioannidis, J. P. (2002). Relation between burden of disease and randomised evidence in sub-Saharan Africa: Survey of research. *British Medical Journal, 324*, 702.

Koltko-Rivera, M. E. (2004). The psychology of worldviews. *Review of General Psychology, 8*, 3-58.

McMinn, M. R., & Voytenko, V. L. (2004). Investing the wealth: International strategies for psychology training in developing countries. *Professional Psychology: Research and Practice, 35*, 302-305.

Mills, E., Foster, B., Heeswijk, R. van, Phillips, E., Wilson, K., Leonard, B., Kosuge, K., & Kanfer, I. (2005). Impact of African herbal medicines on antiretroviral metabolism. *Aids, 19*, 95-97.

Parsonage, M. J., Hart, E., Wilkins, E. G., & Talbot, P. R. (2004). Lesson of the week: A new cause of treatable dementia. *Age and Ageing, 33*, 315-316.

Patel, V., & Sumathipala, A. (2001). International representation in psychiatric literature: Survey of six leading journals. *British Journal of Psychiatry, 178*, 406-409.

Pedulla, B. M., & Pedulla, M. A. (2001). Sharing the wealth: A model for brief mental health volunteer work in developing countries. *Professional Psychology: Research and Practice, 32*, 402-406.

Portegies, P., Solod, L., Cinque, P., Chaudhuri, A., Begovac, J., Everall, I., et al. (2004). Guidelines for the diagnosis and management of neurological complications of HIV infection. *European Journal of Neurology, 11*, 297-304.

Rabenoro, M. (2003). Motherhood in Malagasy society: A major component in the tradition vs. modernity conflict. *Jenda: Journal of Culture and African Women Studies, 4.*

Rohleder, P., & Swartz, L. (2005). "What I've noticed what they need is the stats": Lay HIV counselors' reports of working in a task-orientated health care system. *AIDS Care, 17,* 397-406.

Shisana, O., & Simbayi, L. C. (Eds.). (2002). *Nelson Mandela/HSRC study of HIV/AIDS: South African national HIV prevalence, behavioural risks and mass media: Household survey 2002*. Cape Town: Human Sciences Research Council.

Shweder, R. A., Minow, M., & Markus, H. R. (Eds.). (2004). *Engaging cultural differences: The multicultural challenge in liberal democracies*. New York: Russell Sage Foundation Publications.

Sumathipala, A., Hewege, S., Hanwella, R., & Mann, A. H. (2000). Randomized controlled trial of cognitive behaviour therapy for repeated consultations for medically unexplained complaints: A feasibility study in Sri Lanka. *Psychological Medicine, 30*, 747-757.

Swartz, L. (1998). *Culture and mental health: A southern African view*. Cape Town: Oxford University Press.

Swartz, L. (2002). Dissociation and spirit possession in non-western countries: Notes towards a common research agenda. In V. Sinason (Ed.), *Attachment, trauma and multiplicity: Working with dissociative identity disorder* (pp. 231-239). London: Routledge

Swartz, L., & Drennan, G. (2000). The cultural construction of healing in the Truth and Reconciliation Commission: Implications for mental health practice. *Ethnicity and Health, 5*, 205-213.

Swartz, L., Tomlinson, M., & Landman, M. (2004). Evidence, policies and practices: Continuities and discontinuities in mental health promotion in a developing country. *International Journal of Mental Health Promotion, 6*(1), 32-37.

Tomlinson, M., & Swartz, L. (2002). The "good enough community": Power and knowledge in South African community psychology. In L. Swartz, K. Gibson, & T. Gelman (Eds.), *Reflective practice: Psychodynamic ideas in the community* (pp. 121-133). Cape Town: Human Sciences Research Council.

Tomlinson, M., & Swartz, L. (2003a). Imbalances in the knowledge about infancy: The divide between rich and poor countries. *Infant Mental Health Journal, 24*, 547-556.

Tomlinson, M., & Swartz, L. (2003b). Representing infancy across the world: Does Osama bin Laden love his children? *Culture and Psychology, 9*, 487-497.

Tshabalala-Msimang, M. (2005). Manto on Aids: Nutrition, nutrition, nutrition. Cited in a SA Press Association (SAPA) article dated April 22, 2005, and accessed from www.mg.co.za, June 30, 2005.

UNAIDS. (2001). *Report on the global AIDS epidemic.* Geneva: UNAIDS.

van der Walt, H. M., & Swartz, L. (2002). Task orientated nursing in a tuberculosis control programme in South Africa: Where does it come from and what keeps it going? *Social Science and Medicine, 54*, 1001-1009.

Watson, R. (2004a). New horizons in occupational therapy. In R. Watson, & L. Swartz (Eds.), *Transformation through occupation* (pp. 3-18). London: Whurr.

Watson, R. (2004b). A population approach to transformation. In R. Watson, & L. Swartz (Eds.), *Transformation through occupation* (pp. 51-65). London: Whurr.

Whiteford, G., Townsend, E., & Hocking, C. (2000). Reflections on a renaissance of occupation. *Canadian Journal of Occupational Therapy, 67,* 61-69.

Williams, D. D., & Garner, J. (2002). The case against "the evidence": A different perspective on evidence-based medicine. *British Journal of Psychiatry, 180*, 8-12.

Yen, J., & Wilbraham, L. (2003a). Discourses of culture and illness in South African mental health care and indigenous healing, Part I: Western psychiatric power. *Transcultural Psychiatry, 40*, 542-561.

Yen, J., & Wilbraham, L. (2003b). Discourses of culture and illness in South African mental health care and indigenous healing, Part II: African mentality. *Transcultural Psychiatry, 40,* 562-584.

Mental Health Promotion: The WFMH-WHO Project on Case Studies from Countries

Preston J. Garrison
Secretary General and Chief Executive Officer
World Federation for Mental Health
Alexandria, Virginia, United States

The World Federation for Mental Health and the World Health Organization are very pleased to release a joint publication here in Auckland entitled Mental Health Promotion: Case Studies from Countries. The book describes thirty-five promotion projects from nineteen countries.

The projects were selected from fifty-nine submissions that WFMH gathered from organizations in its network of contacts. Project officer Deborah Maguire collected and processed the submissions. A valued volunteer, Ellen Mercer, helped with the initial review at the Federation's office, as did the late Richard Hunter, former WFMH deputy secretary general. A Federation donor, Mildred Reynolds, supported our participation in the project.

All of the submissions were forwarded to WHO, which selected the thirty-five projects featured in the book. Everyone here at the conference received a copy of the book in the registration package. We also have selected five of the thirty-five projects for awards of distinction, which will be presented by Rosalynn Carter today.

Shekhar Saxena, MD
Coordinator, Mental Health: Evidence and Research
Department of Mental Health and Substance Abuse
World Health Organization
Geneva, Switzerland

This project was a good experience. We came in contact with scores of people working on mental health promotion. In WHO sometimes we tend to be isolated, but here we were pleased to receive fifty-nine case studies from around the world (we expected about fifteen), and we came in contact with very practical people working with very small amounts of money.

Every one of the projects deserves publication. They were a delight to read. It is important for us to listen to people describing, in their own words, their activities in mental health promotion. The book is a tribute to them and to what they are doing on the ground.

It was difficult to choose the projects that will receive the awards for distinction, but we tried to take a wide view of mental health and to recognize diversity. We have selected one project supporting pregnant women, another for teenagers, and a third for elderly people, together with two highly imaginative projects from Iceland and from Turkey.

[Rosalynn Carter then presented certificates of distinction and a small honorarium for each of the following projects.]

- To Hedinn Unnsteinsson, representing the Icelandic Mental Health Promotion Project, for **Geðrækt**. Until 2000 the concept of mental health promotion was unknown in Iceland, except to professionals. Starting with the initiative of a consumer, Hedinn Unnsteinsson, an ambitious project was developed by a group of organizations to improve public knowledge of mental health by a variety of means. This included launching a new word, **Geðrækt** meaning mental health promotion. In two years the concept was understood by more than 60 percent of the population.

- To Margaret Barry, representing the **Mind Out** program. This project was designed to promote mental health among fifteen to eighteen year olds in Irish schools by shaping attitudes about dealing with personal distress, including knowing how and when to seek assistance. Program materials were developed after local consultation and a study of international best-practice information. Evaluation involved a randomized controlled experimental design.

- To Marie Hull-Brown, representing the Mental Health Foundation of New Zealand, for **Meeting of the Minds**. The Mental Health Foundation of New Zealand developed a program through Auckland's library service to provide various mentally stimulating activities for older people. The program, based on the concept of positive aging through lifelong learning, attracted growing numbers of people and expanded its offerings on preferred topics at community libraries.

- To Simone Honikman and colleagues, representing the **Perinatal Mental Health Project** at the Liesbeeck Midwife Obstetric Unit of Mowbray Maternity Hospital, Cape Town, South Africa. This initiative aimed to provide a holistic mental health service for pregnant and post-partum women, with screening, counseling, and referrals for psychiatric care if needed. Additionally, training workshops for staff in all Cape Town obstetric units were offered. In the impoverished Khayelitsha settlement near Cape Town, the prevalence of post-natal depression is 34.7 percent.

- To Bulent and Aysen Coskun, representing the Community Mental Health and Training Centre of Kocaeli University, for a **Public Awareness Training Program**. This program in Kocaeli, Turkey, began with a series of public meetings arranged in tent cities following the earthquake on August 17, 1999, to focus on interpersonal relations after the disaster. As time passed the subjects of the meetings, and their location, changed. The focus developed into a more general approach to interpersonal relations and the well-being of families. Characters and events in popular television series were used as the context for interactive discussion about choices, ways of handling daily issues, and reactions to other people and to events.

Note: The WFMH-WHO book of case studies can be downloaded from a link on the WFMH website (www.wfmh.org). To request a printed copy free of charge, send an e-mail to Dr. Shekhar Saxena at WHO (saxenas@who.int).

Reference

World Health Organization. (2004). Mental health promotion: Case studies from countries. Shekhar Saxena and Preston J. Garrison (Eds.). A joint publication of the World Federation for Mental Health and the World Health Organization. Geneva: World Health Organization.

mental health as a public health issue, the types of evidence that exist in this area, and the feasibility of mental health promotion strategies; examples of the interventions possible and the responsibility of various sectors; and a way forward to activities that can be undertaken immediately within a variety of resource settings. Fifty-seven experts from nineteen countries in WHO's six regions of the world contributed to the report. The contents of the report are as follows:

- Part 1, Concepts, discusses topics such as health promotion, positive mental health, the intrinsic value of mental health, cultural issues, social capital, human rights, and a conceptual framework for action.
- Part 2, Emerging Evidence, looks at objectives and actions of health promotion, evidence and its use in mental health promotion, social determinants, links between physical and mental health, developing indicators of mental health, evidence of effective interventions, effective mental health promotion in low-income countries, generating evidence on effectiveness, and cost-effectiveness.
- Part 3, Policy and Practice, discusses topics such as mental health promotion, sustainable interventions, an intersectoral approach to mental health promotion, and international collaboration. It outlines key recommendations.

The summary report on prevention offers an overview of international evidence-based programs and policies for preventing mental and behavioral disorders. Thirty-seven contributors from ten countries have contributed to this report. The following key messages are presented:

- Prevention of mental disorders is a public health priority.
- Mental disorders have multiple determinants; prevention must be a multipronged effort.
- Effective prevention can reduce the risk of mental disorders.
- Implementation should be guided by available evidence.
- Successful programs and policies should be made widely available.
- Knowledge on evidence for effectiveness needs further expansion.
- Prevention needs to be sensitive to culture and to resources available across countries.
- Population-based outcomes require human and financial investments.
- Effective prevention requires intersectoral linkages.
- Protecting human rights is a major strategy to prevent mental disorders.

The contents of this report are divided into the following sections:

- Part 1, Evidence-Based Risk and Protective Factors, discusses such topics as the concept of risk and protective factors; social, environmental and economic determinants; and individual- and family-related determinants.
- Part 2, Macro-strategies to Reduce Risk and Improve Quality of Life, discusses improving nutrition, housing, access to education, reducing economic insecurity, strengthening community networks, and reducing the harm from addictive substances.
- Part 3, Reducing Stressors and Enhancing Resilience, discusses promoting a healthy start in life, reducing child abuse and neglect, coping with parental mental illness, enhancing resilience and reducing risk behavior in schools, dealing with family disruption, intervening in the workplace, supporting refugees, and aging mentally healthy.

- Part 4, Preventing Mental Disorders, discusses conduct disorders, aggression and violence, depression and depressive symptomatology, anxiety and eating disorders, substance-related and psychotic disorders, and suicide.
- Part 5, The Way Forward, discusses various steps to be taken and conditions needed with regard to policy, capacity building and training, research, advocacy, and resources and infrastructures.

Recent WHO activities, including publication of the two summary reports, primarily involve assisting countries to be better informed on these important issues and to incorporate at least some of these programs into their mental health plans. The primary focus is on low- and middle-income countries, where the need is greatest. In addition, it is anticipated that these reports will be useful to professionals in the mental health field as well as in broader health areas, students, researchers, and all others interested in mental health.

References

Brundtland, Gro Harlem. (2002). The promotion of mental health and the prevention of mental and behavioral disorders. In P. J. Mrazek & C. M. H. Hosman (Eds.), *Toward a strategy for worldwide action to promote mental health and prevent mental and behavioral disorders* (pp. 120-122). Alexandria, VA: World Federation for Mental Health.

Pan American Health Organization. (2001). Mental Health. *128th Session of the Executive Committee.* Washington, D.C.: Pan American Health Organization. CE128.R12.

United Nations. (2004). *The right of everyone to the enjoyment of the highest attainable standard of physical and mental health.* New York: United Nations, UN General Assembly. A/Res/58/173.

World Health Organization. (1974). Psychosocial factors and health. *Resolution of the 27th World Health Assembly of WHO.* Geneva: World Health Organization. WHA27.53.

World Health Organization. (1975). Promotion of mental health. *Resolution of the 28th World Health Assembly of WHO.* Geneva: World Health Organization. WHA28.84.

World Health Organization. (1976). Psychosocial factors and health. *Resolution of the 29th World Health Assembly of WHO.* Geneva: World Health Organization. WHA29.21.

World Health Organization. (1986). Prevention of mental, neurological and psychosocial disorders. *Resolution of the 39th World Health Assembly of WHO.* Geneva: World Health Organization. WHA39.25.

World Health Organization. (1988a). Prevention of mental, psychosocial and neurological disorders in the European Region. *38th Session of the Regional Committee for Europe.* Copenhagen: World Health Organization. EUR/RC38/R7.

World Health Organization. (1988b). Prevention of mental and neurological disorders and psychosocial problems. *39th Session of the Regional Committee for the Western Pacific.* Manila: World Health Organization. WPR/RC39.R13.

World Health Organization. (1992). Disability prevention and rehabilitation. *Resolution of the 45th World Health Assembly of WHO.* Geneva: World Health Organization. WHA45.10.

World Health Organization. (2001a). Regional strategy for mental health. *52nd Session of the Regional Committee for the Western Pacific.* Manila: World Health Organization. WPR/RC52.R5.

World Health Organization. (2001b). *Mental health: A call for action by world health ministers.* Ministerial Round Tables 2001. Geneva: World Health Organization. WHO/NMH/MSD/WHA/01.01

World Health Organization. (2001c). *The world health report 2001. Mental health: New understanding, new hope.* Geneva: World Health Organization.

World Health Organization. (2002a). *The world health report 2002. Reducing risks, promoting healthy life.* Geneva: World Health Organization.

World Health Organization. (2002b). *Prevention and promotion in mental health.* Geneva: World Health Organization.

World Health Organization. (2002c). Strengthening mental health. *Resolution of the 109th Session of the Executive Board of the WHO.* Geneva: World Health Organization. EB109.R8.

World Health Organization. (2002d). Mental health: Responding to the call for action. *Resolution of the 55th World Health Assembly of WHO*. Geneva: World Health Organization. WHA55.10.

World Health Organization. (2004a). *Promoting mental health: Concepts, emerging evidence, practice. Summary report*. Geneva: World Health Organization.

World Health Organization. (2004b). *Prevention of mental disorders: Effective interventions and policy options. Summary report*. Geneva: World Health Organization.

WHO's Global Project on Evidence-Based Prevention of Mental Illness

Clemens M. H. Hosman, PhD
Professor of Mental Health Promotion and Mental Disorders Prevention
Prevention Research Centre
Radbout University Nijmegen and Maastricht University
The Netherlands

This presentation describes the background, content, and conclusions of the WHO summary report *Prevention of Mental Disorders: Effective Interventions and Policy Options* and also poses some questions for further discussion. First, though, I would like to recognize the leadership of the World Health Organization in this project. I have been working for a long time in this field, and the last several years have been very exciting due to several new initiatives to enhance the development, dissemination, and implementation of effective prevention worldwide. Especially I would like to recognize WHO's leadership—particularly that of Benedetto Saraceno and Shekhar Saxena—in putting this issue so strongly on the global mental health agenda.

The issue of prevention in the field of mental health is not a new one. It has been on the agenda for more than a hundred years and is an idea that has been advocated for a long time. But the main reaction, at least through the beginning of the 1990s, has been: "It's wishful thinking." "It's a poorly defined topic." "It's difficult to understand." "There's no scientific knowledge at all on the causes of mental illnesses." In general prevention of mental disorders or poor mental health was treated as a marginal public health problem.

Times have changed, happily. Currently, insight is available into the prevalence and burden of mental illnesses and behavioral disorders across countries and regions. Mental illness occurs in epidemic proportions and has great social and economic impact. Our understanding of the risk factors along the lifespan responsible for such disorders and poor mental health, and also of protective factors, has expanded significantly over the last decades. We still do not have all the scientific knowledge we need, but we have enough to start taking action. There is no reason to say, "Let's wait until we have more knowledge." We have enough knowledge now to do something meaningful in prevention.

A wide range of prevention programs to reduce risk has been developed and evaluated. Evidence is growing of positive outcomes from these programs. It is a fact that dissemination of the programs is beginning across countries. Many best practices and model programs now are traveling around the entire world, and many countries are beginning to adopt and implement the programs. This is a new chapter in the history of prevention.

The WHO prevention report incorporates ten key messages. The first key message, posed by the World Health Organization and many other organizations, targets policy makers: "*Prevention of mental disorders needs to be a public health priority.*" The report is a seventy-page summary of a more extensive book on evidence-based prevention that will be released at a later date (Hosman, Jané-Llopis, & Saxena, in preparation). The authors represent epidemiology, psychology, psychiatry, gerontology, and public health, and come from different parts of the world.

The first issue is how to define *evidence-based* prevention. The first part of the report discusses concepts of prevention, promotion, and the evidence base. The second part presents an overview of evidence-based risk and protective factors in the field of mental health and mental disorder that must be addressed. Parts three and four discuss available evidence-based programs and strategies. The first cluster of programs addresses effects at a macro level, such as nutrition, access to education, economic insecurity, and community networks. The next couple of chapters focus on a range of important stressful life events at one end and, at the other end, phases in life where opportunities exist to increase mental health—and also opportunities, under disadvantaged circumstances, to develop serious problems and eventually mental disorders. This section includes programs that address issues at the start of life and during childhood, such as maternal behavior during pregnancy and early parent-child interactions, child abuse, parental mental illness and family disruption, and programs in schools. It also covers programs in work environments, programs for refugees, and programs for older adults. Then we have a number of chapters that review what we know at this time about possible ways to prevent such mental disorders as conduct disorders and aggression, depression, anxiety disorders, substance-related disorders, and psychotic disorders, and to reduce suicide.

The final section presents conclusions and recommendations. For those of us who have worked on this project for more than three years, this was an extremely interesting learning experience. Eva Jané-Llopis, Shehkar Saxena, and I have talked with many scientists from all over the world, practitioners, and program designers—and we have learned a lot about how prevention works and how it does not work, how prevention can create effects and how prevention can fail. We have translated that knowledge in the last section of the report with the compilation of a range of recommendations on how to develop effective programs and to implement them effectively on a large scale, and the conditions needed to so. Development and implementation of effective programs require dissemination, adaptation and tailoring, evaluation and monitoring, and sustainability. We need to have policy, increased capacity and training, research, a group of advocates, and the infrastructure elements necessary to implement the programs.

This last section points to a significant problem. With increasing numbers of evidence-based programs becoming available, a huge gap exists between our knowledge and the available programs on one hand and our capacity to implement them on the other. If we could generate the conditions and resources to implement them on a large scale, an opportunity would emerge for a public health policy and practice that really could affect mental health and psychiatric morbidity in the population.

The report is focused exclusively on primary prevention—preventing the onset of mental disorders and mental ill health. Within primary prevention we differentiate among universal, selective, and indicated prevention. Universal prevention targets whole populations; selective prevention targets populations at risk; and indicated prevention targets individuals with symptoms but not disorders.

You might wonder why we have prepared a report and book about promoting mental health and a separate report and book about prevention. For some of you, this might not be a surprise, because you say, "Well, prevention is something completely different from promotion." But that's not our view. Of course, our report focuses on risk reduction, because it's about mental disorders. But at the same time, it is based on the view that primary prevention and mental heath promotion are closely related fields. Promotion can be a strategy, among others, to prevent mental and behavioral disorders. Good mental health refers to resilience, to strengths and competencies, that enable a person to cope with the stressors of life. So good mental health represents, among other things, protective factors. Many prevention programs use promotion of mental health as a main strategy to contribute to the prevention of mental disorders. The evidence-based prevention programs reviewed in this report show indeed not only successes in reducing risk factors but also a wide range of positive mental health outcomes, such as increases in cognitive and social skills, emotional resilience, self esteem, and prosocial attitudes and behavior.

The report is summarized in ten key messages, as I mentioned earlier, and I will discuss several of them here. The first message is: *"Prevention should be guided by available evidence."* We need to guide our decisions on practice and policy by the best available evidence for three reasons. First, we need to be accountable for spending public money by doing so in the best way we can. Second, our consumers should be offered support and programs with the best possible perspective on positive outcomes. Third, we know from research that large differences exist in programs' effectiveness and outcomes—ineffective programs, very effective programs, moderately effective programs. There is a lot to improve upon, so we need to base our interventions on a good evidence base.

A debate is ongoing about standards of evidence. The view of WHO, the International Union for Health Promotion and Education, the Society for Prevention Research, and several other leading organizations in this field is to give priority to well-controlled studies. The randomized control model, however, is not always a good fit for health promotion and prevention programs, and we need multiple evaluation methods—qualitative and quantitative. And we need to realize that it is not practical to develop the whole evidence base first and then to make decisions about what programs to implement. In my view and my experience, developing the evidence base requires close interaction between research and practice over many, many, many years. That is important to take into account. It also is important to enhance policies that facilitate a mutually supportive relationship between research and practice.

A crucial question for discussion is, "What does this all mean for low-income countries?" We do not have the resources in low-income countries to do all the research that has been done, for example, in the United States or in Europe. What does "evidence-based" mean for them? During this conference, and in the coming years, we should give the issue a significant place on our prevention and health promotion agenda.

The next key message is, *"Mental disorders have multiple determinants."* In the report we start with an overview of the epidemiology and a discussion of the risk and protective factors that are known in relation to mental illness and poor mental health. One conclusion is that most problems are the outcome of interaction among genetic, neurobiological, psychological, social, and environmental factors. Prevention policies should directly or indirectly address these multiple causes and their interactions along the life span. Consequently, when we want to reduce prevalence and incidence in the community, we need to move to a new generation of comprehensive prevention programs—packages of effective modules that address larger clusters of significant risk and protective factors in a specific community. You may be familiar with the Communities That Care program, a perfect example of this new approach (Hawkins, Catalano, & Arthur, 2002).

In the epidemiology discussion, we addressed the comorbidity issue. It is clear that most problems are not isolated. Considerable comorbidity exists between mental disorders and between and among mental disorders, physical diseases, and social problems. What does this mean? In my view, the big question for the future of public health policy is, "Should we continue, as many governments are doing, with a policy of trying to find the cure for disease after disease?" Is that an efficient strategy? Instead, we might focus more on common risk factors or clusters of problems.

Another key message is, "*Effective programs can reduce risk of mental disorders and mental ill health.*" The report describes a wide spectrum of outcomes that have been found as result of currently available evidence-based programs. We are able to reduce a wide spectrum of risk factors and to strengthen many protective factors. A crucial question is, of course, "Is there any evidence that such programs can also reduce incidence of new mental disorders?" The answer is, "Yes," although the evidence is very limited. I want to give you some examples of programs found to reduce or delay incidence, all of which focus on populations at risk and indicated populations—people who have some symptoms, but not a disorder:

- Anxious children at risk. A program that provided school-based screening and cognitive-behavioral programs in which families were involved produced a reduction in the incidence of anxiety disorders over the next six months from 54 to 16 percent.
- Depression in children of depressed parents. A program found a reduction from 25 to 8 percent in onset of depression in the program's first year.
- Children of divorce. In a program that provided parent training to improve parent/child relationships, after six years 11 percent of the prevention group had mental disorders compared to 23 percent of the control group.
- Cognitive training workshop. For people with a first panic attack, the program found a drop in panic disorder from 13 to 2 percent.

(For original references, see World Health Organization, 2004.)

A final message relates to human rights. Many risk factors and the absence of protective factors are outcomes of violations against human rights (for example, child abuse, violence, discrimination and suppression, inequity, reduced access to education). Protecting human rights may contribute significantly to better mental health and a reduction in mental disorders. We must consider our role and possible active interventions to contribute to better human rights. Success in reducing child abuse through improving early parenting and family conditions, and school programs that help to reduce aggression and violence and that lead to increased prosocial behavior among new generations of children and adolescents are examples of what our field can contribute. Generally speaking, increasing awareness of the long-term impact that violations of human rights have on the mental health of millions of children and future adults around the world should be a priority in our global prevention and mental health promotion agenda.

References

Hawkins, J. D., Catalano, R. F., & Arthur, M. W. (2002). Promoting science-based prevention in communities. *Addictive Behaviors, 27*(6), 951-976.

World Health Organization. (2004). *Prevention of mental disorders: Effective interventions and policy options. Summary Report.* Geneva: World Health Organization.

Promoting Mental Health: Concepts, Emerging Evidence, Practice

Helen Herrman, MD BS
Director of Academic Programs
Australian International Health Institute
Professor and Director of Psychiatry, University of Melbourne
Director, World Health Organization Collaborating Centre for Research and Training in
  Mental Health
Melbourne, Australia

Shekhar Saxena, MD
Coordinator, Mental Health: Evidence and Research
Department of Mental Health and Substance Abuse
World Health Organization
Geneva, Switzerland

Rob Moodie, MBBS MPH
Chief Executive Officer
Victorian Health Promotion Foundation
Victoria, Australia

Introduction

The World Health Organization's (WHO) summary report and book *Promoting Mental Health: Concepts, Emerging Evidence, Practice* (WHO, 2004; Herrman, Saxena, & Moodie, 2005) are produced in collaboration with the Victorian Health Promotion Foundation and the University of Melbourne. WHO recently has defined mental health as a "state of well being in which the individual realizes his or her abilities can cope with the normal stresses of life, can work productively and fruitfully, and is able to make a contribution to his or her community."

Promoting mental health contributes towards overall health and should form an essential component of health promotion. But the concept of promoting mental health is an unfamiliar idea to many people outside the immediate field. Those in the field of public health and health promotion may not be aware of the possibilities for the promotion of mental health, because the concepts of mental health and mental illness are unclear to them. Mainstreaming mental health in health promotion allows the energies applied to health promotion and public health to focus more effectively on this area, and enables a better understanding among professional groups of the specific approaches and rationale.

The scope for promoting mental health is identified by analogy with physical health promotion successes. Mental health is a community responsibility, not just an individual concern, just as many countries and communities have realized for heart health, tobacco control, dental health, and in other areas. The social and economic costs of poor mental health are high, and the evidence suggests that they will continue to grow without community and government action.

Mental health promotion aims to raise the position of mental health in the scale of values of individuals, families, and societies (Sartorius, 1998), so that decisions taken by governments and business improve rather than compromise the population's mental health, and people can make informed choices about their behavior. In addition to its specific interventions, mental health promotion can be completely achieved when policy makers in different sectors, such as education, welfare, housing, employment, and health, make decisions resulting, for example, in improved social connection; reductions in discrimination based on race, age, gender, or health; and improved economic participation. In this context mental health promotion is more than the prevention of mental disorders, although these are necessarily related and overlapping activities. Because the former is concerned with the determinants of health and the latter focuses on the causes of disease, promotion sometimes is used as an umbrella concept covering also the more specific activities of prevention (Lehtinen et al., 1997). The aims of improving mental health and lowering the personal and social costs of mental ill health require a comprehensive public health approach that encompasses the promotion of health, the prevention of illnesses and disability, and the treatment and rehabilitation of those already suffering. Therefore, just as mental health is part of health, so the promotion of mental health is integral to health promotion and public health.

The WHO report is divided into three parts. Part 1, Concepts, addresses mental health in health promotion and the scope of the actions. Part 2 addresses the emerging evidence and the benefits to countries. Part 3 considers policy and practice implications and in particular the many partnerships that support health promotion in any country or community.

Concepts

Part 1 defines mental health as well as health promotion. Mental health as defined above is a state of balance resulting from the action of many personal and external factors—physical, mental, social, cultural, spiritual, and other. Mental health is inseparable from physical health, as implied by the WHO definition of health, and is more than the absence of disease (Sartorius, 1990). Health promotion has been described by WHO as "actions and advocacy to address the full range of potentially modifiable determinants of health." These are actions that allow people to adopt and maintain healthy lives on the one hand, but also create living conditions and environments that support health. Promoting mental health is concerned with the determinants of health. It includes people and organizations outside the health sector as well as within it. The outcomes include changes in behavior related to physical health, improved quality of life, and economic productivity, as well as the prevention of mental disorders.

Decisions in the education, welfare, housing, employment, and health sectors influence mental health. They do so by modifying the determinants of mental health, which can be grouped as social inclusion, tolerance of difference, and economic participation. By economic participation we mean access to education, housing, employment, adequate employment conditions, and sufficient money for personal and family needs. Health promotion in this sense is part of a national suicide prevention plan in any country. The broad approach to social policy and programs to improve mental health through nonhealth as well as health sectors sits alongside other components of a national suicide prevention plan, such as population approaches to substance abuse; controlling access to the means of suicide, such as agricultural poisons or industrial gas; improving the treatment and access to treatment of mental disorders; and the mental health care and protection from self-harm of prisoners.

WHO has presented a number of resolutions at global and regional levels over recent years that have been endorsed by the countries. For instance, the resolution endorsed by the Regional Committee in the Western Pacific Region in September 2001 urges member states:

THEME 2

EVIDENCE-BASED PROGRAMS, POLICIES AND PRINCIPLES

Critical Thinking About Evidence-Based Programs

Paul J. Brounstein, PhD
Senior Public Health Advisor
Center for Mental Health Services
Substance Abuse and Mental Health Services Administration
United States

Scientists go to such great pains to qualify every statement about process or findings, so as to be perfectly, explicitly clear that what they *intended* to say is indeed what they do say. These same scientists have adopted many shorthand ways to communicate—especially with each other—in their written articles and talks to the public or their peers. In this, they often remain blissfully unaware that the precision with which they describe their findings—which may have been derived from technically sophisticated methods in which lots of assumptions had been made—are completely undercut by these shorthand descriptors. This is especially true, and the lack of communication most problematic, when communications are left in the ear of policy makers, program developers, and/or funding agencies. This broader audience may lack the degree of sophistication needed to understand all the nuanced meanings of the shorthand descriptors.

Take, for example, the term "evidence based." When I hear the term "evidence based," I assume that the program or intervention under discussion had at least one (even better, more than one) trial in which the intervention was implemented properly—with high fidelity, evaluated using a sufficiently rigorous research design—and that it produced predictable and internally consistent significant positive results. That's what I hear.

What do prevention program developers hear when they hear the term "evidence based"? Sometimes they hear: "Yes! You can use *our* program as an example of one that is evidence based. Everyone involved in the program knows that it works!" And indeed they do. Everyone involved in the program can point to John or Mary, whose lives have changed dramatically because of their participation in the program. But when program developers are asked for objective or other corroborative data for their program's effectiveness, they often scratch their heads, think hard, and come up with another person's name. Or they may say, "Well, we've never had any money to do a rigorous, scientifically sound study of the effectiveness of the intervention. We just know it works so we keep on doing it."

The point is not that researchers are smart and the average, well-intentioned program developer or implementer is, well, otherwise. No, the point here is that much of what we mean when we talk about evidence-based efforts is in the unwritten, often unheard, subtext.

Another way someone might look at "evidence-based" programs is to say that the effort was built by borrowing and cobbling together principles, activities, and even policies from other programs that had demonstrated their respective effectiveness in sound scientific research studies. The problem here, of course, is that no a *priori* reason exists to believe that these cobbled-together parts will work when taken out of context and applied with a different content—but it is not semantically incorrect to talk about evidence-based programs in this fashion.

In the United States, when we discuss evidence-based, effective prevention or promotion initiatives, we often use a whole set of terms roughly interchangeably. These terms include science based, research based, effective, empirically based—and our old friend, evidence based. But as you can imagine, these terms are far from interchangeable—"effective" says nothing explicitly about the methods used to implement the effort or to gather data. And, as we all know, not all data are created equal. "Research based" says nothing about the quality of the research or the magnitude or valence of the findings. These terms, and the others listed above, are meaningful only because we imbue them with meaning far in excess of the actual meaning conveyed. The key is that because we are discussing "evidence-based" programs, policies, and principles over the next few days, we must be specific as to the meaning of the term.

In addition to the issue of defining and setting up specifiable parameters for "evidence based" (e.g., well-implemented intervention, well-designed and implemented evaluation, and internally consistent, predictable, and positive findings), you might want to attend to a number of related issues over the next few days.

1. How much evidence is sufficient before we declare we are convinced?
   a. What types of studies contribute to our certainty?
   b. What are the respective roles of exact and conceptual replications/adaptations in providing confidence of a causal connection between intervention and outcome?
   c. How much does it matter if the developer is the person replicating or extending the basic research, compared to a third, more objective party?

2. What are the respective roles of efficacy and effectiveness studies in helping us determine what passes for "evidence based"? How much of each do we need?
   a. Efficacy studies may provide greater certainty, by way of findings of strong effects, but at a real cost to generalizability, because of, for example, small sample sizes, controlled environments, highly trained implementers, and "pure cases" (e.g., a person with depression, but without other mental or behavioral disorders).
   b. Effectiveness studies can use rigorous methods of investigation in the applied setting (e.g., providers working in community clinics with individuals having multiple mental and behavioral disorders), which can enhance generalizability, but attenuate effect sizes—sometimes to the point where the research establishment may question whether the effort is worth replicating.

3. What about issues of fidelity and adaptation?
   a. Fidelity is the extent to which program implementation conforms to the curriculum or protocol originally developed for the program. If a program is delivered exactly as intended by its originator, the program has high fidelity. A program whose delivery varies considerably from its intended implementation has low fidelity. Because programs implemented with high fidelity are more likely than those with low fidelity to achieve their original results—results that identified them as effective—fidelity has clear implications for successful implementations.
   b. Adaptation is the extent to which a program undergoes change in its implementation to fit the needs of a particular delivery situation. The apparent antithesis of fidelity, adaptation has the potential to affect program quality. A reduction in quality can result when a program is adapted so drastically that it is not delivered as originally intended. In most instances, however, adaptation will make a program more responsive to its intended recipients. Adaptation can increase a program's cultural sensitivity and its fit within the new implementation setting. Successful adaptation will result in program acceptance by its intended end users, a necessary condition for eventual outcome effectiveness.
   c. Notwithstanding the clear benefits of adaptation, changing a program can weaken the very elements that accounted for the program's original effects. A heavily adapt-

From Research to Effective Practice

intention is to add to collective wisdom; pragmatically, the assumption is that quality evidence-gathering practices that are effective with one group are of benefit to all groups (Alton-Lee, 2003). What one may call excellent can be appreciated, understood, and applied by many.

Tapa Theory

Tapa, or bark cloth made from the inner bark of certain trees, is one of the most distinctive products of the Pacific islands. Common to peoples of South America, Africa, Southeast Asia, the Philippines, and Indonesia, Pacific peoples like to think that the making of tapa has reached its greatest refinement and variety among the islands of the South Pacific. The word *tapa* is derived from the Samoan word *tapa* for the uncolored border of a bark cloth sheet, and the Hawaiian *kapa* for a variety of bark cloth. From New Guinea to Niue, Tonga to Tahiti, Cook Islands to Samoa, Vanuatu to Aotearoa, this is an ancient craft practiced for many thousands of years. And I am only just beginning to understand. My first lesson is the source of the fiber. To make tapa you must strip away the bark to get to the inner bark.

Tapa theory uses the making of tapa as a guiding principle—that effort is to be made to strip away the bark on evidence gathering, so that we might make something helpful, internationally recognizable, and possibly even beautiful. This paper is about the inner dimensions of evidence gathering.

Who Are Pasifika Peoples?

In its contemporary usage, Pasifika means peoples of Pacific-nation heritage living in New Zealand. The term Pasifika is a useful collective concept that includes several distinct ethnicities (e.g., Niue, Samoa, Tonga, Fiji, Tokelau, Cook Islands). Like many minority groups with a migrant heritage, Pasifika could include those recently immigrated to New Zealand as well as New Zealand residents of several generations. Pasifika peoples make up 16 percent of the national population and have the highest birth rate of all groups. By 2030 30 percent of the eligible workforce will be Pasifika peoples. However, overall Pasifika peoples share bottom ranking with Maori on all national social indexes, including education and health. Pasifika health, including mental health, is a priority area in government policy and strategy. It is operationalized on the basis of meeting identified need.

To ensure maximum return on state investment in Pasifika-focused initiatives, New Zealand government agencies have worked with communities and experts to develop guidelines for evidence gathering with Pasifika peoples (see, for example, New Zealand Ministry of Education, 2001, 2004; Health Research Council, 2004; New Zealand Tertiary Education Commission, 2003).

The case of Pasifika peoples is both unique and generic—unique to the particular composition and history of the Pacific nation peoples who have crossed the greatest ocean on this planet for centuries; generic to the experiences of migrant peoples and expanding nations around the world. Together we share the need to continue to expand and modify the body of knowledge around evidence gathering.

Perspectives on Evidence Gathering

Evidence gathering has not always been an impressive process. As with many minority peoples who find themselves studied, the experience and the project leaders, however well intentioned, can be superficial, hurtful, insincere, and short-term.

Some Pasifika people viewed a New Zealand education project focused on boosting learning outcomes in the low socio-economic area of Otara negatively. Assumptions seemed to have been made about what might be generalized from one population group (and hemisphere) to another; commitment to those with whom the researchers worked did not seem to be genuine:

> They send in people who know nothing about Otara; they try to use methods that they believe work in the slums of London, but they will never work in Otara. (New Zealand Ministry of Education, 2001, 20)
> Many people have been burned in the past by research done to further the researcher's career, and people haven't seen the results of the research. (New Zealand Ministry of Education, 2001, 20)

Evidence gathering is about integrity and reciprocity. The methods we use must make sense to the community we seek to serve and have benefits the community can see.

Characteristics of Evidence Gathering

Excellence in evidence gathering has at least three major characteristics: values, collaboration, and balance in inclusion.

Values base. For Pasifika peoples evidence gathering that is geared to authenticity begins by identifying Pacific values and "the way in which Pacific societies create meaning, structure and construct reality" (New Zealand Ministry of Education, 2001, 7).

Collaboration. Excellent approaches to evidence gathering will support local capacity and raise local research capability, integrating local perspectives and skills as central to the evidence-gathering process. This means that for Pasifika peoples, evidence gathering "requires the active involvement of Pacific peoples (as researchers, advisors, and stakeholders) and demonstrates that Pacific people are more than just the subjects of research. Pacific research will build the capacity and capability of Pacific peoples in research" (Health Research Council, 2004, 11).

Balance. Excellence in evidence gathering with Pasifika peoples "encompasses research that involves specific ethnic groups…as well as research that spans Pacific communities (New Zealand Tertiary Education Commission, 2003,1). Evidence gathering will achieve excellence when it recognizes both the homogeneous and heterogeneous nature of population groups.

In total, these three characteristics suggest that evidence gathering can be more than surface-level studies of what is readily observed and can have a sustainable social impact. To be so, evidence gathering must be about early and total commitment to an ethic of advancement and development.

Who Can Be Part of Evidence Gathering?

The commitment to social advancement through evidence gathering is reflected in the range of different positions and who it is that might be part of these projects. For Pasifika peoples, as for many population groups who strive and at times struggle as minority groups, there are at least two positions. The first is focused on entry through ethnicity. This is the position that says that only those of Pacific nation heritage might take part in leadership or as a participant. In the health sector such evidence gathering is "Pacific research" that is "by Pacific, for Pacific" (Health Research Council, 2004, 11).[1]

An alternative perspective is that evidence gathering is most effective as a tool for social advancement when it is inclusive. In this way, for some Pasifika peoples, excellent evidence gathering is "undertaken and presented by Pacific *and* non-Pacific researchers" (New Zealand Tertiary Education Commission, 2003, 1) (emphasis added).

How Evidence Gathering Happens: Pasifika Perspectives

Actions often speak louder than words when we engage in evidence gathering. Too, what we do reveals our actual motivation, concepts about diversity, and commitment to social advancement. Pasifika peoples have been engaged in a range of project types in the mental health sector, as in education and other social sectors. Profiles and key indicators of these project types are described in Table 1.

Table 1: Evidence-gathering project profiles

Profile	Indicators
Notional	Identification as Pasifika project in name only, with no or very low access by project to Pasifika communities and practices
Positive	Some levels of involvement in Pasifika communities and practices; involvement of Pasifika and non-Pasifika; Pasifika expertise at all levels of decision making; focus on organizational or national outcomes
Ethnic	Self-identification as a Pasifika project: "for Pacific, by Pacific"; high levels of involvement in and knowledge of Pasifika communities, practices, and language

Source: Adapted from Durie (1998).

Least effective are those projects that trivialize and exploit Pasifika participation. Such projects are notional in regard to the potential for evidence gathering to reveal reliable, valid information or to contribute meaningfully to social advancement.

---

[1] A critical examination of the merits of this approach will be discussed more fully in my forthcoming paper *Tatou, tatou e: The politics and pragmatics of researching as community.*

For Pasifika peoples evidence gathering project profiles that are positive or ethnic are the priority. These projects are most likely to be community based and committed to Pasifika capacity and capability raising. The context of the project and the level of development of the Pasifika community will determine whether the project will operate from a positive or ethnic profile. It remains, however, that the project design must provide the quality of data that will enable mental health initiatives to contribute to social advancement. This advancement comes on the basis of strengths, not benevolence. Gather evidence as if you mean strengths-based advancement to happen.

Next Steps for Evidence Gathering

Excellence occurs through ongoing refinement. Suggestions for two key aspects of project management in evidence gathering are provided below: refinement in processes internal to a project and refinement in the processes aimed at maximizing positive outcomes when working with distinct population groups.
Working within a project:
- Support development in project management and evidence gathering
- Clarify which project profile is relevant
- Address project challenges through being attentive to values, collaboration, and the balance between inclusive and individual perspectives

Working with population groups:
- Connect—with strategy and policy frameworks
- Consult—early, authentically, and regularly in an ongoing manner
- Compose the project itself to have:
    - Pasifika expertise at all levels of decision making
    - Complementary skills
    - Clearly defined roles
- Adopt the ethic of advancement and development
- Challenge yourself through increased self-awareness about expertise, motivation, and expectations. If you fall short of the ability to engage actively in ways identified earlier in this paper, then think about retirement or changing jobs.

Conclusion

Inspiration comes from those with the courage to go beyond boundaries that would otherwise confine each evidence-gathering project to the mundane, automaton approaches to evidence gathering. Such projects and their managers approach each expedition of knowledge exploration with the will to respond to the unique. They understand the need not only to discover but to create a legacy of skill in enquiry. They understand that their work can and should change how we live in the world. They understand the need to communicate often, openly, and clearly about what is coming to light. They understand that evidence gathering is more than three dimensional.

This paper has explored these dimensions. The community expectations, characteristics of good practice, and profiles of projects have revealed three big ideas:

Are we ready for this challenge? Well, I want to conclude on a positive note. We are at an unprecedented political moment in relation to inclusion. The political and policy climate are aligned, and they are strongly permissive with regard to this agenda for change. There is, of course, much *to* change, but there is also much already in place.

Living South Cover: Indicator of Change

Living South is a free quarterly journal that falls regularly through the letterboxes of people like me, who live in communities south of the Thames. Its content is somewhat "bourgeois." Five years ago this magazine would not have run a cover story on a radical mental health service user organization like "mad pride." But in a recent edition, incredibly, there was indeed a tribute to mad pride, sadly in the form of an obituary to its founder, Pete Shaughnessey.

This is a small but significant indicator of change, just a symbol, but an important little symbol of comparative fairness in a media world that, despite major effort, continues in many popular quarters to peddle misinformation and fuel prejudice.

We are undoubtedly up against it, but progress is being made nationally and internationally. While I may in this brief presentation have won few converts to the argument that policy on the needs of the mentally ill is, at least in some conditions, a necessary determinant of a successful mental health promotion strategy, that, in the end, is not the fundamental issue. The real issue is how we learn to learn from each other, not just across national regions but across continents. Progress on inclusion requires a process that is itself inclusive. I hope that among us we will contribute to that process as a result of this conference.

References

Commins, P. (Ed.). (1993). Combatting exclusion in Ireland, 1990-1994: A midway report. Brussels: European Commission.

Social Exclusion Unit. (2004). Mental health and social exclusion: Final report. London: Social Exclusion Unit, Office of the Deputy Prime Minister.

Achieving the Promise: Implications for the Promotion of Mental Health and Prevention of Mental and Behavioral Disorders

A. Kathryn Power, MEd
Director, Center for Mental Health Services
Substance Abuse and Mental Health Services Administration
U.S. Department of Health and Human Services
Rockville, Maryland, United States

In the second century B.C., the Chinese philosopher Liu An wrote, "A skillful doctor cures illness when there is no sign of disease, and thus the disease never comes." It is a pleasure indeed for me to be here this morning with so many "skillful doctors" who passionately endeavor to ensure that, whenever possible, mental and behavioral disorders never come.

It is also a pleasure to meet people who had such a strong impact on promotion and prevention at SAMHSA's Center for Mental Health Services long before I became director. In 1992, when the U.S. Congress created SAMHSA and its three centers, Beverly Long made sure that the *first* responsibility assigned to the director of CMHS was to "design national goals and establish national priorities for the prevention of mental illness and the promotion of mental health." This ensured that some promotion and prevention activities would occur at CMHS, but apparently it was a visit by my predecessor, Dr. Bernie Arons, to Australia and New Zealand in 2000 that really turned the tide at CMHS. Dr. Arons returned to the States an avid preventionist. So if you hear reverberations of your ideas when you read CMHS's promotion and prevention documents, we thank you for them!

The lessons that he brought home started a major cultural shift within our agency, and prevention now has a respected and growing place on our Center's agenda. I am delighted that CMHS is helping to support this international mental health promotion and prevention conference, and that we are continually looking for opportunities to enhance and extend our collaborative efforts to reduce the burden of disease associated with mental illnesses worldwide. In this vein we are collaborating with the World Federation for Mental Health, The Clifford Beers Foundation, The Carter Center, the World Health Organization, and others to get the Global Consortium for the Advancement of Promotion and Prevention in Mental Health (GCAPP) firmly established as an international promotion and prevention resource. In addition, SAMHSA's Administrator Charles Curie has been working collaboratively with ministers of (mental) health from New Zealand, Australia, and the U.K. to initiate the International Initiative for Mental Health Leadership. The mission of this group is to promote policy innovation that fosters improved mental health around the world.

This session covers the international exchange of research, programs, policies, and guidelines to stimulate implementation of evidence-based programs, recognizing the need for cultural variation and adaptation. I want to tell you about how we're trying to develop the infrastructure for such programs, policies, and guidelines in the U.S. As you may know, a major cultural shift is anticipated in the United States' mental health system, a shift that is international in its origins and comprehensive in its approach to the delivery of effective prevention and treatment services to all Americans.

In February 1977 President Jimmy Carter issued an Executive Order establishing the first President's Commission on Mental Health. It took another twenty-five years before another such commission was created. In April 2002 President George W. Bush issued an Executive Order establishing the New Freedom Commission on Mental Health. His charge to the Commission was to "recommend improvements to enable adults with serious mental illness and children with serious emotional disturbances to live, work, learn, and participate fully in their communities" (New Freedom Commission on Mental Health, 2003, 99).

In July 2003 the Commission issued its final report—*Achieving the Promise: Transforming Mental Health Care in America* (New Freedom Commission on Mental Health, 2003). The Commission stated rather bluntly that our nation's mental health system is "fragmented and in disarray," and that most of our people with mental problems are not in our mental health system. Rather, they are in prisons, the juvenile justice system, schools, child welfare agencies, homeless and living on the streets, or in either public or private disability programs.

The Commission concluded that nothing short of a complete transformation that ensured all these systems would work together would give the people of the United States a truly effective mental health system. The Commission's report defined a visionary end state for transformation, and it advanced six goals and nineteen recommendations to help us get there.

In November 2003 The Carter Center hosted a conference on how to make these goals and recommendations a reality. In her opening remarks, Mrs. Rosalynn Carter recalled the work of the earlier commission and said the following:

> Twenty-five years ago, we did not dream that people might someday be able actually to recover from mental illnesses. Today it is a very real possibility.... For one who has worked on mental health issues as long as I have, this is a miraculous development and an answer to my prayers. (Carter Center, 2003, 1)

The concept of recovery is central to the New Freedom Commission's report. By *recovery*, the Commission did not mean complete wellness for every person who has a mental illness. Rather, it defined *recovery* as:

> the process in which people are able to live, work, learn, and participate fully in their communities. For some individuals, recovery is the ability to live a fulfilling and productive life despite a disability. For others, recovery implies the reduction or complete remission of symptoms. (New Freedom Commission on Mental Health, 2003, 5)

Most importantly, in a recovery-oriented system, the individual or family being served makes the choices and is the agent of control in the healing process.

The key dilemma for us now is, how on earth do we get to a recovery-oriented system in a country where so many people do not understand that mental health is fundamental to *everybody's* overall health, where so many know so little about mental health and mental illnesses, and where so many people dichotomize their thinking into "we who are healthy" and "they who are mentally ill"? This is where promotion and prevention come in.

Although promotion and prevention were not part of the Commission's original, official mandate, the commissioners were very much aware of the findings of the *Global Burden of Disease* study (Murray & Lopez, 1996)—that five of the top ten causes of disability worldwide are mental disorders, and that mental conditions are expected to increase dramatically their share of the world's total disease burden by 2020.

The commissioners also were well aware of the lessons of the first Surgeon General's Report on Mental Health (U.S. Public Health Service Office of the Surgeon General, 1999), which advocates a public health approach that includes prevention as well as treatment. The commissioners knew that, with about 20 percent of the U.S. population—that's about 44 million adults and 14 million children—experiencing mental disorders in any given year, these conditions constitute a public health crisis. And the commissioners understood the preventive wisdom of George Albee's statement that no disease or disorder has ever been treated out of existence.

In short, the commissioners clearly recognized that transformation requires a very broad perspective. To provide good treatment and recovery services for people with mental illnesses, a transformed system must be relevant and meaningful to all 300 million of us in the United States. And it is abundantly clear that we cannot make it relevant and meaningful without promotion and prevention activities.

So when the commissioners wrote their vision statement, they were true to their presidential mandate and focused mainly on treatment and recovery, but they also envisioned "a future when . . . mental illnesses can be prevented."

One of the most urgent recommendations calls for the advancement and continued implementation of our National Strategy for Suicide Prevention (U.S. Department of Health and Human Services, 2001), which was developed in 2001. In the United States alone, we lose 30,000 people to suicide each year, and I just recently heard a staggering statistic from the

World Health Organization: Last year, worldwide, 1 million people lost their lives to suicide. These statistics are truly tragic, for we know that suicide *is* preventable.

Effective suicide prevention—like all prevention activities—hinges on involving multiple sectors of society in prevention efforts. Our National Strategy is built around the imperative that we *fully engage both the public and private sector in its implementation.* This is an unprecedented opportunity for us to educate the public about mental health issues in general and about suicide prevention in particular.

At the heart of SAMHSA's efforts is promoting a national vision of suicide prevention based on the premise that mental health is fundamental to *everyone's* overall health. Through this lens suicide must be viewed as a national public health problem that requires each and every citizen to be part of the solution. It is critical to help people who never think of themselves as public health workers to recognize the vital roles they can play.

The movement towards a public health perspective on mental health requires both the belief that people can recover and that society as a whole must take part in transforming an individual diseased–based model into a systems approach of ensuring health. One of the first steps in accomplishing this transformation is for SAMHSA, with CMHS at the lead, to model the behavior it hopes to see imitated.

To this end SAMHSA has convened a Federal Transformation Working Group composed of senior staff from seven federal departments and fourteen other agencies in the Department of Health and Human Services. This has truly been a multicultural experience; each of these agencies has its own norms, values, procedures, policies, rules, regulations, programs, and so on. Despite our different cultures and missions, however, we have found many commonalities, and we have developed a federal agenda for action that details measurable steps that the federal government will take in the next year as part of a five-year transformation process.

Transformation demands that we be on an urgent mission to overcome the divide between the laboratory and the field—between science and services. We are collaborating with the National Institute of Mental Health (NIMH) on field testing local adaptations of evidence-based practices. In addition we are working with NIMH to develop funding mechanisms and requirements that will enable the field to readily adopt and adapt emerging evidence-based practices in a much shorter time than the seventeen years the National Institute of Medicine says is the average time between innovation and broad-based dissemination and use.

Another initiative that supports our science-to-service mission is SAMHSA's Strategic Prevention Framework. In the public health tradition, the Framework provides an effective process, a direction, and a common set of goals, expectations, and accountabilities for localities to prevent mental and substance use disorders and promote mental health. It emphasizes developing community coalitions; assessing problems, resources, and risk and protective factors; developing capacity in states and communities; implementing evidence-based programs with fidelity; and monitoring, evaluating, and sustaining those programs.

To help communities identify evidence-based programs, we also have the National Registry of Effective Programs and Practices, or NREPP, for short. Created in 1998 by Paul Brounstein and his colleagues at the Center for Substance Abuse Prevention, to review and evaluate substance abuse prevention programs, NREPP uses a sophisticated process to identify existing programs as model, effective, promising, or lacking sufficient current support.

In 2002 we began expanding NREPP to include not just substance abuse programs, but also treatment programs in both mental health and substance abuse—programs for people with co-occurring disorders—and now programs to promote mental health and prevent mental and behavioral disorders.

Introduction: The Media, Human Rights, and Promotion and Prevention in Mental Health

Raymond Nairn, PhD
University of Auckland School of Medicine
New Zealand

Media and mental illness is a topic that has quite a history. If you have the inclination, you can find that the earliest articles on the topic by psychologists and psychiatrists date from about forty-seven years ago—1957 was the earliest I could find. One of the things that is rather disheartening about that literature is that it says, throughout most of that time, that there have been no changes in the depiction of mental illnesses.

I have my own thoughts about why there have been so few changes, but it's clear from many speakers on mental health promotion and the prevention of mental and behavioral disorders that something needs to change. One of the possible answers to the conundrum lies in the connection of human rights with this area of study.

I've been asked by one of my co-researchers to mention that we are underway with a major study in this area, not with mental illness and media and human rights, but with Maori and media and human rights. One of my expectations is that what we will find in New Zealand is that those media depictions have strong parallels with the kind of demeaning, stigmatizing, and disabling depictions that have been so much part and parcel of the media representations of people who live with serious mental disorders.

It is a particular pleasure for me to welcome Mrs. Carter to New Zealand. For the past three years, I have been her guest at The Carter Center as the New Zealand member of the advisory board for the Rosalynn Carter Mental Health Journalism Fellowship Program. I have enjoyed the hospitality. I have been nurtured and welcomed there in ways that I sing praises of whenever I have the opportunity. So it is a real pleasure to welcome Mrs. Carter to my place.

Mental Health Journalism: Reducing Stigma Through Informed and Balanced Reporting

Rosalynn Carter
The Carter Center
Atlanta, Georgia, USA

Ray Nairn, PhD, has meant a lot to the Advisory Board of the Rosalynn Carter Fellowships for Mental Health Journalism and to The Carter Center's Mental Health Program. We work closely with him, and also with Gerard Vaughan of the Like Minds, Like Mine anti-stigma campaign. Trying to overcome the stigma surrounding mental illnesses is something that I have worked on for more than thirty years now. The journalists who receive the fellowships come to The Carter Center at the beginning and the close of their fellowship year. They tell us what they plan to do, and, a year later, they come back and report on what they did.

Jimmy and I founded The Carter Center in 1982 after we left the White House. We have programs in sixty-five countries—the poorest, most isolated in the world, including thirty-five in Africa. We work on peace and health issues. Our work is guided by a commitment that overarches all our programs, to defend human rights and alleviate suffering. We work to prevent and resolve conflicts, to foster democracy, and more than two-thirds of our budget is expended for health purposes. We are working to eradicate a horrible disease called Guinea worm. We are now working on the last one percent of cases. When we began, there were 350 million people affected, and now there are about 30,000. And we could have eradicated it already, if it had not been for the civil war in Sudan. We could not get our health workers into the remote areas where the disease remains. But if we do eradicate that disease, it will be only the second in the world that has been eradicated, and we are excited about that. We also work to control river blindness, schistosomiasis, lymphatic filariasis (elephantiasis), and trachoma. It is an exciting, fulfilling life for us.

Mental health falls within our health programs. It is about our only domestic program—all the others are overseas—and now we have internationalized my mental health program.

I have worked in the mental health area for more than thirty years. When Jimmy was governor, I had a Governor's Commission; when he was president, a President's Commission. Now I have a really good program at The Carter Center. Over the years we have worked on many initiatives to try to overcome stigma.

The most successful initiative, the one I am so excited about, is the Fellowships for Mental Health Journalism program.

We decided that since the media has such great influence on people's opinions about people who have mental illnesses, we needed to develop a cadre of journalists who knew the issues, could have some influence on their peers, and could report accurately. You know you can work and work to eliminate stigma, then something happens that results in a big, sensational, stereotyping headline that just destroys everything you have done. So we began these fellowships in 1997.

Fellowships are open to all working press in any media, either professionally affiliated or freelance. Journalists apply with a subject in mind that they plan to address. They do not leave their jobs, of course, but they do receive a stipend that varies depending on their home country. In September new fellows come to The Carter Center, which is affiliated with Emory University, and outline their project for us. They return the following year to present the finished products or, in the case of more long-term efforts like books and television documentaries, to update us on their progress. Now with both incoming and outgoing fellows reporting, it is the most exciting three days at The Carter Center. I always look forward to it.

We have been thrilled with the caliber of journalists who have applied for and received these fellowships. This year, for instance, we have journalists from the *Los Angeles Times, Washington Post,* and the American *60 Minutes.* They all have been really great! In fact, last year we turned down two Pulitzer Prize winners, only because we had just had fellows who had studied the same subject. This year more than one hundred American journalists applied for six positions.

When we decided that we would internationalize our program, we immediately thought about New Zealand, because we were familiar with the Like Minds, Like Mine program. The director of my Mental Health Program at that time had worked in New Zealand for a short while and knew Ray Nairn. Also, David Satcher, the former U.S. Surgeon General, had been to New Zealand and was really impressed with the anti-stigma program. We chose New Zealand for a number of other reasons: for our initial expansion, we thought it wise to select an English-speaking country. Also there is a large multicultural presence here that mirrors some of the disparities in the U.S. and elsewhere around the world. So with Ray's help the New Zealand fellows were chosen and came to The Carter Center.

I remember that first day. It was September 11, 2001. I was on the way to Atlanta to meet with the fellows and got the message on the two-way radio about the World Trade Center. At that time we thought the first plane crash was an accident. When I arrived in Atlanta, everyone at The Carter Center was glued to the televisions. For a few hours, we were numb, unable to tear ourselves away, until Jimmy finally said, "There's nothing we can do about it. We need to go to work." So we went ahead with our program that day. It was interesting to have the interna-

So what are some of the practical things that we may be able to do? If your own life story is not relevant or of interest to the media, you still may be able to help. If you work in an organization, you may be able to support networks of people who are of interest to the media to talk to and interview.

People will have different needs. For example, some people might need media training if they are not used to talking to the media. Even if people are used to talking to the media, they may benefit from the advice of a communications advisor regarding the issue or story that they plan to discuss.

In addition to supporting people with experience of mental illness to talk directly to the media to get various types of stories told, we in New Zealand also have implemented a number of other media strategies, including educational presentations to trainee journalists, developing better relationships with local working journalists, writing letters to the editor, and complaining about unbalanced media reporting. We also have a partnership with The Carter Center around Mental Health Journalism Fellowships. This has been an excellent project for New Zealand. Through it, over the last four years, eight New Zealand journalists have completed mental health research projects. This also has included two trips for each journalist to The Carter Center and involvement in their wider mental health journalism program. We have had excellent feedback from all the journalists involved, and this also has contributed greatly to a broader range of media stories written about the experience of mental illness. We also have produced a media handbook for working journalists and even coached actors and producers of stage plays on story lines or acting parts about people with mental illness.

In finishing this short talk I would like to show you a couple of the television advertisements that we have produced via the project.

(Mr. Vaughan showed two one-minute television public service advertisements—one launched in 2000 showing pictures of well-known people, international and national, who have experienced mental illness, and the other launched in 2003 showing everyday people through the eyes of their families, friends, and work mates, with the tag line "Know Me Before You Judge Me.")

Media, Human Rights, and Promotion in Mental Health

John Francis
Founder and Publisher, *Tearaway*
Fellow, Rosalynn Carter Mental Health Journalism Fellowship Program
New Zealand

Rosalynn Carter Mental Health Journalism Awards

I would like to acknowledge Mrs. Rosalynn Carter regarding the Rosalynn Carter Mental Health Journalism Fellowships. These awards are a most valuable contribution towards healthy community understanding and responses on mental health issues. I know I speak on behalf of our group of New Zealand fellows in thanking her and the Carter Center for the opportunities they have given us.

Take my own case, and my publication, *Tearaway*. As New Zealand's leading youth magazine, we work hard to bring socially useful messages to our readers. But the Carter Mental Health Fellowship provided a much more clearly defined focus and impetus. As a result we are now running articles on mental health/holistic health on a fairly regular basis. This is a long-term commitment and a direct outcome of the fellowship.

The Challenge: Reduce "Failures," Win "Friends"

It was ironic and totally appropriate on the morning the conference opened that the *New Zealand Herald*, on page 4, had this as its main story: "'First Lady of Mental Health' Advocacy: Rosalynn Carter's crusade has done wonders but there's more to be done." Then on the facing page was this headline: "Failure in court freed man to kill. Insane man's release is blamed on breakdown in communication."

So these are the two realities: Yes, mental health can get positive press—but, since this is not an exact science, there will always be failures that will generate unwanted headlines. The challenge is, therefore, to reduce "failures" and win "friends" via the media. A challenge for organizers of this and similar conferences, where so much that is positive is being showcased and debated, is to create a different balance among the delegates—by stacking it with representatives from the media.

Many in the mental health world see the media as the enemy. Several people at this conference have admitted that the opposite is also true—that there are many within the health professions who create enemies, by their unhelpful attitudes and responses to journalists.

We know this has to change.

Therefore I present to you a little model I've whipped up with the help of one of our cartoonists, Toby Morris. (Actually it's an adaptation from one we designed for another purpose, but it also works well here). This cartoon is based on a motif very familiar to people here in Auckland—the America's Cup yacht race. Our entrant in the race is called Team Media.

Team Media

On the team are all possible permutations of public information channels, including TV/radio, newspapers/magazines, government/community campaigns (such as New Zealand's *Like Minds, Like Mine* campaign), mobile phones, Internet (Anne Leer's www.mindmedia.tv comes to mind here), film, and music/songwriters.

Vision of Holistic Health

The vision must be promulgated clearly and widely if this boat is to steer true, a shared vision (that the media can "buy into" on behalf of its audience/readership) of creating a more just, equitable, healthy, safe society. Guidelines for responsible reporting (e.g., the Scottish "See Me" booklet, available at www.seemescotland.org) must be made available and publicized.

The Stories

Where do they start? Where do they stop? Stories include:

- Debunking myths
- "Ordinariness" of mental conditions. We're not talking about "them, over there"; so many of us are affected in some way.
- An illness is just "one small part of me."
- Well-known people who "know" first-hand, as consumers and/or caregivers
- Growth through adversity
- Holistic health: physical, mental, social, spiritual
- Economic benefits to governments and business
- This information should be woven into any story. Stories should not always be labeled, "This is about mental health."
- Consumers should be used as media experts/consultants whenever and wherever needed.

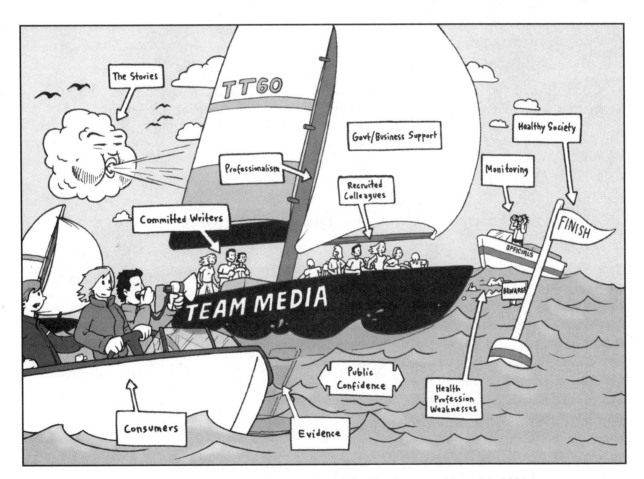

Source: Toby Morris, adapted from *Magazines Exposed,* published by Tearaway Magazine, 2004.

Committed Writers/Journalists

There's plenty of cynicism (read: tiredness) and opportunism out there in "medialand." But there are at least as many:

- People of experience and with social concern, always ready with pen and microphone
- Idealistic "new kids" (the new breed of journalists) eager to address social issues

The new breed in time will be promoted through the ranks and, with the right encouragement, can positively "infect" management.

Recruited Colleagues

How do you eat an elephant? One bite at a time. As more journalists become involved, they can spread the word to colleagues, department heads, sub-editors, etc. We can encourage the spread also to various departments/sections in the media, for instance, within a newspaper or magazine, to the pages on business, children/youth, entertainment/music, and lifestyle.

Good Allies

Good allies include advertising agencies, editors of newspapers' magazine and other specialist sections within a medium, such as youth/alternative press, schools of journalism, women's/men's specialty magazines, community newspapers/radio/TV, and songwriters.

Professionalism

A strong mast is essential to drive the momentum. Media representatives need encouragement to aim for:

- Balanced, fair reporting (that does not ignore the negative stories, but puts things in perspective)
- Use of appropriate sources (not the lazy use of tired old experts)
- News editors allowing their reporters to tell the real story—to let the humanity shine through, rather than using a cheap "hook" for sensationalism or to feed preconceptions
- Guidelines for mental health reporting promulgated through all media organizations

Government/Business Support (Including Media Owners)

Lots of work remains to be done here, but we have a very persuasive bottom-line message to take to government and business: A healthy society means higher productivity with less public cost and lower business overheads. How do we sell this message? Through evangelizing articles in the general media and business press.

What Does Research on the Social Brain Tell Us About Prevention?

Thomas R. Insel, MD
Director, National Institute of Mental Health
Bethesda, Maryland, United States

Over the past two decades, neuroscience research has transformed our understanding of the brain. Among the many changes in our concept of brain function, three insights have been fundamental. First, we now recognize the brain as a dynamic organ, capable of remarkable changes in how cells are connected and even in the number of cells available throughout life. Second, we recognize considerable individual variation in the relationship between brain anatomy and function. Classic maps of the cortex with specific areas for motor and sensory fields are still useful, but only as a broad generalization that varies greatly across individuals. And finally, we now appreciate a stunning level of modularity in the brain, with circuits dedicated to highly specific functions, such as verbs versus nouns or animate versus inanimate objects.

While all three aspects of brain function are pertinent to the promotion of mental health, I will focus on the high degree of modularity with specific reference to how the brain processes social information. We tend to consider social information among the most highly complex forms of knowledge, requiring visual, auditory, and even somatosensory processing. In fact, recognizing friend from foe, kin from predator, and mate from stranger are among the most basic forms of information for survival in the animal kingdom. No wonder then that many species have developed extraordinary abilities to detect social information, usually in the olfactory domain. Indeed, many mammals use a dedicated system, the accessory olfactory system, adapted specifically for social signals, such as pheromones (Insel & Fernald, 2004).

Humans, like other primates, are primarily visual rather than olfactory creatures. One particular area of the visual cortex, the fusiform gyrus and its surrounding cortex, appears to be essential for face recognition. Most people activate this area when looking at pictures of faces, but those with autism fail to show activity in the fusiform area, and those with schizophrenia appear to have a reduced volume of this region. People with strokes infarcting this region develop prosopagnosia, an inability to recognize faces. Connections from this area to the amygdale are believed to be important for higher order decoding of faces, including reading emotion, nonverbal expressions, and gaze.

In the past couple of years, a surprising set of studies in mice suggests that there may be a specific molecular as well as anatomic basis for social information. Mice engineered to lack the genes for oxytocin or vasopressin show a specific loss of social memory apparently without loss of any other aspect of cognition (Ferguson, Young, Hearn, et al., 2000). Oxytocin and vasopressin previously have been implicated in social behavior, including maternal care and pair bond formation or attachment. Mice lacking either of these genes cannot distinguish familiar from novel mice. Indeed, they do not develop a sense of familiarity, responding to all mice as if they are meeting them for the first time. Replacing oxytocin or vasopressin restores the ability to make social memories. In fact, when placed into a tiny subnucleus of the amygdale, oxytocin completely restores social cognition, revealing a remarkable circuitry for social recognition in the mouse brain. The results of these studies with mice lacking these neuropeptide genes are important because they suggest that social cognition is supported by a unique family of molecules, setting it apart from spatial learning, fear conditioning, or habituation.

What does the neurobiology of social information processing have to do with mental health and prevention? Aside from the deficits in social cognition in schizophrenia and autism, important lessons are emerging from the field that we now call social neuroscience. We have known for nearly half a century that there are critical periods in development. Infants born with cataracts can regain normal vision if the cataract is removed in the first six months, but not thereafter. The critical period for language extends further, with six years often used as a period in which children acquire a native language. What about a critical period for social information? The Nobel Laureate ethologist Konrad Lorenz described a critical period for social attachment in Greylag geese. In the hours after hatching, goslings form a preference for the first object they follow, usually the mother, but, as Lorenz demonstrated, they can imprint on a human almost as easily.

Do human children have a similar critical period for attachment? Studies of orphans raised with a variety of institutional caretakers have reported persistent social deficits, akin to autism (Rutter & O'Connor, 2004). If these children are provided with a consistent, caring foster parent in the first two years, there is no evident long-term deficit. Children who remain institutionalized for longer periods may fail to recover full social abilities, just as infants who do not have their cataracts repaired in their first six months may not develop normal vision.

We do not know the brain mechanisms for critical periods in either the visual domain or the circuits for social information. However, recent studies in infant rats have suggested a potential mechanism by which the quality of infant care influences the "mental health" of offspring. After laboratory rats give birth, mothers differ greatly in the degree of licking and grooming afforded their pups. Michael Meaney and his students noticed some years ago that pups receiving high levels of licking and grooming grew up to become adults with less stress responsiveness compared to pups receiving less licking and grooming (Meaney, 2001). Of course, this difference could reflect a genetic difference in the rats. Perhaps mothers with more licking and grooming behavior gave birth to pups genetically less responsive to stress. In a series of cross-fostering experiments, this group showed that it was indeed the maternal behavior and not the biological mother that determined adult behavior. In fact, female offspring receiving high levels of licking and grooming from either a biological mother or a foster mother grew up to show less stress responsiveness and more licking and grooming of their own pups (Francis, Diorio, Liu, & Meaney, 1999).

By itself, the observation that the quality of maternal care influences the adult behavior of offspring is hardly surprising. What is interesting in this research is that the mechanisms for this relationship are now being identified. The decrease in stress responses in Meaney's high licking and grooming rats seems to be due to increased numbers of receptors for glucocorticoids in the hippocampus. These receptors, which sense the circulating stress hormone corticosterone, serve as a brake on the brain's stress circuit. Therefore more receptors mean less stress response. But why does more licking and grooming mean more receptors? The answer appears to be due to what is known as an epigenetic modification of the glucocorticoid receptor gene. This simply means that licking and grooming causes a change in the state of this receptor. Amazingly, this state change appears to occur within a critical period. In the first six days postnatal, the regulatory region of this gene can go from a methylated to nonmethylated state. If methylated through the first six days, it will remain so throughout life and there will be fewer glucocorticoid receptors. Licking and grooming, in ways we still do not understand, remove the methylation tag from this region of the gene and allow the induction of gene expression, with a resulting increase in receptors and decrease in stress responsiveness (Weaver, Cervoni, Champagne, et al., 2004).

In this case, we are beginning to understand the molecular mechanisms by which early experience confers lasting changes in behavior. It is certainly possible that an opposing process occurs in children who have been physically or sexually abused. We know that these children have increased stress responsiveness and have high baseline levels of stress hormones, such as corticotrophin releasing hormone (CRH). It seems highly likely that the chronic elevation of stress hormones has deleterious effects on the central nervous system, including increasing the risk for major depressive disorder. A recent comparison of the outcome of drug treatment and cognitive behavior therapy in depression found no significant effect of medication in the subgroup with a history of abuse, although this subgroup responded to psychotherapy (Nemeroff, Heim, Thase, et al., 2003).

In summary, social neuroscience is revealing the mechanisms by which social experience influences the developing brain and how the brain, in turn, can process social information. Although one is tempted to suspect that molecular and cellular studies will only prove reductionistic, failing to capture the richness of behavior, our experience in the past decade suggests just the opposite. Studies of the molecular and cellular mechanisms of social information have begun to reveal previously unexpected, counter-intuitive insights, from unique molecules for social memory to molecular consequences of maternal care. We have unprecedented traction in modern neuroscience. The task for the next decade will be to channel this traction toward the study of mental health and the prevention of mental disorders.

References

Ferguson, J. N., Young, L. J., Hearn, E. F., Matzuk, M. M., Insel, T. R., & Winslow, J. T. (2000). Social amnesia in mice lacking the oxytocin gene. *Nature Genetics, 25*, 284-288.

Francis, D., Diorio, J., Liu, D., & Meaney, M. J. (1999). Nongenomic transmission across generations of maternal behavior and stress responses in the rat. *Science, 286*, 1155-1158.

Insel, T. R., & Fernald, R. (2004). How the brain processes social information. *Annual Review of Neuroscience, 27,* 697-722.

Meaney, M. J. (2001). Maternal care, gene expression, and the transmission of individual differences in stress reactivity across generations. *Annual Review of Neuroscience, 24*, 1161-1192.

Nemeroff, C. B., Heim, C. M., Thase, M. E., Klein, D. N., Rush, A. J., Schatzberg, A. F., et al. (2003). Differential responses to psychotherapy versus pharmacotherapy in patients with chronic forms of major depression and childhood trauma. *Proceedings of the National Academy of Sciences USA, 100*, 14293-14296.

Rutter, M., & O'Connor, T. G. (2004). English and Romanian Adoptees Study Team: Are there biological programming effects for psychological development? Findings from a study of Romanian adoptees. *Developmental Psychology, 40*, 81-94.

Weaver, I. C., Cervoni, N., Champagne, F. A., D'Alessio, A. C., Sharma, S., Seckl, J. R., et al. (2004). Epigenetic programming by maternal behavior. *Nature Neuroscience, 7*, 847-854.

Two big legacy problems get in the way and create barriers to successful promotion and advocacy. The first is the very definitions of promotion and advocacy. The second is the way in which media is perceived and defined traditionally, primarily as a vehicle to be used for propaganda and public relations. The world has changed profoundly with the advances of communication technology and the growth of the media industries. The media no longer can be referred to as one entity, described with one all-fitting label. We now live in a global media-driven society where geographical borders make little sense. Issues of ownership and control of the media are increasingly difficult to deal with on a national and jurisdictional basis. Media policy and regulation can be dealt with effectively only on an international level. Anyone can set up a TV network today or broadcast anything from anywhere on the Internet.

The world has changed totally in terms of how communication and information are organized and accessed. The early days of propaganda and promotion through simple media campaigns have gone. In many public as well as private sectors, the perception and approach to media are stuck in the 1920s and 1930s, when radio, TV, newspapers, books, and other print media were used, particularly in the United States, very effectively and systematically by those in power to control and censor and shape public opinion to fear the Communists—the big Red Scare—and to mobilize support for World War II through hatred of all things German.

Woodrow Wilson, who was re-elected U.S. president in 1916, is famously credited for having set up the first U.S. government spin doctor and propaganda machine, called the Creel Committee (Committee on Public Information, established April 1917). The success of the Creel Committee had an enormous impact on what since has grown to become a huge public relations industry, with spending on public relations in 2003 of more than $2 billion in the U.S. alone.

But the world has changed and the media no longer are a separate entity to be controlled and manipulated. The media have become an integral part of our society for better and for worse. In many shapes and forms, the media have the power to promote mental health more effectively than any limited government-orchestrated public relations campaign or advertising effort could ever achieve. For example, after the terror attacks struck New York on 9/11, New York State's mental health department spent millions of its scarce budget on commissioning an advertising and public relations company to develop a media strategy that primarily focused on expensive advertising in mainstream media. In my view so much more can be achieved effectively by building and developing creative relationships with media professionals directly.

The Carter Center in Atlanta has a fellowship program for journalists interested in mental health issues. Through this initiative journalists and mental health professionals get to "infect" each other with their respective knowledge and learn of each other's crafts. It is an excellent example of how to promote mental health effectively.

It is very important to discard old models that no longer work. Public relations, advocacy, media, and mental health are big concepts that no longer are what they used to be. The world and the maps we use to understand the landscapes in which we operate all have changed. We need new maps to fit these changing landscapes and new ways to use media effectively to create lasting, positive impact. It is also so important to work across traditionally separate disciplines and professional roles to achieve common understanding of the challenges facing us all during these turbulent times. That is why I am particularly honored and grateful that you invited me as a media professional to speak to you at your conference and also in this way give me the opportunity to learn from you and be infected by your impressive work as mental health professionals.

I look forward to continuing to share our respective knowledge in media and mental health and invite you all to stay in touch. Who knows, maybe we can move some mountains together!

A New Approach at SAMHSA

Charles G. Curie, MA, ACSW
Administrator
Substance Abuse and Mental Health Services Administration (SAMHSA)
U.S. Department of Health and Human Services
United States

Across the globe leaders of mental health systems from time to time have found a door of opportunity to create real change. As stewards it becomes our responsibility to share not only how we found the door, but also how to open it, how to teach people to step through it, and importantly what was on the other side.

When I first began to serve in my position as administrator of the Substance Abuse and Mental Health Services Administration (SAMHSA), our Secretary for the U.S. Department of Health and Human Services, Tommy Thompson, gave me an early and clear directive to lead the agency in a new direction—to find that door. I decided to redefine SAMHSA's vision to capture the notion of consumer- and family-driven care.

I based my approach on the simple and fundamental request of every consumer I had worked with, and our new vision statement became "a life in the community for everyone."

Together with our many partners, SAMHSA is working to ensure that people with or at risk for mental or substance abuse disorders have an opportunity for a fulfilling life—a life that is rewarding, that includes a job, a home, and meaningful relationships with family and friends.

At SAMHSA we work toward our vision through our mission, which is to build resilience and facilitate recovery. To do this, we design our everyday work around the multiple needs of the people we serve. Whether we are setting policy, providing treatment, or delivering mental health promotion or mental illness prevention programs, consumers and families must be our focus when we talk about building resilience and facilitating recovery.

To keep us focused on our vision and mission, I created the SAMHSA Matrix of leadership priorities and cross-cutting management principles. I am sharing the newest version of the Matrix with you today—I like to call it the Matrix Reloaded. The Matrix undergoes revisions to reflect the most current needs of the States, local communities, providers, and consumers and families.

The Matrix was developed around discussions with members of Congress, our advisory councils, the research community, constituency groups, people working in the field, and people working to attain and sustain recovery. It has produced concrete results by focusing SAMHSA staff and the field on planting a few "redwoods," rather than letting "a thousand flowers bloom." And most importantly, it is helping us make the best, evidence-based services available to people in need.

The Matrix priority areas and cross-cutting principles also align with President Bush's agenda and with the agenda of Health and Human Services Secretary Thompson. I want to recognize the support SAMHSA has received from the White House and the Secretary. This kind of support from our highest levels of leadership, along with SAMHSA's clear sense of purpose and the contributions of our partners on all levels, has led to many recent successes.

For example, Secretary Thompson announced in April 2004 the availability of $45 million to implement our new Strategic Prevention Framework at the National HealthierUS conference. HealthierUS is the President's plan to improve overall public health by capitalizing on the power of prevention. The goal is to aid Americans in living healthier, longer lives.

SAMHSA Priorities: Programs & Principles Matrix

Cross-Cutting Principles

- Science to Services/Evidence-Based Practices
- Data for Performance Measurement & Management
- Collaboration with Public & Private Partners
- Recovery/Reducing Stigma & Barriers to Services
- Cultural Competency/Eliminating Disparities
- Community & Faith-Based Approaches
- Trauma & Violence (e.g. Physical & Sexual Abuse)
- Financing Strategies & Cost-Effectiveness
- Rural & Other Specific Settings
- Workforce Development

Programs/Issues

- Co-Occurring Disorders
- Substance Abuse Treatment Capacity
- Seclusion & Restraint
- Strategic Prevention Framework
- Children & Families
- Mental Health System Transformation
- Disaster Readiness & Response
- Homelessness
- Older Adults
- HIV/AIDS & Hepatitis
- Criminal & Juvenile Justice

A Life
In The
Community
For
Everyone

Building
Resilience &
Facilitating
Recovery

The release of the Strategic Prevention Framework on a national scale is profound because substance abuse and mental illness prevention, as well as mental health promotion, now are on a par with other preventable illnesses such as heart disease, diabetes, and other chronic conditions.

I am excited about this effort because it has the potential to bring together multiple funding streams from multiple sources to create and sustain a community-based, science-based approach to substance abuse prevention, mental illness prevention, and mental health promotion.

Alone, each of our prevention programs in the U.S. across the federal government provides a trickling stream of funds. Together I believe we can provide an ocean of change.

In addition to a new and more solid approach to prevention, we also are unearthing new ways to address co-occurring mental health and substance abuse disorders, which is another SAMHSA Matrix priority area.

I have made available more funds for our Co-Occurring State Incentive Grants (COSIG), created a newly operational Co-Occurring Center for Excellence, held a national Policy Academy for States, and broadened our approach to identify and disseminate known effective programs for the prevention and treatment of co-occurring disorders through our National Registry of Effective Programs and Practices (NREPP).

Another Matrix priority area is expanding substance abuse treatment capacity. Unfortunately, the need for treatment in the United States is great. Our most recent survey identified 22 million Americans who last year suffered from substance dependence or abuse due to drugs, alcohol, or both.

To begin meeting this profound need for treatment, President Bush has committed and released funds for our new Access to Recovery program. Access to Recovery, or ATR, promotes choice and accountability in substance abuse clinical treatment and recovery support services. It is based on the knowledge that there are many pathways to recovery, and it empowers people with the ability to choose the path best for them—whether it is physical, mental, medical, emotional, or spiritual.

As a result of this new program, very soon thousands of Americans battling addiction will have the opportunity to choose their treatment options for recovery. ATR is promising and exciting, but it clearly is not business as usual. Instead of SAMHSA requiring another exhaustive list of data requirements, we are asking grantees to report on only seven outcome measures. These measures are recovery based and broader than simply reporting numbers of people served or beds occupied. I'll discuss these outcomes in greater detail in a few moments.

At the same time we are expanding substance abuse treatment capacity in new and innovative ways, we are beginning the process of transforming mental health care in America. In July 2003, the President's New Freedom Commission on Mental Health submitted its final report. The report found that our nation's mental health care system is beyond simple repair. Instead, the Commission recommended a wholesale transformation that involves consumers and families, public and private providers, and policy makers from all levels of government.

I was tasked to review the Commission's report and to develop an action agenda to achieve the goals outlined in the report. As we expected, developing the action agenda has proven to be a tremendous undertaking. My lead staff person for the action agenda is Kathryn Power, director of SAMHSA's Center for Mental Health Services (see the text of her presentation in this publication, page 129).

A hallmark of the action agenda is the unprecedented collaboration and partnership across the federal government to work together and make every effort to keep consumers and families at the center of care. As you know, partnerships are hard work. They take time and energy. I'm

The report went on to say:

> We believe that the eradication of poverty is the first step in primary prevention of mental illness and related social problems. Canada and the United States must urgently confront poverty.
>
> The Council agrees with the statement of Max Abbott, outgoing President of WFMH, who argued that "the gap between the rich and the poor, the powerful and the dispossessed, grows wider and deeper. . . . Poverty in the midst of plenty is an outrage." (report distributed at the 1993 WFMH Tokyo meeting)

Wilkinson (1996) has reviewed a wide range of research that should convince us that the greater the gap in average income level between the rich and the poor in industrialized societies, the worse the mental health—not just because old people live a few years longer in narrow-gap societies, but because there is more poor health and death for all in broad-gap societies. Interestingly, the causes of death in inegalitarian societies include violence, homicide, suicide, and the stresses of social disintegration that lead to biological pathology. Those societies with narrow gaps between the rich and poor enjoy a larger degree of social cohesion. Better health in a society is less the result of expert medical care and more the result of the quality of social life. The rate of crime and violence, and the degree of sickness and emotional distress are functions of the size of the gap between the rich and the poor.

In a speech at the 2004 World Health Assembly in Geneva, Switzerland, former President Jimmy Carter stated, "I want to share with you my conviction that the greatest challenge facing the world is the growing chasm between the rich and the poor, both between nations and people within nations." Carter had many wise things to say in this speech, in which he called attention to the "tremendous magnitude and burden of mental illness around the world." He pointed to the urgent need for family planning, education (especially for girls), and alleviation of poverty.

Another major cause of emotional distress is widespread and rampant sexism—the mistreatment and exploitation of girls and women throughout the world—that must be the concern of any attempt at the reduction of stress. One of the clearest examples is the genital mutilation of millions of girls, largely in Africa. Again this should be well known to the WFMH. At the biennial meeting in Lahti, Finland, Dr. Mawaheb T. El-Mouelhy (1997) gave the invited Albee Prevention Lecture on stresses affecting women. Because of time constraints she focused her remarks on female genital mutilation. Her talk was delivered at the full plenary session. It was followed by active discussion of the urgent need to take action. Finally, Judi Clemens (then chief executive of MIND, England's mental health association) and I (Clemens and Albee, 1997) drafted the following resolution:

> Be it resolved by the assembly of the WFMH that we express our strong
> support for the elimination of all forms of genital mutilation of women as
> a major source of stress leading to physical and mental problems. We support the Minister of Health in Egypt and all others in Africa who have
> proposed outlawing this practice in hospitals and clinics. Proposed: Judi
> Clemens, Seconded: G.W. Albee

The WFMH Assembly passed the resolution unanimously. Subsequently the Board of the WFMH expressed strong support for the resolution and recommended that the Federation's United Nations representatives advocate this position at the UN.

A WFMH Committee on the Commercial Sexual Exploitation of Children chaired by Professor Arshad Husain has had success in calling attention to the danger to children in war-torn lands. A NATO resolution has endorsed a zero-tolerance policy concerning trafficking in persons.

The resolutions on poverty (Tokyo meeting) and genital mutilation (Finland meeting) and on trafficking children are examples of efforts at major social change that have been proposed by the WFMH.

3. **A third major source of stress leading to emotional disorder is being born unwanted.** A major positive contribution to lifelong mental health is being born into a caring, supportive family and community. Prevention efforts begin with infants and children.

The best overall examination of needed efforts at primary prevention was conducted by the Commission on the Prevention of Mental-Emotional Disabilities (1986) chaired by Beverly B. Long. It considered important prevention efforts at stages across the life span. It heard testimony from a wide range of experts in various fields, including genetics, family planning, infancy and early childhood experience, adolescence, marital relationships, nutrition, and aging.

One afternoon, as the members of the Commission sat around a table after listening to a full morning of testimony from experts, someone (I think it was psychiatrist George Tarjan) asked the question: "If we had just one prevention program we could put into place, and knew that it would succeed, which one would that be?"

The question led to some hours of discussion, at the end of which the members of the Commission agreed on an answer: We would opt for a program that would ensure that every baby born anywhere in the world would be a wanted child—a healthy, full-term infant welcomed into the world by economically secure parents who wanted the child and had planned together for her or his conception and birth. (I would add the hope that the baby would be breast-fed by a mother who was not on drugs. I also would ask for good health care and good nutrition for the expectant mother and child. Such an arrival into the world would go a long way toward assuring later healthy relationships, reduced mother and child mortality, reduced developmental disability, and reduced later mental disorders. So would improved education for women and early education for children.)

In a landmark study David, Dytrych, and Matejcek (2003) reported that "being born from an unwanted pregnancy is a risk factor for poor mental health in adulthood" (p. 226). This finding has profound implications for the crucial importance of family planning, birth control, and women's rights—all issues on any prevention agenda.

4. **It is important to recognize the fact that emotional disorders, unlike physical diseases, are *not* the same across the world.** Clearly, those of us from Western industrial nations try to apply our psychiatric diagnostic categories across all societies. But anyone familiar with cross-cultural epidemiology knows that content and frequency of conditions viewed as disorders vary significantly from society to society. Perhaps the best example is homosexuality. This behavior across time and across cultures is sometimes viewed as a normal variant, or a mental disorder, or a criminal violation.

Similarly, the consumption of alcohol and drugs may be culturally acceptable or unacceptable. There are enormous differences in cultural views of depression. In some societies depression is unknown; in others it is a pervasive undercurrent; in others it is regarded as pathology. Buddhism has definitions of mental disorder very different from Islam, Christianity, and Judaism, so we need knowledgeable people from many different cultures to work together on prevention issues.

5. A fifth area that calls out for objective, dispassionate consideration is the current quasi-political view that all mental disorders are brain diseases. This issue, more than any other, will affect our treatment and our efforts at prevention for the next half century. Clearly this position calls for calm, objective consideration and resolution.

I agree with those who argue that most emotional disorders are *not* brain diseases, but I do not want to debate the issue here. All I ask is that we enlist help in evaluating the issue from persons with good scientific training and values, and that we do not accept prematurely a position based on the opinion of authority figures and on economics-based arguments. If, ultimately, it becomes clear that most emotional disorders are *not* diseases, the implications are staggering for treatment and prevention. I am ready for the debate to begin!

Summary

1. One-on-one treatment, while humane, cannot reduce the rate of mental disorders, but the fact that relationship therapy can reduce or eliminate individual emotional disorder shows that many such disorders are not due to organic pathology.

2. Only primary prevention, which includes strengthening resistance, can reduce the rate of disorders. Positive infant and childhood experiences are crucial. Reducing poverty and sexism are urgent strategies.

3. Ensuring that each child is welcomed into life with good nutrition, a supportive family, good education, and economic security will greatly reduce emotional distress. But forces of resistance to family planning, birth control, abortion, and strong religious patriarchal bias must be confronted.

4. Cultural differences in diagnoses must be understood and be part of program planning.

5. Strong differences of opinions about causes—particularly brain disease versus social injustice—must be resolved by unbiased scientific judgment before real progress can be made.

References

Albee, G. W. (1959). *Mental health manpower trends*. New York: Basic Books.

Albee, G. W. (1990). The futility of psychotherapy. *The Journal of Mind and Behavior, 11*(1&2), 369-384.

Carter, J. (2004, May 19). Remarks presented at the World Health Organization's World Health Assembly, Geneva, Switzerland. Retrieved from www.cartercenter.org/viewdoc.asp?docID=1687&submenu=news

Clemens, J., & Albee, G. W. (1997). Resolution at the Membership Assembly. Biennial Congress of the World Federation for Mental Health, Lahti, Finland.

Commission on the Prevention of Mental-Emotional Disabilities. (1986). *The prevention of mental-emotional disabilities*. 2 vols. Alexandria, VA: National Mental Health Association.

David, H. P., Dytrich, Z., & Matejcek, Z. (2003). Born unwanted: Observations from the Prague study. *American Psychologist, 58*(3), 224-229.

El-Mouelhy, M. T. (1997). Violence against women: A public health concern. Invited Albee lecture on prevention. Biennial Congress of the World Federation for Mental Health, October 2004, Lahti, Finland. *Journal of Primary Prevention, 25*(2), 289-292.

Evans, G. W. (2004). The environment of childhood poverty. *American Psychologist, 59*(2), 77-92.

Joffe, J. (1988). The cause of the causes. In Albee, G.W., Joffe, J.M., & Dusenbury, L.A. (Eds.). *Prevention, Powerlessness, & Politics: Readings on Social Change*. Newbury Park, CA: SAGE Publications.

New Freedom Commission on Mental Health. (2003). *Achieving the promise: Transforming mental health care in America. Final report*. DHHS Pub. No. SMA-03-3832. Rockville, MD: U.S. Department of Health and Human Services.

Ryan, W. (Ed.). (1969). *Distress in the city: Essays on the design and administration of urban mental health services*. Cleveland: The Press of Case Western Reserve University.

SPECIAL PLENARY

LINKAGE OF MENTAL HEALTH, PHYSICAL ACTIVITY, AND PUBLIC HEALTH

Physical Activity and Mental Health: The Evidence Base and Beyond

Kenneth R. Fox, PhD
Professor and Research Fellow of Exercise and Health Sciences
University of Bristol
United Kingdom

Introduction

The case for physical activity and the promotion of public health has been built largely around the impact of physical activity on physical health. This case has been established on the increased risks of heart disease, obesity, diabetes, some cancers, and musculoskeletal disorders associated with inactive living (Department of Health, 2004). Evolution has prepared us with musculoskeletal systems that have enabled fast running and endurance walking, primarily to survive threat and to source ourselves with adequate nutrition and sustenance. Perhaps it is not surprising that systems begin to fail if they are inadequately used and maintained. Increasing incidence of sedentary living accompanies material wealth and advancing technology. Fewer active occupations; labor-saving devices in the home, at work, and in the community; increasing dominance and use of the car; increasing diversity and availability of home screen entertainment; and less access to attractive and safe play and recreation areas are the likely intermediaries of reducing activity levels in populations in both developed and developing countries. This trend already is causing dramatic increases in costs in terms of health care and human suffering.

Attention increasingly has been drawn to mental disorders as a major cause of illness and restricted life quality. The World Health Organization predicts that by 2020 unipolar depression will be the second most common cause of disability-adjusted life years. For women and for populations in developing countries, it is predicted to be the leading cause of disease burden. Already, in developed countries, a high proportion of primary-care resources are spent on dealing with mental health problems, which include mild to severe forms of depression, anxiety, drug and alcohol abuse, sleep and stress problems, chronic fatigue, and psychosomatic complaints. Clearly, cost-effective ways of preventing and treating mental disorders are needed.

Evidence Base for Physical Activity and Mental Health

The study of the effect of exercise on mental illness and well-being is relatively recent, and has occurred mainly within the fields of exercise science and health and clinical psychology. The evidence base has been reviewed and summarized extensively (Biddle et al., 2000) and recently updated for the U.K. Chief Medical Officer's report on physical activity and health (Department of Health, 2004). Table 1 summarizes the findings from this latter review.

The evidence base must be described as relatively immature at this point. Few prospective epidemiological studies investigate preventive effects. There are a smaller number of well-controlled randomized trials than we find in other areas of activity and health. Interventions tend to be short (eight to twelve weeks) with little follow-up. There is also a strong bias towards North American populations. Furthermore, until recently the field has not conducted cost-effectiveness

Table 1: Summary of the evidence base for the effect of physical activity on mental illness and well-being

	Prevention		Therapy	
	Evidence	Effect	Evidence	Effect
Clinical depression	Low	Weak	Medium	Moderate
Other mental illnesses	Not enough evidence	-	Low	Weak
Mental well-being	N/A	N/A	Medium	Moderate
Mental function	Low	Moderate	Low	Weak
Social well-being	N/A	N/A	Low	Weak
State of evidence base graded as low, medium, or high, based on volume and rigor of research Strength of evidence graded as weak, moderate, or high, depending on typical effect				

Source: Department of Health. (2004). *At least five a week: Evidence on the impact of physical activity and its relationship to health: A report from the Chief Medical Officer.* London: Department of Health. Full details available at www.dh.gov.uk/publications (pp. 67–71).

studies in health service settings and applied the appropriate statistics. It is clear that rigor and volume of research have been held back by limited availability of research funding, particularly for larger, sophisticated studies. The potential of exercise has not been fully appreciated. Furthermore, the area has not been supported by research sponsorship from the pharmaceutical industry or other commercial organizations. However, the recent additions to the literature have improved considerably, and a broader array of evidence, including that derived from qualitative research, is becoming more accepted. This is important because of the difficulties of attracting and organizing patients with mental illness, as well as the heterogeneity of their conditions and responses.

1. **Can physical activity prevent mental disorders?** Six prospective observational studies have investigated the effect on subsequent depression. These studies indicate a reduction in risk of between 10 and 20 percent. One study covered a period of eighteen years. A recent study has established the effect over an eight-year period with older adults. Also two recent prospective studies suggest that remaining physically active through the elderly years produces a substantially reduced risk of serious decline in cognitive ability, such as dementia and Alzheimer's disease. Although further research is needed, these studies show that exercise has great potential for avoidance of mental disorders, particularly in later adulthood.

2. **Is activity effective in the treatment of depression and other disorders**? Fourteen randomized controlled trials (RCTs) and sixteen other experiments have investigated the effects of exercise on depression. Exercise produced a moderate positive effect (ES=0.72). Four studies show the exercise effect to be as good as psychotherapy and two as good as drug therapy over a six-month period. Positive effects have been seen from aerobic exercise, resistance training, and yoga. Although qualitative research has shown benefits, only limited quantitative research has been conducted with other mental illnesses, such as anxiety, panic attacks, obsessive-compulsive disorders, and schizophrenia.

From Research to Effective Practice

3. **Can activity improve mental well-being?** The answer to this question is a convincing yes. The question has been addressed mainly through acute responses to exercise and also to longer-term training studies and their effect on subjective well-being, mood, and self-perceptions.

Large-scale surveys confirm a moderate association between physical activity and indexes of subjective well-being. Furthermore, large numbers of experimental studies with a range of populations support a positive acute effect on mood for moderate-intensity exercise, even from bouts of walking for ten minutes.

Exercise can improve global self-esteem, but the relationship is fairly weak and inconsistent. It does improve physical self-perceptions including body image, perceived strength, fitness, and sports competence. About 70 percent of studies show these changes. Improvement is found in all populations, but is most likely in those who are initially low in self-perceptions.

4. **Can activity improve mental function?** This question has been investigated through the effects of exercise on cognitive function in older adults, academic performance in children, sleep, reactivity to stress, and anxiety levels. Recent robust data from trials has emerged that exercise can assist older people to maintain cognitive function through executive processes such as decision making and short-term memory.

Epidemiological studies indicate that exercisers report better quality sleep and that a single exercise bout is associated with increases in length and quality of sleep even in good sleepers. Two recent RCTs indicate that exercise programs improve sleep in poor sleepers.

There is a convincing volume of evidence that exercise can reduce state anxiety following a single bout and also that trait anxiety levels can be reduced through a regular program of exercise. Some evidence shows under experimental conditions that reactivity to stressors (as measured by blood pressure and other biomedical indicators) can be reduced with fitness training.

Although there is an association between academic performance and sport and activity in children, there is no reliable experimental evidence to support a causal link. Similarly, there is little robust evidence linking physical activity with productivity at work.

5. **Can activity improve social well-being?** There has been considerable political interest in the capacity of activity and sport to reduce crime and the effects of deprivation and inequality on people, and to increase sense of community. Such programs are difficult to evaluate and currently there is no substantial evidence base to establish the impact of exercise on social well-being. There is scope for research in this area, as there seems to be a potential benefit, particularly for older people and the trend for society to become more isolated and "cocooned" as walking has reduced.

Guidelines for Exercise for Mental Health

Currently no generic guidelines exist for exercise for mental health. There appear to be no consistent physiological or endocrinological mechanisms for determining mental health outcomes. It is likely that multiple mechanisms are operating and that the dominant process at any time will be dependent on the intensity of the exercise, the setting in which it takes place, and the preferences and characteristics of the individual. Research so far has indicated that aerobic, rhythmic exercise of moderate intensity such as dance, brisk walking, and cycling is successful, and also some evidence exists to indicate that resistance exercise can have a positive effect. Research has been too focused on gym-based activity, and more studies need to be conducted on expressive activities such as dance, daily walking and cycling to work, adventurous activities such as sailing and surfing, and recreational pastimes such as gardening and nature walking.

Reactions to the Evidence Base

The evidence is still regarded as relatively weak by many sectors, and skepticism remains among the medical and psychiatric fraternity. Perhaps because of the absence of cost-effectiveness evidence, central health policy makers until recently have been slow to advocate the use of exercise either as a preventive or treatment medium. But there is a very strong intuitive interest in exercise and a strong belief at the grassroots level that it has a critical role in the enhancement of well-being. This is reflected in the growth of many small projects and schemes that have used various forms of activity, such as community center sports, health walks, and leisure center classes to improve mental health.

Where Do We Go from Here?

- Rambling, nature walking
- More epidemiological evidence establishing reduced risk of mental illness
- More RCTs to establish the effectiveness of exercise in real settings (e.g., primary care, workplace, schools)
- Studies to address the effects of exercise and physical activity modality, dose, and setting
- Studies focusing on different mental conditions
- Studies investigating service acceptability and satisfaction
- Studies attempting to isolate mechanisms and test out theoretical tenets
- Acceptance of a diversity of research approaches (e.g., case studies, qualitative designs)

Final Thoughts

Sedentary living is largely a product of environmental change rather than individual choice. Psychologists cannot solve inactivity on their own. Central and regional policy is needed to make environments user friendly for activity. This will require the engagement of departments of health, education, transportation, and planning. In the meantime sufficient evidence supports policy that utilizes exercise as a therapy for improving well-being in those who have mental illnesses and those who do not. Once engaged, the evidence clearly shows that individuals will

promotion of mental and public health (Biddle, Fox, & Boutcher, 2000). Taken together the results also provide a strong argument for the promotion of mental health through regular exercise in general and membership of a health club in particular, for those members of society who are able to afford such membership. Many large companies and institutions have established health clubs on their premises. In view of findings related to decreased work absenteeism and increased productivity and general wellness (Biddle, Fox, & Boutcher, 2000), this trend is likely to continue.

Findings support earlier research on universal, essential, diverse, and contextual aspects of the exercise experience and its community effects (Edwards, 2002b). Biddle, Fox, & Boutcher (2000) and Edwards (2002b) have suggested various explanatory dynamics and mechanisms as to why physical activity that is sometimes physiologically identical to the physiological response of psychological stress promotes psychological well-being: detoxification of stress-related compounds; outlet for anger and hostility; a form of moving meditation; harmonization of essence, energy, and spirit; body, breath, and mind, especially in the form of the bionic, bio-electric energy of *chi*; enhanced feelings of self-esteem, self-efficacy, and mastery; periodic solitude and introspection; social support; human touch; reduction of muscular tension; endorphin theories; autonomic, biochemical (e.g., catecholamine), and hyperthermic changes; increased coping skills and somatic awareness (e.g., visceral feedback); training for competition, improved exercise facilities and environment; improvement in sleep and rest; and greater fitness to fight stress and disease. Unraveling of such multifactorial dynamics is a great future challenge, requiring holistic, systemic, collaborative, and synergistic research involving various interdisciplinary investigations.

The findings supported earlier research on the value of various forms of physical activity, exercise, and sport for the promotion of mental and public health (Biddle, Fox, & Boutcher, 2000). The findings also support and extend earlier studies on the general beneficial effects of moderate, aerobic, resistance, and team sport–oriented physical exercise on mental health and psychological well-being. These findings provide further motivation for the recommendation that health professionals in general and mental health workers in particular should routinely consider referrals of persons with mental health and/or stress-related problems to health clubs as well as recommending regular, moderate exercise suitable for and enjoyed by the particular client or patient concerned.

Psychotherapeutic Implications

In terms of psychotherapeutic implications, the lived body is mediator and anchor in the world. In dialogue with the world, it is a source of pre-reflective intentionality, meaning, and goal-directed behavior. Building on positive past experiences that have been bodily re-experienced as anchors is the phenomenological base for remedial breathing, progressive relaxation, systematic desensitization, visualization, and imagery used in exercise psychology, crisis intervention, solution-oriented counseling, multicultural counseling, and psychotherapy. This implies that researchers and practitioners in the field need to take great care in exploring and explicating various meanings of mental health, physical activity, and exercise before, during, and after therapeutically focused investigations and interventions.

Discussions with participants in the study in health clubs particularly pointed to two primary factors, which may be described as feel-good and social support factors. These factors are known to be related to mental health. Psychosocial support acts as a buffer for stressful life events. The research was limited to a psychosocial perspective on stress, with special reference to the perceptions and/or experiences of life events and coping with the stress of such events. Stress itself is an extraordinarily diverse phenomenon with biochemical, physiological, psychological, social, and spiritual concomitants with different effects on different people at different times and in different contexts. This research provided evidence towards the preventive and promotive mental health effects of physical exercise.

Empowerment

Promoting mental health through physical activity means an empowered context. Empowerment implies increased experienced control over the environment ranging from distal influences, such as politics and economics, through proximal influences, such as domestic and work situation, to personal factors, such as beliefs and feelings. Trickett (1996) has described community psychology in terms of contexts of diversity within a diversity of contexts. Along with recognition and celebration of diversity in choice of physical activity, exercise, and sport, and media encouragement of physical activity, appropriate financial support and empowerment initiatives are needed for people and contexts as well. Various academic, professional, governmental, and nongovernmental organizations are involved in supporting South African physical activity, sport, and exercise programs. The Sports Trust, chaired by Bruce Fordyce, former world ultra-marathon record holder, famous for his nine consecutive wins in the 90-kilometer Comrades Marathon, deserves special mention for its wonderful work in formerly disadvantaged communities. Besides Bruce Fordyce, some other noteworthy individuals who have advanced the mental health, physical activity, and public health link in South Africa include politicians Nelson Mandela, Steve Tswete, and Ngconde Balfour; academics Tim Noakes and Justice Potgieter; Sam Ramsami for elite sport; Ali Bacher for cricket; Irwin Khosa for soccer; and Silas Kunune for rugby.

Primary Health Care

The development and application of primary health care and the public health evidence base to improve the health of populations has grown considerably over the past three decades. Education with regard to the benefits of positive health behaviors such as regular physical activity in various contexts is internationally practiced in public health promotion campaigns. This research provides further support for this movement. This presentation is concerned with a preventive and promotive model of mental health, which has provided a valuable framework for contextualizing some physical activity research and interventions in South Africa. The research overview also is intended as a resource for other African and international research and interventions in the mental and public health fields with special reference to physical activity research and interventions in developing countries.

Community Psychology Implications

Great need remains for further qualitative research interventions into physical activity, exercise, and sport. Individual physical activity prescriptions by health professionals must be based on some form of qualitative enquiry. Many qualitative research studies have been criticized for simply providing descriptions, however thick, dense, or in-depth these may be. Yet, if participants chosen for their special experience of such a problem share both descriptions of and solutions to this problem in an ongoing action-reflection research spiral, this significantly increases the probability of effective problem solving for improving human life.

Conclusion

Physical activity, exercise, and sport have great potential for promoting health in general, and mental health and psychological well-being in particular, in their positive emphasis on survival, health, and strength through managing stress, coping with crises, and developing competencies, skills, supplies, and resources such as regular exercise and membership in some form of a health, sport, or exercise association.

Finally, the research has provided further evidence for a relationship that has received experiential and cultural recognition for millennia. Physical activity, exercise, and sport promote mental and public health. Given the limited percentage of the population engaged in regular, beneficial physical activity, the ongoing challenging task is to improve ways to promote such knowledge and behavior for the benefit of all.

Note: This research was supported by a South African National Research Foundation Grant for the project entitled "Methods of Health Promotion" and SPARC (Sport and Recreation New Zealand).

References

Biddle, S. J., Fox, K. R., & Boutcher, S. H. (2000). *Physical activity and psychological well-being*. London: Routledge.

Caplan, G. (1964). *Principles of preventive psychiatry*. New York: Basic Books.

Edwards, S. D. (2001). Promoting mental health: Community effects of the exercise experience. *International Journal of Mental Health Promotion, 3*(4), 7-15.

Edwards, S. D. (2002a). *Health promotion: community psychology and indigenous healing*. KwaDlangezwa: Zululand University.

Edwards, S. D. (2002b). *Promoting mental health through physical exercise*. KwaDlangezwa: Zululand University.

Edwards, S. D. (2003). Physical exercise and psychological wellness in health club members: A comparative and longitudinal study. *South African Journal for Research in Sport, Physical Education and Recreation, 25*(1), 23-33.

Edwards, S. D., Ngcobo, H. S. B., Edwards, D. J., & Palavar, K. (2005). Physical activity, psychological well-being and physical self-perception. *South African Journal for Research in Sport, Physical Education and Recreation 27*(1), 75-90.

Jahoda, M. (1958). *Current concepts of positive mental health*. New York: Basic Books.

Ryff, C. D. (1989). Happiness is everything, or is it? Explorations on the meaning of psychological well-being. *Journal of Personality and Social Psychology, 57*(6), 1069-1081.

Trickett, E. J. (1996). A future for community psychology: the contexts of diversity and the diversity of contexts. *American Journal of Community Psychology, 24*, 209-234.

immutable and both treatment and preventive interventions as ineffective. Such views tend to work strongly against monitoring and incorporating the findings of research, and in an emergent field such as this, the views may contribute to a lag between research and its implementation.

We also need to recognize that although the evidence base is growing, it is very patchy and not yet very strong. For universal prevention we need evidence that establishes that risk factors are known. We also need evidence that known risk factors are modifiable. When we look at the origins of the public health discipline, we can see that the methods of infectious disease epidemiology do not translate well into understanding the complexity of mental disorders. The classic intervention of John Snow in halting an epidemic of cholera in 1854 by removing the handle of the Broad Street water pump is hard to replicate. Mental disorders are not like cholera: Disorders such as schizophrenia and anxiety disorders may not be a single entity. Risk factors are complex and multi-factorial. Most risk factors have relatively weak effects. Moreover, many of the risk factors that have been identified are extraordinarily difficult to change.

In saying this I am not casting aspersions on the work of others. My own research into bulimia nervosa is fairly typical. Over several years' study into the apparent epidemic of bulimia nervosa in the 1980s, my colleagues and I identified the impact of several risk factors. At that time there was mounting evidence of a wide range of factors that might predispose young women to developing this disorder: gender, adolescence, puberty, culture, family environment, genes, socio-economic status, family breakdown, sexual abuse, parenting style, and parental mental disorder.

After several years of research it was possible to conclude only that:

> Beyond being female and adolescent, our knowledge of risk factors is fragmentary and incomplete. The strongest evidence of predisposing factors suggests a contribution of both genetics, biology and environment. Occurring at an increased rate in young women at the onset of sexual maturity, eating disorders are more likely in an adverse family environment in which sexual abuse has occurred, or a disturbed family environment in which there was either parental psychiatric disorder or a parenting style with low caring and nurturing but high levels of rules and control, or with low school achievement. (Bushnell, 1997, 336)

When we consider the complexity of parenting styles or sexual abuse—or, more broadly, the issues of poverty, poor housing, or inequality—clearly there is no single "pump handle" to remove. Furthermore, we need to understand more about how risk factors interact to increase vulnerability to mental illnesses, and to continue to broaden the scope of both research and interventions toward a multisectoral approach that includes promotion of resilience as well as reduction of risk factors.

We know from studies of the general population that rates of mental disorder in New Zealand are comparable to many other Western-style countries. The three big groups of disorder are mood disorders (mainly depression), substance use disorders (mainly alcohol-related disorders), and anxiety disorders (see Table 1). The Ministry of Health's modeling, based on this kind of data, suggests that about one person in five in the general population has a diagnosable mental disorder in any six-month period.

Table 1. Six-month prevalence of mental disorders: Percentage of adults in the New Zealand general population with a DSM-III diagnosable disorder

Disorder	Overall	Male	Female
Affective disorder	9	6	12
Substance use disorder	9	15	3
Anxiety disorder	8	5	12

Source: M. A. Oakley-Browne, P. R. Joyce, J. E. Wells, J. A. Bushnell, & A. R. Hornblow. (1989). Christchurch Psychiatric Epidemiology Study: Six month and other period prevalences. *Australian and New Zealand Journal of Psychiatry, 23*, 327-340.

We also know from the modeling of burden of illness undertaken by Murray and Lopez (1996) that the relative burden of mental disorder is expected to increase over the next fifteen years. Already, treatment services fail to address the needs of most persons with mental disorders, and most people with mental health problems either get help from their general practitioner or not at all. This raises the possibility that primary care–based services might function also as a platform for delivering selective preventive interventions. I would like to consider data from two local studies that support consideration of the role that primary care may play.

The first is a study by Sarah Roberts (2005) that shows that men whose partners have post-partum depression are themselves at substantially greater risk of psychological problems. Roberts contacted about a thousand women who had just had a baby and determined if they had post-partum depression. She then recruited 58 male partners of the women with post-partum depression and 116 partners of women without post-partum depression. She was able to show that the men with partners who were depressed were at about three times the risk of developing depression as measured by a Beck Depression Inventory greater than 13 (OR 3.1, 95% Confidence Interval [CI] 1.0-9.5). There was a similar risk of distress as measured by a GHQ greater than 5 (OR 2.6, 85%CI 1.1-6.0) and somatic symptoms as measured by a SPHERE Soma6 score (OR 2.8, 95%CI 1.0-7.4). While there is considerable awareness of the risk of post-partum depression among new mothers, this data suggests that consideration of the whole family may be indicated, especially if the new mother does have post-partum depression.

Secondly, I would like to look at mental disorder in primary care. The Mental health and General Practice Investigation (MaGPIe study) has explored the way in which people with psychological problems are dealt with in New Zealand general practices. The study has shown that 18.5 percent of people who are seen by their general practitioner will have a diagnosable mental disorder in the month prior to consultation. It also has shown that this 18.5 percent consists mainly of three groups of disorder—depression, anxiety disorder, and substance use disorder—and that there is a great deal of comorbidity among these three disorders (MaGPIe Research Group, 2003).

Although a prevailing belief exists within the literature on primary care that general practitioners (GPs) miss about half the psychological problems that their patients have, these GPs were good at identifying psychological problems, provided they had some degree of prior contact with the patient (see Table 2).

From Research to Effective Practice

Table 2. "Any" psychological problem identified by general practitioners in patients with a CIDI common mental disorder

Number of Consultations in Last 12 Months	General Practitioner Identified "Any" Psychological Problem (percentage)
0	28.8
1-2	56.2
3-4	65.4
5+	80.2

Source: The MaGPIe Research Group (2004). Frequency of consultations and general practitioner recognition of psychological symptoms. *British Journal of General Practice, 54,* 838-842.

Rates of mental disorder among Maori patients of GPs were higher than among non-Maori (see Table 3). Overall, Maori women patients were twice as likely as non-Maori women patients to have a diagnosable mental disorder. The rates of anxiety, depressive, and substance use disorders were all higher for Maori than for others seen by GPs. Treatment for psychological problems was offered by GPs at similar rates to both Maori and non-Maori. Although differences between Maori and non-Maori were observed in terms of social and material deprivation, higher rates of mental disorder among Maori patients of GPs compared to non-Maori cannot be accounted for by these differences alone. Interventions to address Maori mental health (whether by reducing risk factors for mental disorder; by promoting disclosure, early recognition, and intervention; or by ensuring access to acceptable and effective treatments) may need to take those factors explicitly into account.

Table 3. Mental disorders among Maori and non-Maori New Zealanders seen by their general practitioner

Ethnicity/Gender	N	Relative Risk	95% Confidence Interval
Maori men	28	1.07	0.4-2.5
Maori women	53	2.02	1.5-2.8
Non-Maori men	249	0.86	0.6-1.2

Source: The MaGPIe Research Group. (In press). Mental disorders among Maori people attending their general practitioner. *Australian and New Zealand Journal of Psychiatry.*

By comparing the independent assessment of mental disorder (using the Composite International Diagnostic Interview [CIDI]) for each participant at the time he or she was recruited into the study (time 1), then 12 months later (time 2), it is possible to get some ideas about the course of illness and rates of treatment. Of those well at time 1, 80.1 percent were well at time 2 and only 4 percent were treated, suggesting that not a great deal of inappropriate treatment is occurring.

Of those with a disorder in the last month at time 1, 64.1 percent had a disorder at time 2. Only 50.1 percent were treated during this year. This suggests that, provided there is continuity of care, GPs are good at spotting mental health issues, but that treatments often are either not delivered or delivered in such a way that they do not greatly alter the course of the disorder.

These data have implications for training. Primary care is strategically placed to integrate prevention and promotion, but the existing workforce is trained to deliver individual patient care and may be struggling even to do that in an optimal manner. Thinking at a population level requires knowledge, attitudes, and skills different from those held by the present primary care workforce.

It can be argued that three different sets of skills are required to enable effective prevention and promotion to happen: conceptualizing and planning prevention and promotion activities; planning and conducting both research and evaluation; and delivering programs through a diverse range of health, social, and other agencies. In order to foster the development of such an infrastructure, we need to utilize the existing (physical) health prevention and promotion infrastructure, promoting greater interaction between mental health and public health for training, to facilitate research and evaluation, and for models of program delivery.

New Zealand recently has adopted a policy framework that spells out the need for mental health prevention and promotion. This framework provides an excellent base from which to work. I believe we need both national and local initiatives that respond to this framework. This approach would be helped if the main postgraduate funding agencies could be persuaded to align their objectives with government policies. The Ministry of Health's Clinical Training Agency (CTA) is notorious for running its own agenda, and it has become almost impossible to get the Ministry of Education to fund new tertiary programs that they believe should be within the purview of the CTA, whether or not the CTA will agree to fund them itself.

It is important not to reinvent the wheel and to use existing infrastructure wherever it is possible to do so. This may require both a charm offensive on our public health colleagues and the provision of some incentives to get them involved in the development of training for mental health promotion and prevention. This would be reinforced by the development of international collaborations, but it remains vital that local people have ownership and investment in new initiatives, and that there is room to ensure adaptation of training for local cultures.

References

Bushnell, J. A. (1997). The prevention of eating disorders. In Ellis, P. M., and Collings, C. D., *Mental Health in New Zealand from a Public Health Perspective: Research Report No. 2.* Wellington: Ministry of Health.

The MaGPIe Research Group (J. A. Bushnell, D. McLeod, A. Dowell, C. Salmond, S. Ramage, S. Collings, P. Ellis, M. Kljakovic, & L. McBain). (2003). Psychological problems in New Zealand primary health care: A report on the Mental health and General Practice Investigation (MaGPIe). *New Zealand Medical Journal, 116,* 1171, U379.

The MaGPIe Research Group (2004). Frequency of consultations and general practitioner recognition of psychological symptoms. *British Journal of General Practice. 54,* 838-842.

The MaGPIe Research Group. (In press). Mental disorders among Maori people attending their general practitioner. *Australian and New Zealand Journal of Psychiatry.*

Murray, C. J. L., & Lopez, A. D., eds. (1996). *The global burden of disease: A comprehensive assessment of mortality and disability from diseases, injuries and risk factors in 1990 and projected to 2020.* Cambridge: Harvard School of Public Health on behalf of the World Health Organization and the World Bank (Global Burden of Disease and Injury Series, v I).

Oakley-Browne, M. A., Joyce, P. R., Wells, J. E., Bushnell, J. A., & Hornblow, A. R. (1989). Christchurch Psychiatric Epidemiology Study: Six month and other period prevalences. *Australian and New Zealand Journal of Psychiatry, 23,* 327-340.

Roberts, S. L. (2005). The psychological health and expressed emotion of men with partners who have postpartum depression. PhD thesis. University of Otago, New Zealand.

Development of Training and Expertise in the Promotion of Mental Health: Let's Get Real

Graham Martin, MD, FRANZCP, DPM
Professor and Director of Child and Adolescent Psychiatry
The University of Queensland, Australia

The first thing to say about mental health is that it has been going on for a long time. It is not an invention of the 1960s U.S. mental hygiene movement, not a hip new way of repackaging the prevention of mental illness, and not just a novel topic in university curricula. It is an essential part of what it means to be human. It may come as a surprise that there are people who have given not a scrap of thought to their mental health, and yet lifelong are mentally healthy people. They are generally happy people with a specified role in life, surrounded by the rituals of ordinary everyday family life. They have a clear sense of their life's work, contribute to their immediate community, are prepared for some of life's crises, and they eventually die with a sense of completion and fulfillment surrounded by those they love. Many of these folk are quite ordinary. They have limited means but live within them, have a limited horizon but think it is beautiful, do not have aspirations that are unlikely to be met, do not have access to electronic wizardry (but then are not poisoned by the detritus of modern-day advertising, the shallowness of repeated sitcoms, or media insistence on providing the worst of the daily international news in graphic detail). Their diet may have deficiencies, but they compensate with supplements whose sources are passed down through generations of oral history. Their oral hygiene may not be the best, but that does not stop them from acknowledging all people with that most basic of human connections, the smile. They are not restless, frustrated, anxious, traumatized, or depressed.

The second thing to say is that there are many people who promote mental health without having heard that it is important. The young mother who holds her pregnant belly and talks gently to her unborn child is developing a relationship that culminates initially in that first weeping smile of recognition after the birth, when the child, laid on the breast, opens his or her eyes in peace and holds the maternal gaze. The young father playing soccer who dribbles the ball past a four year old, but then avoids frustration in the child by dribbling back, pretending to be tackled, falling over with drama—letting the child run away with the ball, much to the amusement of all. The parent who gives up time to go into school, unpaid, to help his or her child and others' children with reading. The ordinary teacher in an ordinary school where they might never have heard of the whole school approach to mental health, who, nevertheless, praises the child struggling to take the first steps toward the idea of symbolism inherent in learning algebra. The bloke listening attentively to a workmate "spilling his guts" about a failed relationship while they both work the production line.

I think secretly we *all* know how to promote mental health. The problem is remembering.

So why all the fuss? Why this current fascination? My best guess would be that worldwide we are failing to keep pace with the burden of mental illness (Murray & Lopez, 1997). There have been myriad advances over the last twenty years, billions poured into "mental health" research, and hopes of a cure for even the most serious of illnesses being just round the corner. However, even with the new hope from the early explorations of the human genome, we know that mental illness is increasing and that the cost burden is going to wipe out health budgets after 2020 if a radical change does not occur.

The most holistic model to help our understanding of the origins of mental illness is that of "stress-vulnerability" (Falloon et al., 1998). It appears today that stress is getting out of hand. Whether we look at stressors from the biological point of view (pollution, fast foods) or the psychological (pace of life, aspirational expectation), the social (reduced connectedness, family fragmentation) or the cultural (loss of groundedness, loss of meaning), as humans, we increasingly are stressed out. As is clear from the existing research, this translates into restlessness, frustration, anxiety, post-traumatic states, depression, drug and alcohol abuse, and the precipitation of other psychiatric disorders. It seems that we are unable to stop the progression, whether at a personal, community, national, or international level.

So we have turned to the "vulnerability" side of the equation. If we are always going to be under ever-increasing stress, can we be better prepared to manage it? If we think about what we know of other aspects of life for a moment, it does appear that there are models or examples we can use. They are mostly based in what seems to be central for human beings—the wish to be physically healthy, well, successful. One example of this relates to the billions of dollars in vitamins and minerals swallowed every year by the population in the belief that we will be better protected from a number of minor irritants like the common cold. We could call this "ensuring optimum nutrition" or "ensuring environmental responsiveness" of the internal environment. Another example is that of inoculation. Many of the major infective scourges of the world have been reduced by population-based inoculation—either in childhood or preparatory to traveling to an area where the risks are high. A different trick in the face of a known risk is to use protection. Three common examples would be boiling water before drinking in suspected places of pollution, the use of the condom in avoiding sexually transmitted diseases, or more recently the use of sunscreen or sun suits to avoid excess exposure to ultraviolet rays. Another trick is that of practice. If we think of the training of soldiers preparatory to going to war, we would not send them unless they knew how to use a gun—that is, to look after it, take it apart to clean it for maximum efficiency, know how to load it, know the possible range, and have practiced over and over to gain accuracy. But there is another aspect of this training and practice. The soldier has to be prepared to shoot someone on command in combat (and not believe it to be murder).

We all know about these solutions. They are as common as putting on a seat belt for driving, and knowing that if you drink and drive you are an idiot. Similarly, I would argue that every single one of us knows deep down that mental health, in terms of emotional well-being, prepares us for adverse circumstances, ensures an optimum response, is protective in situations of risk. In some circumstances the gaining of aspects of mental health involves inoculation. As we mature, for instance, we manage more and more complex adverse circumstances. Our internal system (in this case, the mind) has been challenged and knows how to respond. Perhaps two aspects of what I was talking about before that we do not deliberately do are to prepare as if we were going into a battle zone (and life in many ways can be conceptualized as a battle zone), and we do not consciously believe that we need to practice our mind skills.

At this point you may ask: "What has all this got to do with training?" I need to point out that the perspective I have taken is a very individual one. This is deliberate on two grounds. First, we are all individuals, however strongly we may be connected to our families or our culture. Ultimately we dream alone, and ultimately we die alone, even if surrounded by those who care. One part of what we are trying to achieve in mental health promotion is the personal optimum for all individuals, given their unique genetics, their individual life trajectory, the sum of their experiences, and the family and cultural context in which they live. We are not trying to make everyone the same. Not everyone will suffer mental illness (even if the percentages keep creeping up). But given that we cannot predict with any accuracy, yet, who will get a mental illness, every one of us should have the mental preparation, and preparedness, to deal with such an adverse event in the best way known.

The second ground for taking this individual perspective is that it goes to the heart of teaching and training. I don't know many people who can listen to a conference presentation or attend an intensive teaching session about policy and come out with the ideas anchored in such a way that they could do the presentation. But when teaching is anchored in individual or personal examples, when it resonates with the internal world of the student, listeners are more easily able to rebuild such a lecture or seminar and find their own solutions—from the individual level right through to the public health perspective. Furthermore, while I believe it is important for professionals in a field to know about relevant policy and government strategy, most of them want someone else to be involved in developing it. They just want to do their job, preferably one on one, preferably during daylight hours and not on weekends, and preferably without having to write anything. Similarly, for many professionals the mere mention of the public health approach leaves them confused; they just glaze over. It is hard enough to get many professionals in the mental health field to think about the systemic implications of an illness and the need to work with family members, let alone think about the community or cultural level. And the national level is best left to politicians, bureaucrats, and high flyers!

Let me give you some idea of what I think emotional well-being is about before we look at some specifics about training. I think it is about self-knowledge and self-awareness. More than that, it is about taking pleasure in who you are. So: "I know that I am—and I take great pleasure in it."

It is about meaning that is life affirming. That is: "I feel that my life has meaning—I am worthwhile and have some purpose." This may be at the level of individual relationships, but increasingly I think we are coming to learn more about the place of spirituality and that sense of connectedness to something higher.

An essential part is connectedness. Despite what I have said about dreaming and dying alone, connectedness is a big part of what makes us who we are. We are, in part, reflections of how others see us. So: "I feel connected to place, people, and process—I belong—I am committed to those who depend on me." The last part of this is about the reciprocity that exists in relationships. An integral part of mentally healthy beings is their commitment to those with whom they are connected.

Mental health is about skills, particularly the ability to turn thought into action, appropriate to the context. So: "I know what I am able to do—and I contribute whatever I can." Inherent in this is a sense of optimism—a "can do" approach—that is a strong part of the solution-focused approach. I came across a wonderful statement relating to this the other day, which may or may not make sense to you. You don't have to struggle to solve a problem. What you just have to do is: "Remember how you solved this problem last time." It is probably a Buddhist Koan and has a context in a belief about past lives. But I have to tell you, it seems to work. Try it.

Finally, I have taken every step along the way to prepare myself for what is to come—that is, "I am prepared." We prepare for everything else we do that makes us who we are. Why should we believe that mental health just comes along without training and practice?

So with those thoughts, I want to spend the last few minutes breaking up training in mental health and its promotion into some essential questions: Who? What? When? Where? Why? How? How much? In fact, though, here I focus on the Who and the What.

Who?

Given the mantra that seems to be emerging from the mental health promotion movement that "it is everyone's business," we could have a serious problem. But if I am right about the innate skills that may exist, we do *not* have to train everyone. We have to identify where mental health is being naturally promoted and ensure that that we don't get in the way of those behaviors that Antonovsky called salutogenic (Lindstrom & Eriksson, 2005). Let me suggest two examples. If Tom Insel was right in his wonderful presentation on the brain, we simply have to support "licking and grooming mothers." We might have to do more for those who do not lick and groom so much, perhaps training them to do so more and ensuring that maternal stress levels are kept low for this group. If I translate that into the human environment, then what we know is that positive attachment increases both the numbers of cells and the numbers of connections between cells in the prefrontal cortex of the baby, and it is in this place that so many important higher cognitive functions are developed—judgment, empathy, compassion, to name a few. But in mothers at risk because of young age, socio-economic adversity, depression, lacking in partner or grandparent support, this may not be so easy. To provide the best brain substrate for the future for a child to reach his or her optimum, it is crucial to get this bit of "epigenetics" as right as we can at the start. Postnatal care so often stops at six weeks. This needs to be extended, and the professionals involved in supporting this and providing parent education must understand the long-term implications of what they do. If we are serious about this translation of research into practice, then a serious look at the economic support process for new parents needs to occur. One-off subsidies are nowhere near sufficient.

Another example would be the natural mental health promotion that goes on in schools. Teachers would not call it this, even if they recognize the long-term implications of the process. But if you look at a list of individual protective factors, such as in the Australian monograph on promotion, prevention, and early intervention (Commonwealth Department of Health and Aged Care, 2000), it is immediately obvious that teachers are doing a considerable amount in building protective factors toward future mental health. Some of that has been enhanced and clarified in Australia with such programs as MindMatters, in which curriculum-based courses have been developed on such issues as resilience. Professional development has been a major part of the program—simply helping teachers to do what they already do, but better.

I believe we can take a life trajectory and identify clear points along that trajectory where promotion under lots of guises is occurring with a wide range of others doing the job. As a movement we have to do nothing more than acknowledge, support, and avoid interfering. Equally in the same exercise we will find gaps to be filled.

What?

Our courses have been developed with an Australian government grant. They are targeted specifically at professionals working across health, the community, and public health.

I only have time to make one point that I believe to be central. First, I do not believe that mental health promotion is just a public health intervention, something remote and for others to do. I believe it is a way of thinking, and it is this that has become central to our graduate and post-graduate teaching. It may not be appropriate for all mental health professionals from whatever discipline to consider their role in public health. It is, however, crucial for them to have unpacked the construct of mental health (as has been done in the policies and strategies I have mentioned) and know how to work with their clients to develop strengths towards the kind of resilience that holds up under adversity. Let us take the most important example, that of someone with a mental illness. When the crisis is over, a management plan is in place, and the time for transfer back into the community comes, the promotion of mental health gives the best

From Research to Effective Practice

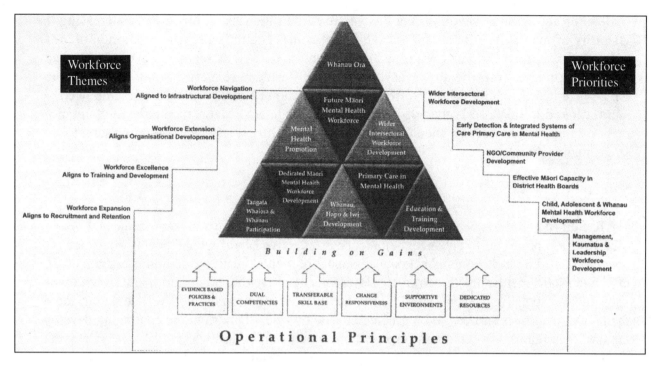

Fig. 1. Nga Aronui Framework

As depicted in the framework, eight key workforce pathways (each depicted within a triangle) have been identified for the future development of the Maori mental health workforce.[3] The pathways represent an innovative and holistic approach and recognize the dynamic components that contribute to strong and effective workforce development.

Pathway seven (depicted in the third level of triangles on the left) acknowledges the importance of mental health promotion to Maori mental health workforce development. The strategic direction of the pathway encompasses the aim to enhance the capability of Maori to encourage supportive living, learning, and working environments that foster positive mental health outcomes.

The promotion of well-being and the objective of enhancing the capacity of people to live full lives underlie the importance of mental health promotion and moving towards whanau ora (maximizing health gains for families). Promoting mental health and whanau ora can happen anywhere "where people live, work, play, party, relax, shop, study, pray, meet, exercise, or receive treatment."[4]

The destigmatization of mental health by mental health providers, wider Maori health and social service sectors, tertiary and secondary training institutions, and wider Maori communities is critical to strengthening mental health promotion and enhancing the capacity of tangata whaiora and whanau to make informed life decisions and enhance their mental health and well-being.[5] The promotion of holistic well-being (as outlined in Te Whare Tapa Wha), the use of Maori models of health (such as Te Pae Mahutonga[6]), and freely accessible information about Maori mental health and well-being also are essential to mental health promotion.

Therefore, pathway seven of Kia Puawai Te Ararau focuses on proactively increasing the visibility of mental health and understanding of mental health issues, the promotion of holistic mental health and whanau ora based on prevention as well as recovery, and greater access to information about resilience, resourcefulness, self-esteem, relationship building, supportive environments, parenting skills, life skills, prevention of mental illness, and empowerment. Linked to this also is the need for accessible dedicated Maori mental health human resource support services to encourage and support healthy workplace programs such as stress management.

Summary

Te Rau Matatini has been working in a number of different ways in using dedicated Maori pilot research programs to enhance the practice of effective Maori mental health workforce development. The inclusion and acknowledgement of mental heath promotion is essential for effective Maori mental health workforce development; strengthening Maori mental health services to be responsive to mental health need and greater understanding of well-being outside of the mental health sector need to be progressed side by side. Supporting the continuing development of communities, workforces, organizations, youth, and Maori whanau all have synergies with the promotion of mental health and well-being and share the common overall goal of whanau ora, supporting families to achieve their maximum health and well-being.

Notes

[1] Te Puni Kokiri. (1996). *Nga Ia o the Oranga Hinengaro Maori: Trends in Maori mental health 1984–1993.* Wellington: Author.

[2] Durie, Mason. (2004, February 9-11). Kahui Pou Book Launch. In *Te rau tipu Maori child and adolescent mental health workforce development conference proceedings.* DVD. Palmerston North: Te Rau Matatini and The Werry Centre.

[3] The pathways have been numbered for ease of reference and are not ranked in a particular order.

[4] Mental Health Foundation. (2004). *Making a positive difference in people's lives: A recipe book for promoting mental health and well-being.* Draft. (Auckland: Author), 16.

[5] Joubert, N., & Raeburn, J. (1998). Cited in Mental Health Foundation (2004).

[6] Te Pae Mahutonga outlines elements of modern health promotion, which include four key tasks: mauriora (cultural identity), waiora (physical environment), toiora (health lifestyles), and te oranga (participation in society), as well as the two pointers, Nga manukura (community leadership) and te mana whakahaere (autonomy).

From Research to Effective Practice

CLOSING SESSION

Thank You to the Host Organization

L. Patt Franciosi, PhD
President
World Federation for Mental Health
United States

It is my pleasure to introduce this closing session where we review the activities of the past three days. I would like to offer warm thanks to our hosts from the Mental Health Foundation of New Zealand for their generous welcome and the thoughtfulness of the arrangements. This conference has had an unusual spirit of grace and hospitality. Those of us from abroad have learned much about new developments in promotion and prevention in this part of the world, and if by the end we have only had time to learn a few words of the Maori language, we have enjoyed becoming familiar with its cadences and waiata (songs). Thank you for all you have done to make this an exceptional meeting. In every respect it has surpassed expectations, and we have taken another big step forward in advancing the cause of promotion and prevention.

At this point, it is appropriate to look at the work of the last few days and appreciate what has been accomplished. Our speaker is Peter McGeorge, well known to the Mental Health Foundation here and also to the World Federation for Mental Health. He will offer an overview of the conference. We also will have an announcement from Beverly Long, and after that Clemens Hosman has something to say. Lastly, we will hear concluding remarks from Alison Taylor, chief executive of the Mental Health Foundation of New Zealand, and the person who led the hard-working local team that made this such a special event.

Overview of the Conference

Peter McGeorge, MB ChB, FRANZCP
Oceania Vice President
World Federation for Mental Health
New Zealand

Kia Orana tatou
Talofa lava
Nisa bula vinaka
Malo Lelei
Taloha ni
Fakalofa atu
Tena kotou, tena kotou, tena kotua katoa

I am a board member and the regional vice president for Oceania of the World Federation for Mental Health, a board member of the Mental Health Foundation of New Zealand, and a mental health professional. We are all originally migrants to our country, Aoteoroa/New Zealand. My father's family traveled here from Scotland; my mother's family, of the Marama tribe, came here from the Cook Islands. I am a husband and the proud father of three young men.

Over the past three days we have been on a journey of discovery. Blown by the winds of our aspiration for a peaceful, just, and harmonious world, we have sailed in the spirit of the ancient navigators of Polynesia to find new places and ways in which the human spirit might flourish.

The ancient navigators traversed the huge distances of the Pacific in search of new territories and, later, as a means of maintaining complex relationships involving gift exchange and habitation. They defined and came to know currents, swells and tides, the weather patterns, the stellar constellations, and the habits of birds and fish that enabled them to establish coordinates of location and the ways in which others might follow. On these journeys the visionaries, the master navigators, and the tohunga, or shamans, sustained the hopes of and quelled the fears of their fellow sailors—warriors, chiefs, and pioneer families.

In a similar spirit we have, over past decades, embarked on perilous journeys into the unknown, where at first we had only the stars to guide us and our visionaries, such as George Albee and Beverly Long, who happily have been with us at this conference, to urge us forward. And we did so at first through faith and intuition, and later by the maps we began to inscribe of the psychological and social spaces that had become, like the Polynesian navigators of the Pacific, our oceans of realization. Now we have not only the maps, we have claimed territories. We have proven their existence to our fellows and have begun the process of establishing relationships and the means by which we might provide equitable sustenance for our people.

Join me in recovering and affirming the journey of our conference.

It was an honor to be invited to speak on behalf of you all at the powhiri, or welcome, at Orakei—the Marae of the Ngati Whatua iwi, or tribe. They are the Mana Whenua, the people of the land, for the Auckland isthmus and those further north. In becoming one with them, our conference was always going to be well grounded. And so it came to be—and all the more so because we were so well supported by the New Zealand government, with Minister of Health Annette King and Associate Minister Ruth Dyson. Adding to the mana or spiritual status of the conference was the patron of the Mental Health Foundation, the previous Head of State Sir Paul Reeves, and former First Lady of the USA Mrs. Rosalynn Carter.

These things matter to the people of Aoteoroa/New Zealand and the people of the Pacific. We are increasingly a people-based society whose rituals parallel and give expression to the combined history of our people.

In a similar fashion the cartography for the conference was laid out by the conference organizers: the World Federation for Mental Health, the Carter Center, the Clifford Beers Foundation, and the Mental Health Foundation of New Zealand, making sure that human process dominated the structure and proceedings of what we have all enjoyed.

This conference did not happen by accident. It has had direction and purpose in terms of advancing the benefits of mental health promotion and the prevention of mental and behavioral disorders in a systematic way. The matrix was based on developmental stages and the core issues focal to promotion and prevention. This said, we are still like the ancient navigators of the Pacific with more to define than has been defined and territories to claim than have been claimed.

At least, however, and perhaps to the amazement of some, the key stellar constellations and land masses have begun to be defined. Standing on the prow of our canoe, or waka, with keen eyes on the horizon are the pioneers such as George Albee and Bev Long. In the rear of the waka, with their hands on the helm, are the new pioneers like Clemens Hosman, Mason Durie, and the representatives of a range of international organizations that either are or are to be part of the promotion and prevention (P&P) consortium: the World Federation for Mental Health, The Carter Center, The Clifford Beers Foundation, the International Union for Health Promotion and Education.

At the policy forum that preceded the conference, the scene was set for the days to come by warriors such as Charles Curie, David Morris, Thomas Insel, Helen Herrman, and Janice

From Research to Effective Practice

Wilson, with questions being raised regarding the nature and forms of "evidence," where the most gains could be made in terms of policy development and implementation, and also whether a life-stage focus or a more inclusive community focus is best for the allocation of our limited funding.

These questions and others were picked up after the formal conference opening by Mrs. Rosalynn Carter, Shekhar Saxena of the World Health Organization, Thom Bornemann, Beverly Long, Rob Moodie, and Eva Jané-Llopis. International advocacy and collaboration, the gains of P&P compared with treatment, the use of Internet technology to establish databases of what works, and innovative approaches to social inclusion whetted our appetite for the journey ahead. Rob Moodie's succinct comment about not needing a randomized control trial for a parachute stuck with me.

In line with the emphasis given to the needs and status of indigenous people in New Zealand, Mason Durie presented what I'm sure will be one of the papers that will endure in your minds, as did the swells and currents of the original navigators for future sailors and settlers. His elegant thoughts on indigeneity gave cause for us to question our assumptions about socio-economic status as the dominant factor in social disadvantage. He was to be beautifully supported the following day by Kathie Irwin speaking of the pioneer work of Te Kohanga Reo, or Maori language nests, in New Zealand. If Kathie, Materoa Mar, and Kayleen Katene are products of the Maori renaissance their ancestors will be truly proud!

Leslie Swartz from South Africa began to share the experience of his country after Mason. It was a tongue-tip taste of the great wisdom that has been accumulated in that country and the complexities of the tasks faced in less developed areas of the world.

On Wednesday afternoon Shekhar Saxena, Clemens Hosman, and Helen Herrman launched the work they had done with Rob Moodie and others on case studies in P&P—ocean maps for the future—and then we were treated to an evaluation *tour de force* by Margaret Barry of the Department of Health Promotion of the National University of Ireland, Galway. I thought to myself that while an academic, she had spent a good deal of time with real people in real situations—enough at least to allow her to make maps that didn't let follower sailors end up on the rocks. I thought there was even a good chance of the kumara, or sweet potato, growing where she had been!

Full of modesty and with great beauty and clarity, we then had a further caution sounded in researching and working with Pacific people by Airini of the Education Department of Auckland University. Do you remember her metaphor of the Tapa cloth and how you had to strip the outer bark of certain trees to get to it? This was a map to rival the advice given to Captain James Cook on dealing with the indigenous people he would meet on his journeys.

Our minds bulging with maps and our hearts with aroha, or love, inspired by singing and passionate, focused people, on Thursday we had a true navigator of the territories of social inclusion speak to us in the person of David Morris. And then we had Kathryn Power talk to us about the relationship between P&P and service development for people with mental illnesses. For those of you who work in the latter field, Kathryn's dynamic personality and commitment came to us like a refreshing breeze—a zephyr to fill our sails for our work back home and a perfect transition to the focus that was given to the rights and needs of service users in the next session on the media and human rights.

It was inspiring to hear again from Mrs. Carter and to have her messages powerfully reinforced and expanded by Liz Sayce, director of the Disability Rights Commission in the United Kingdom, about the central importance of how the media can best represent the rights and experience of consumers. Gerard Vaughan, in commenting on the presentations, then spoke of New

Zealand's experience with its anti-stigmatization campaign, and John Francis presented his cartoon of the Team Media. Others rounded out the media messages the following day. But do you remember the Like Minds, Like Mine TV presentations? It made us very proud of our ancestors who discovered this country.

For me a highlight of the conference was the fortuitous session that allowed consumers and indigenous people to speak of their concerns about the P&P movement. The preservation of diversity and personal experience is critical in any high-level strategy for the future.

On Thursday afternoon more treats for our three kite (pronounced kitty) baskets of knowledge, with Thomas Insel's remarkable summary of the latest brain and genetic research and later Charles Curie's presentation of the work of the Substance Abuse and Mental Health Services Administration in the United States. (I must apologize to speakers Ken Fox, Steve Edwards, John Bushnell, Graham Martin, and Kirsty Maxwell-Crawford, whose presentations I was unable to hear prior to my presentation.)

But I was able to have the privilege of being in the audience when George Albee spoke. It is only right that when the waka touches shore that a Chief of the Mana (status) of George should have a special place in the ceremonies. Thank you, George, for once again specifying the key issues, with such passion, wisdom, and commitment, the varieties of ways in which mental disorders are recognized and expressed, the evils of sexism, and above all else, the need to have children who are wanted in this world.

How would I summarize the main issues for the way forward?

- Continuing collaboration through the consortium, which Clemens Hosman will describe
- Multilingualism (being able to speak in terms of, and recognize the languages of, different schools of knowledge in mental health P&P)
- Intellectual rigor
- Re-integration of the mind-body-spirit division
- A broad view of evidence, taking into account the measurable and experiential parameters
- Mindfulness of the needs and rights of service users and indigenous peoples

In concluding I would like to thank all the speakers, the chairs, the presenters of workshop sessions, the organizers, and in particular Mrs. Rosalynn Carter, Sir Paul Reeves, Thom Bornemann, Alison Taylor, Materoa Mar, Michael Murray, and the World Federation for Mental Health. You provided us with fun and opportunities to bond. But above all I think you have done an excellent job in achieving your objective, namely to explore, map, and bring back for later travelers knowledge of the territories from research to practice in the ocean of the promotion of mental health and the prevention of mental and behavioral disorders. You have been true navigators for us all!

May your journeys home be safe and your reunions with your loved ones tender.

Tena kotou, tena kotou, tena kotou katoa.

At the podium during the conference's closing session, Beverly Long announced her retirement as chair of the Global Consortium for Promotion and Prevention in Mental Health, formerly the Biennial Conference Committee. She told the audience that Clemens Hosman of Radboud and Maastricht Universities had been selected to serve as the new chair, along with L. Patt Franciosi, president of the World Federation for Mental Health, as vice chair. Prof. Hosman offered the following remarks.

PRESENTATION ABSTRACTS

PRESENTATION ABSTRACTS

1.1   Research on Promotion and Prevention Worldwide: Older People

Opportunities for Cost-Effective Prevention of Late-Life Depression: An Epidemiological Approach

Filip Smit
Trimbos Institute
The Netherlands

Background. Clinically relevant late-life depression has a prevalence of 16 percent. Through its burden of disease and unfavorable prognosis, it is further associated with substantial societal costs. From the public health perspective, depression prevention may thus be an attractive, if not imperative, means to generate health gains and reduce future costs. The research question is how to target depression prevention at high-risk groups in order to generate the maximum health gains against the lowest cost.

Methods. Prospective cohort study of factors that predict the onset of depression in a large (N=2,200) unselected sample of older people (55-85 years at baseline) in the community. Clinically relevant depression was measured with the Center for Epidemiological Studies Depression Scale. For each of the risk factors (and their combinations), indexes of potential health gain and the effort (costs) required to generate those health gains were calculated.

Results. In every five cases of clinically relevant late-life depression, one case is an incident case. Consequently, depression prevention must play a key role in reducing the influx of new cases. This is best done by targeting prevention at older people who have depressive symptoms, experience functional impairment, and have a small social network, in particular women as well as people who have attained only a low educational level or suffer from chronic diseases.

Conclusion. Targeting prevention on the selected high-risk groups could help to reduce the incidence of depression and is likely to be more cost-effective than alternative approaches. Our paper further shows that we have the methodology at our disposal to conduct ante-hoc cost-benefit analysis in preventive psychiatry. This helps to set a rational research and development agenda before embarking on testing the cost-effectiveness of interventions in time-consuming and expensive trials.

Risk Factors for Depressive Symptoms in Older Chinese Migrants in Auckland: Implications for Prevention

Max Abbott, PhD
Professor, Psychology and Public Health
Auckland University of Technology
Auckland, New Zealand

Depression is the major psychological problem affecting older people and the risk factor most often associated with suicide. In the U.S. older foreign-born Chinese have significantly higher suicide rates than their U.S.-born counterparts and other older people. Given the increase in numbers of older Chinese migrants, the investigators sought information about depression in this population, including identification of risk factors. One hundred sixty-two Chinese migrants aged 55 years and older living in the community were interviewed using a Chinese version of the Geriatric Depression Scale and measures of stressful life events, morbid conditions, self-rated health, acculturation, social support, and service utilization. Twenty-six percent met criteria for depressive symptomatology. Risk factors included time in New Zealand, low social support and satisfaction with support, low New Zealand cultural orientation, language and acculturation difficulties, reliance on public transportation, self-rated poor health, cardiovascular disease, having an illness in the past year, higher doctor consultations, and difficulty accessing health services. Although the overall prevalence of mental disorder for this sample appears to be similar to that of older people in the general population, the findings extend understanding of the adjustment and mental health of migrants and identify focal points for prevention. Social support and aspects of acculturation appear to be particularly relevant in this regard.

Meeting of the Minds: A Library-Based Program Promoting Positive Aging

Marie Hull-Brown
Mental Health Foundation of New Zealand
Auckland, New Zealand

In response to requests from older people for more mental stimulation in our approaches to positive aging, in 2001 the Mental Health Foundation and Age Concern Auckland approached Auckland City libraries' access specialist to seek support for a program to "stretch older people's minds." This program fit well with the libraries' "Lifelong Learning" policy and their marketing strategy to deliver improved access to library services for older people. Consultation with community librarians resulted in the planning of hour-long programs for older people, with a variety of themes relevant to the interests of the local community. Every month each of the sixteen community libraries would host a program called Meeting of the Minds. During October 2001, the first month of the project, twelve of the libraries took part, with programs ranging from Fun with Word Games to growing salad vegetables and fruit in containers. The three themes that proved most popular with persons attending were celebrating people and their cultures, including genealogy, local history, traditional festivals, and different cultural experiences; acquiring new skills and knowledge, particularly computer literacy; and reading for stimulation with invited authors speaking about their books, book clubs, and interactive discussions about selected books. An evaluation, both quantitative and qualitative, was conducted between April and July 2002 to assess whether the program was encouraging positive aging and increasing access for older adults to library services and collections. The findings were positive, and the programs are now an established feature in the libraries' calendar. Two years later, a second survey provided further information about this project and will be examined to assess the program's place in New Zealand's Positive Ageing Strategy.

1.2 Research on Promotion and Prevention Worldwide: Preschool

Preventing Externalizing Behavior Problems from Early Childhood: Pilot Research for a Universal Parenting Program in Primary Health Care

Dr. Jordana Bayer
Royal Children's Hospital
Melbourne, Australia

Objective. In an integrated approach to reducing externalizing behavior problems, primary prevention strategies would be partnered by targeted secondary prevention and skilled tertiary services. We report pilot findings from a universal preventive parenting program aimed at 8- to 15-month-old children designed to be sustainable in the primary care setting.
Design. Pre-post pilot study of program delivered by child health nurses
Setting. Well-child clinics, Melbourne, Australia
Participants. Fifty-seven mothers of infants attending their 8-month developmental visit
Main outcome measures. Child Behavior Checklist (CBCL/1.5-5) at 18 months; Parent Behavior Checklist at 12 and 18 months
Results. Ninety-five percent of mothers reported that they would recommend the program to friends. Nurses found the program feasible to conduct in a busy primary care setting. Information about strategies to encourage positive behavior and manage misbehavior in young children were rated as "quite" to "extremely" useful by 89 percent and 91 percent of mothers, respectively. Maternal perception of an infant as "difficult" at 8 months predicted toddler behavior problems at 18 months (r=.41, p<.001). When compared with mothers who attended the whole program, mothers who did not were more likely to report greater continuity of temperament difficulty at 8 months to behavior difficulty at 18 months (r=.32 vs. r=.58 respectively). Furthermore, mothers of 18-month-olds reporting behavior problems were more likely to report higher levels of stress/anxiety/depression (r=.5, p=.01).
Conclusions. A brief universal program of anticipatory guidance to prevent toddler externalizing behavior problems was useful and acceptable to mothers, and feasible in the primary care setting.

Maternal Perception of Infant Temperament and Psychosocial Risk Factors

Veronika Ispanovic-Radojkovic
Institute of Mental Health
Belgrade, Serbia and Montenegro

Objective. The aim of the study was to explore the relationships between maternal perceptions of the temperament of their 3-month-old babies and the presence/absence of risk factors for psychosocial problems in children. The research is a part of the European Early Promotion Project, a multicenter study of the effects of early intervention in primary health care.
Sample. The sample consisted of 141 mothers with a 3-month-old baby living in Belgrade, Serbia. They were recruited by trained home visiting nurses during their regular visits to families with newborns. Each family was assessed as "in need" (44 percent) or "in no need" (56 percent) of further support. Families with severe psychosocial risk (psychotic illness of parents or

severe developmental difficulty of the child) were not included in the study.

Method. Perceptions of infant temperament were assessed by the mothers completing the Infant Characteristics Questionnaire (Bates, 1992), and risk factors were determined by maternal interviews conducted by independent research psychologists. An operational grouping of risk variables and an index of cumulative risk was developed specifically for the study in Belgrade.

Results. Maternal perception of negative temperamental features of their babies (fussy, difficult, inadaptable, unpredictable) significantly correlated with the following risk factors: poor financial situation, discordant marital relationship, lack of social support, father's indifferent or negative attitude towards the baby, and a poor mother-child relationship. A strong positive correlation also was found between the number of risk factors and negative temperament. There was very good agreement between the assessment of family risk as conducted separately by the home visiting nurses and the independent researchers.

Treatment of Noncompliant Behavior Among 4- to 8-Year-Old Children: Results from a Norwegian Replication Study

Bo Larsson
RBUP
Department of Neuroscience
ABUP, Trondheim, Norway

In the present controlled trial, 127 families with a child aged 4 to 8 years with a diagnosis of ODD or CD, participated in an evaluation of Webster-Stratton treatment. The families were randomized into basic parent training (PT), PT combined with child therapy (CT) (the Dinosaur school), or a waiting list condition (WL). The study was conducted at two sites in Norway. One important purpose was to examine how these North American treatment procedures would work when offered to families with an ODD or CD child in another country and culture. Since the Eyberg Child Behavior Inventory (ECBI) was used as a screening measure, it was first standardized specifically for the two sites.

Ninety percent of the children received a diagnosis of ODD and the rest a CD diagnosis; 80 percent of the children were boys, and about two thirds were 6 years or older. The children in the CT condition received treatment in groups of 4-6 children for 18 sessions covering about 4 months, whereas the PT groups typically included about 10-12 parents who received treatment lasting 12-14 sessions (2 hours weekly). Four families dropped out early from the PT groups. The results showed that mothers consistently rated higher levels of behavioral problems on the ECBI for their children as compared to fathers. Overall, behavioral problems among children in the two active treatment groups were significantly more improved than for children in the WL group (effect sizes ranged from 0.63 to 0.72). After treatment about half of the parents in the two active treatment groups rated their children's functioning within normal variation, as compared to 28 percent of those in the WL group. Similar results were obtained on the Child Behavior Checklist for aggression and externalizing problems, in addition to a reduction of internalizing and total problems. Positive parenting and monitoring practices among parents increased significantly in the two treatment groups.

Early Childhood Care and Mental Health

Bonnie Pape
Canadian Mental Health Association
Toronto, Canada

A recent Canadian project has been studying the question of how knowledge from the literature about mental health promotion translates into practice in daycare settings. The Canadian Mental Health Association, in partnership with the Hincks-Dellcrest Institute (a child and adolescent mental health research and treatment facility in Toronto, Canada), examined whether daycare centers can be settings for promoting the mental health of young children and how knowledge from research about mental health promotion and prevention of mental disorders can inform policies and practices of child care providers. The research was conducted using two interdependent methodologies: a literature review and a telephone survey. The partners conducted an extensive literature review of community daycare in the context of mental health promotion and a telephone survey in which staff in 80 daycare centers across Canada responded to a questionnaire about their policies and practices in regard to the promotion of mental health. The survey questions were informed by the literature, while the report of the literature review in turn is animated by quotes and examples from the survey. The result is a comprehensive picture of the research and rationale for promoting the mental health of young children in child care settings and the actual mental health promotion practices taking place in some of these settings. Findings are documented in both the report of the literature review as well as a booklet of ideas and strategies, translating the research knowledge and results of the survey into plain language written for daycare practitioners. This presentation discusses the project rationale, methodologies, and findings, as well as successes and challenges, and introduces the project's practical tool for daycare providers to help them understand and implement mental health promotion practices in their work. The presentation looks at ways in which this project's goals and objectives can inform the transfer of mental health promotion knowledge to practice more generally and in other contexts such as home care for seniors.

1.3   Research on Promotion and Prevention Worldwide: School Age

Preventing Children's Mental Health Problems by Treating Parents' Substance Abuse Problems: It Works Best for Younger Children, Not for Adolescents

Brian T. Yates
American University
Washington, D.C., United States

It is widely recognized that children who live with substance-abusing parents often manifest significant emotional and behavioral problems. Unfortunately, many children are raised in families in which a parent abuses alcohol or other drugs. Given these children's elevated risk for psychosocial adjustment problems, the substance abuse treatment community has been urged to intervene actively with these children, not only to treat any current adjustment difficulties, but also to help prevent future problems that often emerge as these children enter late adolescence and early adulthood.

The "bad news" is that only a small proportion of parents entering substance abuse treatment allow their children to participate actively in any interventions provided by the programs. However, the "good news" is that, with custodial school-aged children, working with substance-abusing parents in couples therapy has positive effects on children's short- and long-term emotional and behavioral adjustment, even without the active participation of the children. As such, many have touted couples therapy for substance-abusing parents as a viable method of helping their children.

What remains unclear is whether couples therapy for substance-abusing parents has the same positive effects on children who are in different developmental stages. It is plausible that parents' improvement in responses to treatment would have a greater impact on preadolescent children than adolescent children, as the latter are more likely to be comparatively more influenced by their peers than by their parents. We compared the outcomes of couples therapy for substance-abusing men and their nonsubstance-abusing female partners with respect to effects on their custodial children. In our sample of couples (N=136), parents had an adolescent (i.e., ages 13-17) and preadolescent custodial child (i.e., ages 8-12). As hypothesized, we found a stronger relationship between parents' 1-year post-treatment outcomes and the outcomes of their pre-adolescent children compared to their adolescent children. Compared to the preadolescent children, adolescents in this sample had significantly higher levels of emotional and behavioral problems during the year after their parents ended treatment and used more mental health and substance abuse services.

Depression Awareness Campaign Project Proposal: The Color of My Emotions Drawing Contest

Ya Hsing Yeh
John Tung Foundation
Taipei, Taiwan

Goals of the Program
1. Raise depression awareness among children and teenagers
2. Share our field-tested prevention model with other Chinese-speaking societies and countries
3. Provide our project's experience and statistics to develop a better prevention and treatment model for our adolescents and their families and schools

Method and Design
1. All students aged under 15 were invited to submit their painting on the "color of my emotions."
2. Students chose one of the following themes for their paintings: What are the colors of my feelings?
What are images of my depression? What are the things I do to make me feel better? What would you share with others when you are depressed?
3. The contest was announced through press releases, mail, the Internet, flyers, and school bulletins.
4. A panel of judges reviewed all submissions and winners were announced.
5. Award-winning paintings are to be used for mental heath promotion activities, including reprint, exhibition, and mass media circulation.
6. The entire project, from planning through execution and evaluation, will be reviewed for depression prevention model development.

Residents' satisfaction with the climate around their neighborhoods for Taichung County in 2002 was higher than in 1999. There were significant differences in residents' satisfaction with the possibility of losing the natural environments for Taichung County and Cha-Hwa County between both surveys. The green fields, leisure spaces, and safety of walking on the streets around their neighborhoods were the subjects of three other survey questions. This study showed that residents were least satisfied with the safety of walking on the streets for the three locations in both years. Because of bad road conditions and more disturbances in these three areas, the residents had the same level of dissatisfaction in 1999 and 2002. Unfortunately, residents' satisfaction for Taichung County was worse in 2002 than in 1999. More police to reduce crime was the highest priority for the future for the three local governments.

Primary Mental Health Care: An Issues Paper Presented by the New Zealand Mental Health Advocacy Coalition

Kayleen Katene
Mental Health Advocacy Coalition
Wellington, New Zealand

The common mental health (including drug and alcohol) conditions are:
1. Very high prevalence, affecting 25 percent of New Zealand's population at any point in time, 33 percent of general practitioner (GP) attenders, and up to 50 percent of people with chronic medical conditions
2. Leading causes of disability and disease burden, resulting in significant mortality, and exacting an enormous cost (human, social, and financial)
3. Most often not detected and/or not treated effectively
4. Yet very treatable, with recovery rates of 80 percent or more for most conditions if detected early and treated effectively
5. Relatively low cost of treatment, leading to the conclusion that the very high disability, burden, and cost are direct consequences of lack of detection and access to effective treatment.

Relevant literature regarding the range of issues in the provision of effective primary mental health care is reviewed, including literature regarding the substantial co-morbidity of chronic medical conditions and mental health conditions and related very poor outcome. A series of recommendations regarding development of primary mental health care is made. In particular, it is proposed that development of sustainable systematic approaches to effective primary mental health care delivery should be a central element of the current primary care agenda arising out of the Primary Care Strategy. The case is made that this is the single development that will contribute most to achieving the population health objectives outlined in the New Zealand Health Strategy.

Living With Terrorism: Media and Mental Health Before, During, and After Terror Attacks

Anne Leer
Financial Times Prentice Hall & MMG
London, United Kingdom

Terrorism has become one of the most pressing and disturbing issues of our time. World leaders warn of real dangers and vulnerability. Governments and industries are joining forces in the war against terrorism. Billions of dollars are being spent every day on recovery after events and on strengthening the preparedness for terror attacks. Most of the funds are being spent on the protection of societies on a physical level, and little is being spent on securing preparedness, prevention, and recovery in terms of managing the effects of terrorism on people and mental health.

The recent series of terror attacks around the world following 9/11 has taken place in a social landscape where the impact of mental health problems on people's lives, business, and economic performance is already enormous. Prevalence rates of mental health problems approach one in four individuals worldwide, with 500 million persons estimated as underserved in terms of mental health care provision, and the cost of mental health problems to governments and industry in North America and Europe soaring to more than $200 billion in 2004. An appropriate response to what the UN has called an "unheralded crisis in public health" requires a concerted effort across the public and private sectors in which media, mental health, science, and education have a crucial role to play.

Terrorism cripples communities around the world. In New York City alone an estimated 3.1 million residents experienced substantial emotional distress, and many are still suffering from nightmares and debilitating mental health problems. Two decades of research into community and individual reactions to traumatic stress have provided ample evidence of the consequences of such disasters. Much could be achieved in terms of both prevention and cure if mental health issues were part of an integrated response to how society copes with terrorism.

It is not bullets and bombs that will win this new global war; it is people. The best weapon in the war on terror is an intelligent and powerful use of media and education to arm people with knowledge and healthy minds. The mental health care sector has much to contribute at this moment in time and an enormous task on its hands in promoting a global mental health agenda. Without a focus on mental health millions of people will suffer; prevalence rates will continue to soar; and societies will weaken in terms of their ability to deal effectively with terrorism that is now recognized internationally to be the biggest global threat to world stability.

We live in a global media society, and the media increasingly play a critical role in how people as well as governments and business deal with the fear, stress, and trauma of terrorism. Yet so far little has been done to encourage mental health and the prevention of chronic behavioral disorders through the effective use of media. It is time we change this situation and make the media a powerful vehicle for public mental health.

Promotion of Refugee Mental Health: A Community Empowerment Model

Nyunt Naing Thein and Elena Fowler
Auckland Refugees as Survivors Centre
Auckland, New Zealand

Auckland Refugees as Survivors Centre (RAS) is a nonprofit agency established to work with refugee survivors of torture and trauma now residing in New Zealand. The primary activities of the RAS Centre have been providing refugees with mental health assessment, short-term therapy, and onward referral. RAS comprises a multidisciplinary team, so therapy can involve a combination of individual, couple, or family counseling; body therapy; and group therapy. There has been growing awareness that the mental distress of refugee clients frequently is the result of the challenges of resettlement as opposed (and/or in addition) to a history of torture and trauma. In order to provide clients with the best outcomes, stronger links need to be built with the wider refugee communities. The challenge to mental health presented by resettlement has been the impetus behind the implementation of a new model promoting mental health in refugee communities. In 2003 the RAS community team (social worker, community worker, and administrator) initiated the Community Empowerment Program (CEP) employing 11 people from eight different ethnic communities to work as community facilitators (CF). Currently the CF Team runs 12 information sessions covering eight communities. In addition to addressing resettlement challenges by providing information in a culturally appropriate environment, facilities for capacity building and training opportunities are identified. As trust develops the group setting also serves as a social support network. The CF works to empower group members and advocate for improved social services and educational and employment opportunities. The CF also plays an important role in educating RAS clinical and body therapy teams and staff from external organizations about refugee experiences and cultural beliefs and practices. This paper covers the theories that inform the CEP, the RAS model of mental health promotion, and key achievements of the CEP as captured by the New Zealand Ministry of Health's Community Project Indicators Framework.

Better Mental Health Promotion Practice as a Result of Researching "Depression" with Ethnic Minority Groups

Sandy Clark
East Metropolitan Population Health Unit
Perth, Australia

Depression is increasingly recognized as a global health problem, yet little conclusive research has been conducted into the most appropriate strategies to use in the prevention of depression. Likewise, there is even less research in Australia about the understanding that people of culturally and linguistically diverse backgrounds have of the conditions encompassed by the term "depression." The authors have been involved in a Healthway-funded project to investigate the understanding of depression among a number of migrant and refugee communities. This project employed a combination of methods, namely focus groups and in-depth interviews, in order to investigate the meaning of depression in seven ethnic minority groups (Eritrean, Somali,

Sudanese, Ethiopian, Croatian, Bosnian, and Chinese) and the perceived relevance of present health promotion information to these communities. Focus groups involving the targeted communities were conducted and information elicited about participants' understanding of depression with a view to developing meaningful mental health promotion programs for the different community groups. Information derived from focus groups was supplemented, where appropriate, with information from in-depth interviews. The results of the three-year research to date indicate that current health promotion is inappropriate for these communities. Social and cultural determinants peculiar to these groups, such as migration and settlement issues, as well as their concerns about family members still living in war zones or refugee camps, require new methods of delivering mental health promotion. Such methods require working with other sectors (housing, police, and nongovernmental agencies) in partnership with the communities themselves, because most of the research findings relate to environmental, economic, social, and cultural factors. Feedback of the results of the focus groups and interviews has been provided to the various communities. This feedback process has enabled the research team to work with the communities to address some of the problems and issues raised in the original research.

1.6 Poster Sessions

Role and Problems of Private-Sector Organizations in Preventing Child Abuse in Japan

Kazuyo Nakazoe
Kagawa Prefectural College of Health Sciences
Japan

In Japan in 2001, 23,738 consultations about child abuse were conducted in Prefectural Child Consultation Offices across the country; the number of consultations was 15 times more than those conducted a decade ago. As child abuse becomes a more serious problem in child-rearing each year, public organizations, such as Child Consultation Offices, are supposed to take on an important role in this matter. However, it is unlikely that they will meet the public's expectations because they lack human resources and expertise.

It also is difficult to bring about successful outcomes in prevention of child abuse and protection of abused children, and also in care for abusers, as a result of lack of collaboration among such disciplines as health care, medical care, welfare, education, and others, and because public agencies take an approach of impartiality and neutrality.

Government personnel, as well as alternative resources, are not sufficient to meet individuals' needs or to tackle the diverse problems of the community. Expectations of NPOs and volunteer organizations have been growing in recent years due to their flexible approach and diverse services. In Japan in the 1990s, private-sector organizations that focused on prevention of child abuse began to provide such services as telephone consultation, group support for abusers, education of local inhabitants, and personnel training. Private-sector organizations engaging in child abuse services share the same problems: finances, human resources, and the situation of head offices. Each is essential to sustainable activities.

We represent one of the regional NPOs for child abuse, Child Abuse Prevention Network Kagawa, in which we have been participating from its inception. We discuss the roles the organization has taken and the problems it faces.

Implementing and Sustaining School-Based Suicide Prevention: What Do We Need to Know?

Carole Hooven
University of Washington
Seattle, Washington, United States

Effective prevention research bridges the gap between scientific trials and "real world" practice by building community/school partnerships and by understanding and working with barriers to individual- and system-level change. Nowhere is this more true than in the field of suicide prevention. The CAST-Plus program is a high school–based adolescent suicide prevention program that has successfully met the challenge of implementing suicide prevention in twelve high schools in the northwestern and southwestern United States over the last two years. During this time, a systematic investigation of the process of adopting and integrating suicide prevention practice in each school building also was conducted, with a goal of identifying the factors key to sustaining the prevention program and practices. Guided by innovation diffusion theory, confidential qualitative interviews were conducted with identified key informants, using a snowball nomination strategy from informant to informant.

Interviews focused on a high school's perceived need and readiness for suicide prevention programming, student mental health needs and how they were attended to, and barriers and readiness for change. In addition to increased understanding of building-specific dynamics related to change, the result is a rich portrait of the structure, cultures, challenges, and concerns of American high schools as they grapple with responding to this important and all-too-frequent issue for adolescents.

Differential Efficacy in Reducing Suicide Risk among Adolescents

Jerald R. Hurting
University of Washington
Seattle, Washington, United States

Over the past five years, using randomized trials, we have shown fairly strong and consistent response to a short indicated suicide risk prevention intervention. The program strategies consist of identifying youth at risk of suicide behaviors using a valid screen, intervening with a short one-on-one interview to further assess risk and provide brief motivation and skill building in the individual, and activating the individual's social network to provide additional support (e.g., family and caring adults at school). Work presented by Thompson et al. (*Journal of Public Health*, 2001) and Randell et al. (*Journal of Child & Adolescent Psychiatric Nursing*, 2002) has demonstrated efficacy in this approach for adolescents aged 14 to 19 in reducing depressed affect, suicide ideation, and suicide threats; results suggest reductions are sustained for at least a 9-month period.

This paper re-examines data from two sets of studies, specifically the data for differential response to these short one-on-one interventions, and assesses the specificity of the intervention. Initial results using latent growth mixture modeling have demonstrated three classes of individuals. One group reduces its risk behaviors as demonstrated previously. A second group reduces behaviors but had initially relatively lower levels of risk. And, a third group seems to fail to respond or fail to reduce its risk behaviors. We explore what initial factors may identify membership in these different responses to the preventive interventions.

The analysis uses more than 500 high school–aged youth who were randomly assigned to the intervention or to usual care; parental consent and youth assent were obtained prior to assignment. Youth respond to a baseline questionnaire and have repeated measures at 1 month, 2.5 months, and 9 months post-baseline and intervention. Self-report behaviors include the depressed affect (CES-D).

Initial Evaluation of a Transition to a Secondary School Program for Australian Indigenous Students

Carmelita Almain
Tropical Public Health Unit
Queensland Health
Cairns, Australia

Many students find the transition from primary to secondary schooling stressful. The stress associated with this transition is compounded for indigenous students who often face moving away from their families and communities to larger urban or regional areas for high school education. Reaction to such dislocation is hypothesized to contribute to the low school retention rate in this population. Dropping out of school has negative implications for an individual's economic and social advancement as well as his or her physical and mental health.

The Taking Big Steps (TBS) program was developed in consultation with members of indigenous communities in Australia's north. The program offers strategies to assist school personnel, parents, and most of all young people to prepare for transition to secondary schooling. The program consists of a workshop conducted in communities for school personnel, parents, and students approaching transition. The materials used are an information booklet, a video, teacher's note, and transparencies.

To date, 131 TBS workshops have been conducted in schools in Far North Queensland, including the Torres Strait. A total of 1,490 students from years 6, 7, and 8, and 185 parents have participated in the program. Further workshops have been conducted for service providers in nongovernmental organizations. Feedback on the level of satisfaction and appropriateness of program material was extremely favorable, with 80 percent of participants indicating that they understood and learned about transition. Although it is too early to report retention rates, this paper presents data on the appropriateness and relevance of the program as rated by students and parents. Additional data on the extent to which the program has been a catalyst for community-initiated activity around transition is also presented.

Developing a Video Film for Facilitating a School-Based Inoculation Program to Prevent the Start of Smoking by Children in Yogyakarta Municipality, Indonesia

Yayi Suryo Prabandari
University of Newcastle
Newcastle, New South Wales, Australia

The proportion of smokers in the male population of Indonesia is around 75 percent and the country is the fifth largest nation in terms of numbers of smokers. The number of children smoking in Indonesia has increased over the last decade. Previous studies indicated that Indonesian smokers wanted to quit, but their dependency impeded their success.

Smoking prevention programs that use a psychosocial approach appear promising. Moreover, evidence shows that smoking-inoculation programs are effective in reducing the number of teens who begin smoking. A pilot work using a rapid assessment procedure was applied to assess a smoking inoculation program's material and instruments adapted from San Diego, California. Pilot work in 2000 among junior high school students, teachers, and health promotion providers indicated that all participants considered smoking prevention an urgent issue, and a modified smoking inoculation program could be implemented in Indonesia. It used interactive media, such as video film. The objective of this study was to develop a video film for facilitating implementation of a smoking inoculation program.

A participatory approach was chosen for developing a video film about smoking prevention. Fourteen student senate representatives from five junior high schools in Yogyakarta municipality participated in this study. Three communication media experts facilitated the process. Three meetings and several small group discussions were conducted during the process. The main ideas of the video story were based on the students' suggestions, and some students acted in the video.

Video production took two and half months. The first version ran 35 minutes. After three focus group discussions among junior high school students, the video was shortened and revised. Although it faced some difficulties in its implementation, involving students in the process was promising, because they knew exactly what young people wanted. The process of video making, including meetings, small group discussions, and focus group discussions took four months. Students were enthusiastic about their participation in the video process.

Childhood Performance Anxiety: Management Through Negative Self-Talk Reduction

Erigoni Valss
Sydney, Australia

The aim of this study was to examine whether training 10-year-old, primary school–based children in a modified version of the FRIENDS program (an evidenced-based, cognitive behavioral approach) to reduce the physical symptoms of anxiety and negative self-talk prior to a class presentation was effective. Fifty-one children were recruited from two public primary schools in the Sydney metropolitan area. Twenty-nine year-5 children from one of the schools were trained using the modified FRIENDS program (Barrett, Lowry-Webster, & Holmes, 2000), and the remaining twenty-two children from the second school received anxiety education alone. Pre-

and post-training assessments were conducted using the Social Anxiety Scale for Children-Revised (SASC-R) (Greca & Stone 1993) (elementary school–level version) and the Negative Affect Self-Statement Questionnaire (NASSQ) (Ronan and Kendall, 1994) for 7 to 10 year olds. In comparison to the anxiety education group, the FRIENDS group showed significantly greater reductions in negative self-talk at post-training assessment and prior to class presentation. These results support the universal inclusion of such training programs in the primary school curriculum.

Is Early Intervention Effective for Young Children with Autism Spectrum Disorder (ASD)?

Carolyn J. Doughty
Christchurch School of Medicine and Health Sciences
Christchurch, New Zealand

This poster presentation summarized the evidence for the effectiveness of behavioral and skill-based early interventions that are used to prevent, manage, or treat autism spectrum disorder (ASD) in young children. The information presented is not restricted to a single intervention, but instead refers to a number of interventions with a similar theoretical basis and/or comprehensive programs that utilize either an intensive behavioral or social-developmental approach.

Databases (Medline, PsychInfo, Embase, and CINAHL) were searched systematically for studies published between January 2000 and June 2004 inclusive in the English language, including primary (original) research (published as a full original report) and secondary research (systematic reviews and meta analyses appearing in the published literature). Of the ten articles appraised, five were secondary studies and five were primary studies. The latter included one cohort study and four controlled studies. Of the controlled studies two were randomized controlled trials (Level II) and two were comparative studies with concurrent controls but no random allocation (Level III-2), according to the NHMRC hierarchy of evidence. The secondary research included reviews that either summarized or critically appraised studies of the highest quality, with the exception of one review, which included a mix of study designs. The intensity and duration of the intervention offered was documented only in some of the studies and sample sizes were mostly small.

Given these and other limitations, the primary studies appraised generally provide only very preliminary evidence about the effectiveness of behavioral and skill-based early intervention. Nevertheless, two of these studies were graded as Level II, according to the NHMRC hierarchy, which reflects high-level evidence.

Most of the primary studies reviewed here document some improvement associated with intervention; however, it remains to be determined if any one early and/or intensive intervention program is more effective than another program. Furthermore, direct empirical evidence that early compared to later intervention has a specific positive benefit is not yet available. At best there appears to be consensus among experts in the field that developmental principles support the notion of early intervention. More research in this area is needed urgently, and the conclusions of this review should be revisited as the results, particularly of current and ongoing trials, become available.

Flipper Card: An Innovative Information Strategy

Chris Scanlan
Barwon Health
Victoria, Australia

Background. Anecdotal evidence from teachers and youth workers indicates a lack of relevant information resources for young people. A literature search of mental health promotion, help-seeking behavior, and social marketing provided a series of guiding principles upon which to base an innovative mental health information strategy. These principles included:

1. A universal strategy that maximizes coverage and reduces associated stigma of mental illness (Raphael)
2. The use of schools as a base for preventative programs and the incorporation of programs into school curricula (Raphael, Hopkins)
3. The need for projects to "speak to young people in their own language" and that messages must be presented in a "catchy and easily remembered format" (Hopkins, Mixon)
4. The value of young people's participation in the project (Hopkins)
5. Young people's increasing use of online counseling and telephone help lines to seek help and assistance (Rickwood, Kids Helpline)

Objectives. A fresh and exciting strategy was developed in Barwon South West Region of Victoria, a "Flipper Card" with the aim of improving young people's mental health literacy and knowledge of available services.

Method. A search for existing resources focused on products with effectiveness, innovation, and youth usability. The flipper card best met these criteria. It had been used successfully in school-based health promotion campaigns for numeracy and literacy. Information on the card includes positive mental health messages, facts about adolescent mental health, and service listings that young people can access.

The presentation of the card is bright, colorful, and attractive, combining photographs and graphics to engage young people.

The project was funded through Rotary and overseen by a management team, with people from clinical services, disability services, youth health services, and mental health consumer organizations. Students at the local TAFE College undertook the design and artwork of the project. Ten thousand copies of the card have been distributed to students in years 9/10 across Geelong with a mental health education program. A pre- and post-test questionnaire was distributed to participating schools.

Results. Three thousand post-test questionnaires were sent to eleven participating public and private schools. The response rate was 30 percent. Seventy-nine percent of students agreed it was important to have written information on mental health. This is supported by 83 percent of pre-test correlation. Seventy percent of the sample had read the card, and 65 percent stated that their friends also had read it, which indicates peer acknowledgment of the card and/or discussion of information contained on the card. When asked if the card were a good way of getting mental health information to young people, 71 percent answered yes. This result is very encouraging in relation to adolescents' perception of user-friendly health information. In response to a question about whether the adolescent or a friend would use the card to seek help, 44 percent responded yes. Taking into account that young people, especially males, do not actively seek help for mental health problems, this result is positive.

Conclusion. This flipper card has made an impact with young people and schools. The project is expanding to all schools in the Southwest Region, Victoria. Further research will be conducted to gain insights into adolescent help-seeking behavior and the effectiveness of the information strategy.

Postpartum Support International: Beyond Talk into Action

Jane Honikman
Santa Barbara, California, United States

The focus of this presentation is to describe the development of perinatal social support networks around the world. Postpartum Support International's mission is to promote awareness, prevention, and treatment of mental health issues related to childbearing in every country worldwide. Its membership consists of professionals and nonprofessionals who have successfully integrated their expertise into models of care in a variety of community settings. Training materials have been developed that explain how to organize self-help family-support networks. This presentation highlights the values and role of social support systems, clarification of the major maternal mood and anxiety disorders, public policy, and the impact of maternal depression on the family. It is aimed at exploring practical hands-on solutions for achieving the well-being of families in all cultures and socioeconomic groups.

Models of Madness: Can "Schizophrenia" Be Prevented?

John Read
University of Auckland
Auckland, New Zealand

"Schizophrenia is a chronic, severe, and disabling brain disease." This is the opening statement of the U.S. government agency, the National Institute for Mental Health, in its public information website, www.nimh.hih.gov/publicat/schizoph.pdf. Such an opinion can be found in most "educational" material, from psychiatric textbooks to drug company–sponsored pamphlets. This paper summarizes the research showing this statement to be false.

This research shows how the dominant biogenetic ideology ignores the childhood events that can lead to psychosis, has increased stigma, and has inhibited primary prevention. It is documented in *Models of Madness: Psychological, Social and Biological Approaches to Schizophrenia* (Read, J., Mosher, L., Bentall, R., eds. London: Brunner-Routledge, 2004).

The heightened sensitivity, unusual experiences, distress, despair, confusion, and disorganization that are currently labeled "schizophrenic" are not symptoms of a medical illness. The notion that "mental illness is an illness like any other," promulgated by biological psychiatry and the pharmaceutical industry, is not supported by research and is extremely damaging to persons with this most stigmatizing of psychiatric labels. The "medical model" of schizophrenia has dominated efforts to understand and assist distressed and distressing people for far too long. It is responsible for unwarranted and destructive pessimism about the chances of "recovery" and has ignored—or even actively discouraged discussion of—what is actually going on in these people's lives, in their families, and in the societies in which they live.

Perhaps most cruelly of all, the belief that "schizophrenia" is an illness and therefore life events and circumstances can play no role in its causation, has led to the awful conclusion that nothing can be done to prevent it. Rather than lobby governments to fund primary prevention programs that could improve the quality of life for children, adolescents, and their families, biological psychiatry gives politicians a perfect excuse for doing nothing.

It is argued, on the basis of the research presented, that the causes of what psychiatrists call "schizophrenia" are just as much based in adverse childhood experiences as are other mental health problems, and that psychosis is, therefore, equally amenable to primary prevention programs aimed at enhancing the safety and emotional well-being of children and their carers.

Multicultural Mental Health Australia

Felicity Zadro
Parramatta, Australia

This presentation provides an overview of Multicultural Mental Health Australia (MMHA), an Australia-wide program working to improve the quality and accessibility of mental health services for Australians from diverse cultural and linguistic backgrounds. Under the National Mental Health Strategy (NMHS) and the National Suicide Prevention Strategy (NSPS), MMHA is responsible for a range of national activities that underpin and support the national focus on multicultural mental health and suicide prevention. Key activities include national communication services such as the MMHA website, newsletter *Synergy*, e-bulletins, information dissemination, policy advice, and training.

In 2003 MMHA worked with the Australian Health Ministers' Advisory Council National Mental Health Working Group to develop a "Framework for the Implementation of the National Mental Health Plan 2003-2008 in Multicultural Australia." The Framework will be published in 2004.

This poster illustrates MMHA's population health approach to developing the issues of multicultural mental health and suicide prevention through strategic alliances and networks with national mainstream programs, state and territory mental health services, specialist services, consumers, carers, and the community sector and the ethnic media. It also highlights MMHA's extensive mental health promotion and cultural competency resources for consumers from diverse backgrounds, their friends, families and communities, and the service providers who work with them.

Understanding How Technical Assistance Can Assist Schools and Communities in Building Capacity for Mental Health Promotion and Youth Violence Prevention

Deborah Haber
Education Development Center, Inc. (EDC)
Newton, Massachusetts, United States

For decades, technical assistance providers have been funded by federal agencies in the United States to assist schools and communities in meeting goals and outcomes aimed at enhancing the health, mental health, and education of children, youth, and families. In today's environment, such providers are further charged not only with supporting these groups to meet their goals, but also to meet them by identifying and developing ongoing capacity for implementing evidence-based programs and strategies with fidelity. What have we learned about useful and effective technical assistance (TA)? How do these learnings apply to today's trends? How have the roles of TA provider and TA consumer evolved? In this workshop, we discuss how the approach used by the National Center for Mental Health Promotion and Youth Violence Prevention, funded by the Substance Abuse and Mental Health Services Administration (SAMHSA), draws from research, experience in the field, and work with more than 160 practitioners as they seek to move research to practice. The TA services of this SAMHSA-funded Center are built on a broad and holistic definition of TA that takes into account all of the ways people, systems, and communities can be supported to create and sustain change. Today's challenges help to focus the roles, responsibilities, and practices for both technical assistance providers and technical assistance consumers. We know that the process is not linear, precise, or fully predictable, and that the developmental needs and stages of agencies and practitioners impact the kinds of TA they require as they seek to make lasting change. There is, however, a foundational knowledge base that, when utilized creatively, can make a difference. Clarifying, applying, and transforming this foundation is the basis for the Center's promising approach to TA and the core of this presentation.

Right From The Start

Marilyn Barnes
Home-Start National Inc., Australia

Home-Start National Inc., with a funding grant from Telstra, has established an early intervention project aptly named Right From The Start, which will provide pre- and postnatal support to families who are expecting a baby and are identified as being vulnerable to psychosocial risks such as loneliness, depression/postpartum depression, mental health issues, and a variety of other social issues that could affect the quality of life of the unborn child and the family unit generally.

The prime focus of the Right From The Start project is to enhance the attachment process between the parents and the expected baby, and to emphasize issues such as early brain development, self-esteem and problem solving, postnatal depression, in utero communication, and the importance of dads becoming involved as a supportive and caring family component.

The involvement of dads within the family unit has long been recognized by Home-Start National as an area that needed to be highlighted to ensure that dads also take on and understand the importance of their role as fathers, supporters, and life partners with the expectation that their input will be valued by their partner, strengthen family ties, and provide a stable platform from which the child can grow and flourish.

Home-Start National's Right From The Start program will link trained volunteers with families for two hours a week and will offer friendship and practical support such as transportation to medical and prenatal classes. Volunteers also will provide information on parenting and community resources, role-model parenting skills, and encourage or enhance parental confidence. Most importantly, Home-Start National volunteers possess the ability to "lend an ear" and listen to the concerns of the families—and often that's all it takes to get it "Right From The Start."

As a preventive program, this program supports parents before crisis occurs by recognizing the early warning signs of mothers at risk of postpartum depression and by offering assistance to the family as a whole.

Post-natal Depression: beyondblue's Response

Nicole Highet
beyondblue: the national depression initiative
Hawthorn West, Australia

As part of beyondblue: the national depression initiative's work in the area of promotion, prevention, and early intervention and research, a number of initiatives and resources have been developed in the area of post-natal depression specifically. First, beyondblue has funded a National Postnatal Depression Program, which aims to develop and evaluate a screening program, within existing primary healthcare settings, to identify women who may be at risk of prenatal and postnatal depression.

The broader objectives of the program are to improve community awareness of depression, enhance partnerships between women and primary healthcare providers, professional bodies, and maternity services and to build capacity by encouraging strategies aimed at improving knowledge about depression assessment and treatment.

In addition to this, beyondblue has established a national consumer and carer initiative: blueVoices, with a specific reference group in the area of postnatal depression. The reference group, beyondbabyblues, promotes the lived experience of postnatal depression and provides a vehicle for advocating the needs and experiences of women and their families who may experience postnatal depression.

Together these initiatives play a key role in promoting and increasing community awareness about postnatal depression and its impact on individuals and their families, as well as addressing issues surrounding information and service provision. This presentation highlights the key developments and outcomes in this area and the significance of this work to date.

Community-Based Rehabilitation of People with Mental Illnesses: SEVAC's Initiative in India with the Support of Development Cooperation Ireland & Misereor

Prativa Sengupta
SEVAC Mental Hospital & Rehabilitation Centre
Kolkata, India

Like the rest of the world, a sizable number of the Indian population is afflicted with varied psychiatric problems. But only 10 percent of them have access to the mental health care delivery system. Just one bed is earmarked in mental hospitals/psychiatric wards of general hospitals for a population of 40,000. This reality proves that the community itself has always extended some sort of care to most persons with mental illnesses in India. But the paradox is this, that the concept of community-based rehabilitation in the form of projects or programs has not been tried adequately in India. In response to this realization, SEVAC, an Indian nongovernmental organization based in Kolkata, implemented a service project for a period of three consecutive years in collaboration with the CBR Forum, a unit of the Misereor. A total of 210 moderately stable clients were selected from the Out Patients' Department of SEVAC for this purpose.

The salient objectives of the project were:

1. Ensuring regular psychiatric check-up and uninterrupted treatment for the selected clients
2. Providing them with psychosocial training
3. Engaging them in meaningful work
4. Providing psychoeducation to family members of the selected clients
5. Generating mental health awareness at the community level to fight stigma and ignorance

At the end of the third year it was noticed that most of the clients who were able to comply with the treatment protocol and procure necessary medicines were able to lead a quality lives and retain their positions in their respective families as meaningful individuals. Recently, in collaboration with Development Corporation Ireland, SEVAC has been implementing a project entitled Operation Dignity to spread mental health education at the community level with an aim to promote the human rights of mental patients by facilitating their community-based rehabilitation. In this poster the impact of the aforementioned project is highlighted.

2.1 Evidence-Based Programs, Policies, and Principles of Effective Promotion and Prevention: Preschool

Webster-Stratton Treatment for Behavioral Disorders: Before and After Parent Groups

Graham Clifford
Medisinsk Teknisk Senter
Trondheim, Norway

In conjunction with a randomized clinical trial and evaluation of Webster-Stratton's treatment program for families with young children affected by behavioral disorders, a qualitative research project was conducted to elicit parents' accounts of their situation before, during, and after treatment. Our paper reviews the findings from twenty qualitative interviews with parents. This paper complements a paper submitted by Larsson and Mørch that deals with results obtained in the treatment trial. Preliminary findings include parental descriptions of children who had displayed angry, aggressive, and/or very active, restless, and reckless behavior, often from an early age. Many were trapped in a cycle of scolding and punishment, leading to increased anger and defiance on the part of the children. Strained relationships between some parents contributed to the child's problems and/or were worsened by the stress of raising a child with behavior problems. Sibling relationships also were frequently difficult, including fighting among siblings, multiple siblings with behavior problems, and parents' difficulty in adapting techniques from the course to only one child, given the reality of a family situation where other siblings had needs, including the need for more attention because of parents' focus on the "problem" child. Other than preschool, which many parents found helpful, most families had received little help prior to the program. Parents participating in Webster-Stratton's parent-group treatment were very satisfied with the parent training course.

Parents were particularly satisfied with the opportunity to meet and exchange experiences with other parents facing similar problems, helping to reduce their isolation and feelings of guilt, and increase their self-confidence and morale. Many parents expressed the desire for continued contact with other group members after the course. Some also gained increased understanding of their children's situation and techniques for improving their interaction with the children. Techniques included reduced scolding and punishment and increased emphasis on attention, praise, and positive reinforcement. Parent satisfaction with the course appeared to have little direct relationship with improvement in their child's behavior during and after the course. Some parents reported having continuing difficulties with their child and other aspects of life two years after treatment. Some had difficulty continuing to practice course principles and methods after the course. Some were pessimistic about the children's future, feeling a need for ongoing assistance. Others were more optimistic, expressing confidence that they were better equipped to meet future challenges.

Mainstreaming Infant Mental Health

Pam Linke
Child and Youth Health
Adelaide, Australia

Child and Youth Health (CYH) in South Australia is a statewide organization with responsibility for family and children's health services. Over the last two years a universal home visiting program has been instituted using a needs-based questionnaire for the home visiting nurse, in partnership with parents, to work out the best pathway for that particular family and infant's needs. One of the options from this assessment is a two-year home visiting program delivered by nurses with multidisciplinary support. The home visiting program is based on Australian and overseas research (Elmira program in the U.S. and Queensland health program). The South Australian program also combines an infant mental health focus with the nursing anticipatory guidance and responsiveness to parent and infant needs and issues. Criteria to enter the program include population-based criteria—social isolation, Aboriginality, and teenager parenthood— together with negative maternal attributions to the infant. Other clinical criteria apply to a smaller number of participants, where they are not linked with one of the above, and include domestic violence, birth injury or abnormality, previous welfare reports, drug use, postnatal depression, and mental illness. Nurses providing the program are selected on relationship, sensitivity, and warmth criteria, as well as on nursing skills and experience. Training for nurses using the program includes the Family Partnerships model of parent support developed by Professor Hilton Davis in the U.K. and the attachment-based Circle of Security and STEEP programs. Nurses use video reflection with parents as part of the intervention. Nurses are supported by a social worker or psychologist infant specialist through a fortnightly case conference and fortnightly individual reflective consultation. In the first year of rollout the program is being provided to 600 families in two metropolitan and two country areas. This program has meant major work changes for CYH staff, which has provided some challenges but has had an enthusiastic response from staff involved. The presentation discusses challenges and opportunities provided by the initiative.

Making Parenting Programs Accessible: Baseline Results of the Every Family Initiative

Matt Sanders
Parenting and Family Support Centre
University of Queensland, Australia

Aim. The Every Family Initiative is Australia's largest population-level trial of an evidence-based, multilevel parenting strategy. The aim is to reduce the prevalence of anxiety, depression, and conduct problems in young children and their families during the transition from preschool to Year 1.

Methods. The project employs a randomized cluster experimental design involving 30 socio-demographically matched catchment areas (10 high-intensity, 10 medium-intensity, and 10 low-intensity intervention communities). High-intensity communities will have access to a wide range of parenting services. Medium-intensity communities will receive fewer services, and low-intensity communities will have minimal exposure to parenting interventions. The main outcome measure is a parenting survey, conducted via computer-assisted telephone interview (CATI), that will be completed by a random cross-section of 4,500 parents on two assessment occasions. The first CATI was conducted with parents of 4- to 7-year-old children in July 2003 and the second CATI will be conducted with parents of 6- to 9-year-old children in July 2005.

Results. Baseline data from the 2003 CATI are presented and implications discussed. It is hypothesized that post intervention, parents in the high-intensity areas will report a greater reduction in the prevalence of children's mental health problems compared with parents in medium- or low-intensity areas.

Kids' Skills: An Educational Method for Working with Unhappy Children

Hooshmand Ebrahimi
Association of Persian Kids' Skills
Shiraz, Iran

Kids' Skills, developed at the Finnish Brief Therapy Institute, is an educational method for helping children to learn skills and overcome problems. The method can be used in schools and any setting where children are cared for, including the home. According to the philosophy of Kids' Skills, which is a positive approach to mental health, a child's problem can be seen as a symptom of lacking a basic skill that the child needs to learn. Therefore, the first task of Kids' Skills is converting the child's problem into a corresponding skill to be learned. This paper discusses the principles of Kids' Skills and describes the tasks involved, such as converting a problem into a skill, agreeing on the skill to learn, exploring the benefits of the skill, naming the skill, choosing a power creature, obtaining supporters, building confidence in success, planning the celebration, defining the skill, going public, practicing the skill, dealing with frustration and disappointment, celebrating success, and teaching others. Then it uses the systematic tasks of Kids' Skills for teaching the skill of "becoming happy again" to an unhappy girl for overcoming her problem of "loss and grief." She is an 11-year-old girl whose classmate died of heart disease two months earlier and soon thereafter she started to be sad. In the process of learning, the unhappy girl invites "happiness" as a nickname for the skill and chooses one of the protagonists of fairy tales as a power creature to help her to learn.

United States. ESMH programs are reducing barriers to student learning, reaching underserved youth, stimulating prevention activities in communities, and assisting in the achievement of valued student, family, and school outcomes. The field is young, however, and there is much work to do along a number of fronts. One of the most important needs for the field is to develop and implement systematic strategies for quality assessment and improvement (QAI), which, in our framework, subsumes empirically supported practices. The presenter reviews experiences in QAI as learned through a local program operating in 22 Baltimore schools, a national center for mental health in schools (Center for School Mental Health Assistance, see http://csmha.umaryland.edu), and through a recent large research grant from the National Institute of Mental Health.

Using Interactive Computer Software Applications to Promote Mental Health in Students Transitioning from Primary to High School

Reg Davis
Central Coast Health
Wyong, Australia

Research. Following a community consultation held on the Central Coast of New South Wales in 2001, in response to the National Action Plan for Promotion, Prevention, and Early Intervention for Mental Health, transition from primary to high school was identified as a period of high mental health risk for students. Between Years 6 and 7 school performance and satisfaction deteriorates, students' self-regard declines, and it is a time of significant uptake of drug and alcohol use. Focus groups of 150 Year-6 and Year-7 students identified specific areas of concern for students in transition, including getting organized, transportation, making friends, managing bullying, and knowing where to get help.

Effective practice. In response to the community consultation and focus groups, the Central Coast School-Link Project, a partnership between NSW Departments of Health and Education & Training, decided to develop an interactive educational CD ROM as a fun, engaging, and informative resource that could be used as part of transition program activities in class and individually with identified at-risk students. The resource "OutaSite: Intergalactic Guide to High School" has a space theme where students travel through a virtual school environment meeting challenges and having to resolve problems and dilemmas with a mental health theme.

The resource includes games, quizzes, and mental health information about such issues as bullying, stress and anger management, conflict resolution, and making friends. The resource has an extensive teacher's area that includes demonstration transition programs used by a wide range of local schools and support material, such as student booklets, that can be printed for classroom use. An evaluation in two schools of 120 students indicated significant improvement overall pre-post test in students' perceived readiness for high school, knowledge of where to get help, confidence in getting themselves organized for school, handling transportation issues, managing difficult situations at school, and making friends. Three thousand copies were produced for distribution through School-Link and school departmental welfare staff.

OmSorg: Dealing with Bereavement—Implementation of Action Plans Towards Children Experiencing Loss and Grief at All Danish Schools

Per Borga and Dige Jes
Danish Cancer Society
Copenhagen, Denmark

One of the basic conditions in working with bereaved children is that their surroundings—school and after-school settings—are supportive and helpful so teachers are prepared to help children in need.

The project OmSorg (Dealing with Bereavement) is a nationwide, practical school-based intervention for children experiencing loss and grief. The aim is to inspire and support teachers in helping grieving children. This is done by offering educational materials and giving lectures, consultation, and courses, and by political lobbying.

Experience shows that the more engaged teachers feel in acting on their concerns, the better help is provided to children in need. Therefore, one of the main tasks of the project has been to encourage teachers to establish action plans for their interactions with children experiencing loss and grief.

Thus far during the six-year intervention, schools have realized the necessity and benefit from establishing these plans. A randomized survey among all Danish public schools (grades 0-10) shows development in the number of schools with written action plans to support children experiencing loss and grief: November 1997, 4 percent; November 1998, 12 percent; May 2000, 32 percent; November 2001, 56 percent; January 2003, 73 percent; February 2004, 86 percent. Amazing progress in establishing action plans over a short period of time has taken place with almost no backup or support from local, regional, or national government agencies.

2.3 Evidence-Based Programs, Policies, and Principles of Effective Promotion and Prevention: Working Age

The Compass Strategy: Promoting Mental Health Literacy to Help Prevent Serious Mental Illness in Young People

Maree Sidey
Orygen Youth Health
Parville, Australia

The Compass Strategy is a community awareness and education program conducted in parts of metropolitan Melbourne and rural Victoria, Australia. It is designed to promote early help seeking for first-onset depression and psychosis in young people through increasing the community's mental health literacy.

The focus is on promoting early help seeking as a means of indicated prevention and early intervention, because early treatment has been found to increase the likelihood of recovery and reduce the risk of relapse in these disorders. A contributing factor to delayed help seeking is the general public's limited knowledge about early signs of illness, benefits of early treatment, and sources of help.

This paper describes the development, implementation, evaluation, and preliminary dissemination of The Compass Strategy. Using the Precede-Proceed Model (Green & Kreuter, 1999) as a foundation for forming a sound evidence base, it has drawn upon a range of bodies of knowledge including psychiatric epidemiology, health promotion, health education, and public health. Local consultation and partnership with young people, parents, community service providers, and mental health service consumers from the culturally and linguistically diverse target area of more than thirty different nationalities has helped refine its development and ensure effective implementation.

The program includes a multimedia campaign, website, telephone information line, video, and mental health first-aid training package. The multilayered design of the evaluation has included:

1. Process evaluation measures of the reach and effectiveness of implementation of campaign modules
2. Impact evaluation using a cross-sectional telephone survey of 1,200 young people to measure changes in mental health literacy pre and post campaign
3. Outcome evaluation measuring duration of untreated illness and rates of help seeking. Results to date are promising. Radio and newspaper advertising, local dissemination of printed materials, and the website were the most effective campaign elements. There have been small but significant improvements in population mental health literacy during the fifteen-month campaign. Preliminary impacts on help seeking have occurred, and duration of untreated illness continues to be measured.

Results are encouraging considering that most health promotion campaigns can take many years to show improvements in health literacy and behavior. The program is continuing to evolve in response to the evaluation. Preliminary dissemination to other regions is currently underway.

Reference

Green, L., & Kreuter, M. (1999). *Health promotion planning: An educational and ecological approach.* Mountain View, Australia: Mayfield Publishing Company.

Building on Strengths: A New Approach to Mental Health Promotion in New Zealand/Aotearoa

Peter Burton
Ministry of Health
Christchurch, New Zealand

"Building on Strengths," published by the Ministry of Health in December 2002, outlines the National Policy Framework for mental health promotion in New Zealand. The document is a challenge to the health and social service sectors to explore and understand the role they can play in promoting the mental health and well-being of New Zealand citizens. In this presentation we provide a brief account of the strategy, the evidence underpinning its development, the thinking behind the document, and its contents. We also review how the strategy is intended to be used to implement the notions of empowerment, partnership, and participation that are central to the policy framework and approach. We draw parallels between the mutually reinforcing links of these key attributes of the strategy and the rights of indigenous Maori people to be more involved in the planning and delivery of Maori health and well-being services. The presentation is primarily an examination of the Ministry of Health's process around development and early implementation of the strategy. It draws on lessons the organization has learned and that will be pivotal in enabling relationships between the center and the community.

Domestic Violence and Depression: Its Impact on Parenting Adolescents

Kevin Corcoran
Graduate School of Social Work
Portland State University, United States

Teenage pregnancy rates have declined during the past decade but remain a social problem due to its association with depression, poorer health, tobacco use, and other problems. Moreover, a substantial number (about 33 percent) of teen mothers are in violent relationships. The presenter discusses the results of two recently completed Center for Substance Abuse Prevention-funded studies with teen parents on substance use prevention, depression, and domestic violence. Domestic violence was defined by actions in response to violence or the threat of violence by a partner or family member. In the first study of 286 pregnant or parenting adolescents, approximately 33 percent appeared to be in violent situations within the past six months. Similar results were found with the current study, where the rate of violence or threat of violence was 28.5 percent. These figures unfortunately are quite stable. In the first study, the rates continued to be 30 percent, 30 percent, and 32 percent at 6, 12, and 18 month follow-ups, respectively. The rates increase over time, with approximately 17-20 percent new cases at the follow-ups. The responses to violence and its threat vary considerably. They also vary in terms of how likely the youth is to be free of violence in the future, and depression. For example, in our first study of those who experienced domestic violence, only one third called the police, while 79 percent avoided the threatening or violent family member, reflecting 11 percent and 27 percent of the total sample, respectively. Calling the police was not associated with domestic violence a year and a half later (chi-square=1.5, ns), while avoiding the other was associated (chi=8.6, p<.01). This definition of domestic violence also was associated with higher rates of depression, poorer health, more adverse impact on oneself due to alcohol and drugs, and more adverse impact on the partner due to alcohol or drugs. In both studies, over the course of 18 and 12 months, respectively, the adverse impact of violence on substance use decreases over time. Depression, however, does not. This suggests, and is explored thoroughly in the presentation, that domestic violence may cause a clinical condition of depression within a short period of time. The implications for mental health providers, police, and social service agencies are considered.

Cannabis and Psychosis: Cross-Sectional Analysis of an Early Psychosis Intervention Service in South Auckland

Karl Marlowe
Counties Manukau District Health Board
Auckland, New Zealand

Background. In two birth cohort studies in New Zealand of more than 3,000 children, cannabis was found to be a significant factor in the development of psychotic symptoms by age 26. Of greater importance is the association of a five-times relapse rate after the onset of psychosis with ongoing cannabis use, found in a separate cohort of patients with psychosis.
Aim. The Early Psychosis Intervention Team (EPIT) in South Auckland covers a low sociodemographic adult population of 108,890 with significant rates of psychosis. The aim is to identify historical and current cannabis use associated with early psychosis in this unique cultural mix. This will lead to the development of a specific preventive intervention.
Results. This is a cross-sectional description of the patient population in February 2004. Of the 30 patients enrolled, 21 had a diagnosis of schizophrenia, 5 schizoaffective disorder, 2 schizophreniform disorder, and 2 bipolar disorder. The ethnic make-up was 57 percent Maori (n=17), 23 percent Pacific Islander (n=8), 13 percent Pakeha/European (n=4), and 7 percent other (1 Vietnamese and 1 Indian). Fifty-six percent had a family psychiatric history (77 percent with a psychotic disorder). The duration of untreated psychosis (DUP) on average was 17 months, with 50 percent less than or equal to 12 months and 20 percent with a DUP equal to or greater than 36 months. Seventy-seven percent (n=23) had prior use of cannabis (87 percent before age 16), with 26 percent (n=6) discontinuing use during contact with EPIT. Of those continuing use, 61 percent (n=11) were using at least weekly.
Conclusion. EPIT can have an impact on the use of cannabis for patients enrolled. Future research aims to develop a specific intervention targeting the continued use of cannabis for persons in the service and to test its clinical effectiveness. Decreasing long-term morbidity of this vulnerable high-risk population is of primary importance for an early psychosis intervention.

Promoting Parent Mental Health in Serious Child Illness: The Strong Parents–Strong Children Program

Helen Jerram, PhD
Registered Psychologist
Strong Parents–Strong Children Foundation
NZ Charitable Trust
Auckland, New Zealand

The Strong Parents–Strong Children program is a stress and illness management course for parents who are managing serious child illness. The program was developed through doctoral studies, with the help of John Raeburn, School of Population Health, Faculty of Medical and Health Sciences, University of Auckland, by Helen Jerram, herself a parent of a long-term survivor of cancer. Consultation with Starship Children's Hospital and collaboration with parent support groups was critical to the program's development. Risk to parent mental health, particularly that of mothers caring for very sick children with disabling sequelae, was the rationale. The program, with the assistance of the Mental Health Foundation of New Zealand, is used with trained parent implementation in Auckland health and community settings, including Starship, with ongoing evaluation and support. The program consists of six weekly sessions with six-month follow-up. Content focuses on common stresses faced by parents and was derived from two sources. The first was a series of preliminary studies that involved interviewing parents from a variety of cultural backgrounds, pediatricians, and charge nurses. Parent interviews using a semi-structured interview format provided a generic bank of parent-ranked stresses encountered while managing on a daily basis. The second source was the psychological literature describing optimal approaches in child development and stress management. Draft sessions with feedback and the completed program were trialed, using a wait-list control design (Kazdin, 2003), with fifty-eight parents, fifty-one of whom were mothers. Evaluation was by standardized and author-developed measures. Analysis of covariance found significant post-test changes in healthier directions for mean scores on key variables, including well-being, happiness, and emotional support, for the study group when compared to mean scores for the control group. Group process and session helpfulness were rated highly; personal goals were largely attained. Attendance and parent recommendations to other parents in similar situations were high. The Strong Parents–Strong Children program can be seen as contributing to maternal mental health as well as to parent daily management in serious child illness, and is implemented entirely from the parent perspective.

This community resource is available through the Mental Health Foundation and the Strong Parents–Strong Children Foundation (Charitable Trust). For further information: www.spsc.org.nz; www.mentalhealth.org.nz

Promoting Career Management and Mental Health with Preventive Group Intervention

Jukka Vuori
Finnish Institute of Occupational Health
Helsinki, Finland

In the rapidly advancing working world, individuals face several critical transitions during their occupational career. Many young people fail to attain adequate vocational qualifications for the demands of work life, and even young workers with a vocational degree often experience unsatisfactory employment and poor work socialization, which may lead to mental health problems. Job loss among workers has become a common phenomenon that endangers mental health. In addition, many workers must retire early due to work-related burnout and depression or other harmful work experiences. This presentation examines the effects of preventive group methods on careers and mental health during the various phases of occupational careers. Three group interventions are presented that use MPRC-group training principles: active learning process, inoculation against setbacks, group support, and trainer referent power. The aim is to promote an active role and critical skills during the transition phases of a career. The effects of two group interventions on both employment and mental health outcomes among vocational school graduates and among unemployed workers are presented. Preliminary results of the effectiveness of a third group intervention, aimed at preventing drop-out from vocational education among graduates of comprehensive schools, are shown. All three effectiveness studies had randomized field experimental designs. The participants were 1,265 unemployed workers during the period 1996-1997, 520 graduates of vocational schools during the period 2000-2002, and about 1,200 graduates of comprehensive schools during the period 2003-2005. Participants randomized to the experimental groups participated in preventive career management groups for five days. The studies had long-term follow-ups for up to two years, which showed sustained beneficial effects on employment and career outcomes. Preventive effects on symptoms of depression became significant in the two-year follow-up. The group method for unemployed persons already has been disseminated nationwide in the Finnish service systems, and the method for vocational school graduates has been widely disseminated in vocational schools. The results and applicability of the preventive principles during workers' later careers in supporting career management and preventing burnout, symptoms of depression, and early retirement due to work-related causes are discussed.

Interventions for Separated and Divorced Persons: A Meta-analysis

Bernd Roehrle and Janina Hartmann
University of Marburg
Germany

The number of divorces worldwide is increasing. For many people this critical life event is an important risk factor for the development of mental disorders. A number of studies show that divorce frequently is accompanied by a variety of psychological, psychosomatic, and physical impairments for the affected people. Only a few studies report on the effectiveness of coping programs. A quantitative overview of various forms of interventions for separated and divorced persons is given. Overall effectiveness seems to be reasonable. Results concerning a variety of technical arrangements, group composition, and operationalization are presented.

2.4 Evidence-Based Programs, Policies, and Principles of Effective Promotion and Prevention: Miscellaneous

Some Reflections on the Future of Promotion and Prevention in Mental Health

L. de Graaf
Mental Health Europe
The Netherlands

The promotion of mental health and the prevention of mental disorders (together here called "promovention") is an enormous task. This presentation describes some factors that facilitate and other factors that limit the impact of "promoventive" interventions. Factors that limit the impact are:
- Lack of consensus on the definition of promovention
- Sheer size of the target group
- Massive spread of new risk factors due to socio-economic conditions, disasters, etc.
- So-called zero-sum developments, where the decrease of risk factors is neutralized by simultaneous increase of other risk factors or decrease of protective factors
- Tenacity of hereditary biological factors

These aggravating factors are counterbalanced, however, by several favorable factors:

- Increasing acknowledgement of the importance of mental health for general well-being, for the economy, and for the stability and coherence of our society
- Scientific progress, which makes evidence-based programs possible for promovention
- Many allies who contribute to promoting mental health, sometimes without being aware of it
- Increased importance of all sorts of prevention in affluent countries
- Decreasing acceptance of violence as part of the process of civilization

The presentation ends with some conclusions and some proposals for action.

Criteria for Assessing Applications to Registries of Evidence-Based Prevention Programs

Chris Ringwalt
Pacific Institute for Research and Evaluation
Chapel Hill, North Carolina, United States

The Department of Education and other federal- and state-level agencies in the United States increasingly are requiring the implementation of evidence-based programs by the schools and community-based organizations whose substance abuse and violence prevention efforts they support. In response, several agencies have established lists of "model" or "effective" programs, including the National Registry of Effective Programs and Blueprints for Violence Prevention, sponsored by the Substance Abuse and Mental Health Services Administration and the Office of Juvenile Justice and Delinquency Prevention, respectively. Each of these agencies also has published a set of criteria by which applications to these registries are judged, and which pertain both to the quality and results of program evaluations. In addition, the Society for Prevention Research recently has promulgated its own set of criteria concerning methodology appropriate for both efficacy and effectiveness trials of prevention programs. In this presentation we specify these various criteria and examine and discuss their commonalities and differences. We then examine the process used by the National Registry of Effective Programs to review applications for model program status, drawing on the presenter's experiences as coordinator of such applications for workplace-based programs. We conclude with recommendations for the development and implementation of such registries, and a discussion of the political pressures they must be able to withstand if they are to establish and maintain their credibility and integrity.

Translating Research Knowledge to Policy and Practice

Janine Smith
Telethon Institute for Child Health Research
West Perth, Australia

Objective. The study explored how researchers translate research knowledge into policy and practice, specifically determining successful conditions and barriers within the Population Science Division of the Telethon Institute for Child Health Research in Western Australia. **Design.** Qualitative study design guided by the principles of grounded theory. Data was collected between January and May 2004 and included a review of the literature and a series of formal interviews.

Reynolds Adolescent Depression Scale (RADS). Results show that 18 percent of females and 9 percent of males had cut-off scores that indicated a high likelihood of significant psychopathology from depression. Multivariate analysis demonstrated that family connection, parental presence, and neighborhood and peer connections all were protective against depression. Indicators of socioeconomic hardship, witnessing violence at home, physical and sexual abuse, and experiencing bullying at school all were significant risk factors for depression. The cumulative effect of exposure to adversity was related strongly to depression symptoms, but was moderated at all levels of adversity by caring and supportive social environments. The findings from this study show that social environments are linked strongly to symptoms of depression among high school students in New Zealand. Furthermore, caring and supportive social environments act to buffer the effects of socioeconomic hardship and violence victimization and highlight areas for primary and secondary intervention to prevent depression and improve outcomes for young people in New Zealand.

Designing and Delivering an International Mental Health Promotion Program for Young Children

Chris Bale
Partnership for Children
Surrey, United Kingdom

Most mental health promotion programs for children are national or local in scope. Zippy's Friends, a school-based program for six and seven year olds, is unusual in having been designed from the outset to be international, and suitable for use with children of different abilities and cultures. More than 20,000 children now have completed the program, and the presentation traces its seven-year development from research to effective practice in different countries. Zippy's Friends teaches young children how to cope better with everyday adversities. The principles and policies that underpin the program are introduced. Extensive international evaluation has demonstrated that, compared to children in control groups, children in the program show improvement in their abilities to cope with adversities; increases in cooperation, self-control, assertiveness, and empathy; and decreases in problem behaviors such as hyperactivity and externalizing. These benefits apply equally to boys and girls and endure after the program is completed. The key findings of the evaluation are presented. Zippy's Friends was piloted first in Denmark and Lithuania, and now is being launched in other countries by a range of local partner agencies. It will run in schools in at least nine countries by late 2004. The presentation explains how the program is promoted internationally and how partner agencies are selected. It reviews the practical issues involved in delivering a program in different countries, including the need to ensure cultural appropriateness, and demonstrates how different stakeholders (governments, educators, mental health professionals, teachers, and parents) all are involved in its successful delivery.

Youth Clubs: Psychosocial Intervention to Prevent Mental Health Problems in Adolescents

Veronika Ispanovic-Radojkovic
Institute of Mental Health
Belgrade, Serbia and Montenegro

Background. The implementation of youth clubs started during the years of war in the former Yugoslavia (1991-95) with the aim of supporting the psychosocial recovery and integration of thousands of young refugees in Serbia, but also to prevent problems in local adolescents exposed to chronic adversity in a deteriorating social context. The youth clubs are one of the psychosocial programs carried out by the Institute for Mental Health in Belgrade since 1992 and conducted throughout Serbia with the support of INTERCARE, a Dutch humanitarian organization. The youth clubs were set up in secondary or boarding schools and consisted of recreational and creative activities (games, music, literature, painting) and sociotherapeutic groups.

Evaluation study. This was done to test the hypothesis that the youth club intervention significantly decreased symptoms of psychological distress (anxiety, withdrawal, and aggressive behavior) and the degree of traumatization, and increased the self-esteem of the adolescents involved. The sample was made up of 1,106 students (813 boys, 293 girls) from nine boarding schools in Belgrade, aged 15-18 years; 158 were refugees. The adolescents (N=128) who participated in youth club activities for at least 6 months formed the experimental group, while the others (N=978) formed the control. The following instruments were used: Youth Self-Report for ages 11 to 18 (Achenbach et al., 1991), Adolescent Self-Construction (Wolf, Davis et al., 1996), War Trauma Questionnaire (Wolf, 1994), and Impact of Event Scale (Horowitz et al., 1979). The evaluation of the effects of the intervention was made by repeated measures before and after the intervention.

Results. The young people who participated in youth club activities reported improved understanding of themselves (78 percent) and others (63 percent), and easier communication with peers (60 percent). A significant increase in self-esteem occurred in all adolescents. A decrease in psychological problems also was significant, especially in refugees (shown in boys on the Achenbach Withdrawal and Anxiety-Depression scales, and in girls on the Withdrawal and Social Problems scales). The level of traumatization decreased among nonrefugees, but not among the highly traumatized refugees.

What is the Evidence for the Effectiveness of Behavioral and Skill-Based Early Intervention in Young Children with Autism Spectrum Disorder (ASD)?

Carole Doughty
Christchurch School of Medicine
New Zealand

Problem behaviors and specific skill deficits are a common concern for parents of young children with autism, because they can become major barriers to effective education and social development. Typical problem behaviors may include physical aggression, self-injury, property destruction, pica, stereotypy, defiance, and tantrums. For this reason behavioral interventions often are used to promote both social and adaptive behavior in children with autism. Experimental analysis of behavior has led to the application of basic psychological principles of learning to human behavior, and applied behavioral analysis (ABA) refers to the application of these principles to improve socially important behaviors. They can include specific approaches (for example, Lovaas Therapy/ABA) that are used to help children acquire or change behaviors (or skills) by reinforcing adaptive responses and suppressing nonadaptive responses, or they may form part of a broader social-developmental treatment and prevention program. Historically treatment programs for children with autism have had a much greater focus on developing or supporting the demonstration of specific skills rather than the promotion of relatedness and attachment. However, tertiary prevention intervention models, which prioritize the developmental dimensions of social communication and emotional regulation, are gaining recognition. Comprehensive or integrated treatment programs also may seek to include components of speech and language therapy, or children may already be receiving these services as part of their usual care. Assessing the efficacy of early intervention for autism is not straightforward. Researchers only recently have begun to address systematically the inherent methodological issues and problems that arise in attempting to conduct trials for treatment of a disorder that is rare and has a very early age of onset. To date experts have recommended early diagnosis and intensive therapy to improve a child's ability to communicate, adapt to change, and develop social skills. Intense, specialized, integrated programs purport to be among those that produce the greatest gains. These programs build upon a child's interests, offer a predictable schedule with parental involvement, teach tasks in a series of simple steps, actively engage a child's attention in highly structured activities, provide regular reinforcement of appropriate behaviors, and aim towards generalization of skills across environments. The focus of this paper is to highlight the most *recent* and *best* evidence for the effectiveness of behavioral and skill-based early interventions for tertiary prevention in young children with ASD.

Mental Health Information for Young People, by Young People: Reality Check

Steve Druitt
Mental Illness Education ACT
Australia

A problem identified by young people about youth-friendly printed information and websites is that it is often someone else's idea of what they like, and actually does not engage them at all! Reality Check, www.realitycheck.net.au, is a new youth mental health website developed in Canberra, Australia. The development process for this site has been guided completely by young people. Focus and feedback groups with young people came up with some surprising answers. Draft designs for the site were rejected as over-designed or an "old people's idea of what we like." On the other hand, young people related well to some stories of older people's experience with mental illness and treatment, and these now form an important part of the site's content. This presentation introduces Reality Check and looks at the development process, showing the value of user feedback along the way. It also looks at the consumer and carer storytelling model that is the basis of the site and of the community education delivered by the host community organization, Mental Illness Education A.C.T. Mental Illness Education A.C.T. is a community organization that provides support and education to consumer and carer presenters to tell their stories and important factual information to schools and other community groups, with the main aim of reducing stigma.

The Paying Attention to Self (PATS) Project: Dissemination and Evaluation of a Peer Support Program for Adolescents Who Have a Parent with a Mental Health Problem

John Hargreaves
Centre for Adolescent Health
Melbourne, Australia

Research indicates that young people with a parent affected by a mental illness are at greater risk of developing mental health problems themselves. Given the increased incidence of mental illness throughout the Western world, it is critical to develop programs that have a prevention or early intervention focus. Such programs have the capacity to reduce the burden of disease and develop a positive trajectory for this population of young people. Paying Attention To Self (PATS) is an innovative program working towards these aims. PATS is a peer support program for adolescents aged 13-18 years who are affected by parental mental illness, coordinated by the Centre for Adolescent Health, Murdoch Children's Research Institute/Royal Children's Hospital, Melbourne, Australia. PATS aims to increase adolescents' knowledge of mental health and illness, to improve their help-seeking behavior and coping strategies, and to improve connections with their peers, family, and community. The program has been disseminated to seven locations across the state of Victoria in rural, inner city, and suburban contexts. An extensive process and outcome evaluation is being conducted exploring the key components necessary to establish programs in different community settings and identifying the impact of the program on young people and their families. This workshop provides an in-depth outline of the peer support approach utilized in PATS and discussion of the process of community consultation, program dissemination, and evaluation design. Issues affecting young people in this situation and ideas around supporting them are explored. Some initial data concerning this group of young people and the impact of the PATS program also are discussed.

Developmental Trajectories of Depressive Symptoms Among Indigenous Adolescents and Their Family Covariates: A Longitudinal Study

Chyi-In Wu
Institute of Sociology
Academia Sinica
Taiwan

This study investigates the associations among parenting, family relationships, and trajectories of depressive symptoms among indigenous adolescents in northern Taiwan. Data were collected through face-to-face interviews using a structured questionnaire. A total of 155 indigenous students from junior high schools were recruited in this three-wave panel with initial data collection in 2000. This study uses a latent growth mixture modeling approach to identified trajectory classes for depressive symptoms. In addition, it uses family covariates to distinguish among trajectory classes. It is primarily concerned with identifying factors that cause indigenous adolescents in Taiwan to escalate the severity of depressive symptoms. The proposed model identifies possible causal mechanisms and specifies the manner in which these phenomena are correlated with each other.

3.2 International Exchange and Cultural Variation: Working Age

Epidemiology of Postnatal Depression Among Pacific Mothers in Auckland: A Research Base for Effective Practice

Max Abbott
Auckland University of Technology
Auckland, New Zealand

Postnatal depressive disorders (PND) are commonplace globally, with significant adverse impacts on the well-being of mothers and partners and the development and mental health of children. Although widespread, there are prevalence variations in different populations. It has been suggested that PND is a culture-bound syndrome associated with Westernization and modernity. Effective prevention practice requires understanding of factors associated with the development of disorders in particular sociocultural contexts. This paper examines findings from 1,288 migrant and non-migrant Pacific Island mothers. Data were collected at 6 months postpartum as part of the Pacific Islands: First 2 Years of Life (PIF) Study. Using the Edinburgh Postnatal Depression Scale, 16.5 percent of mothers were assessed as probably experiencing depression. Prevalence rates varied from 7.6 percent for Samoans to 30.9 percent for Tongans. Risk factors, additional to ethnicity, included low Pacific Island acculturation, first birth, stress due to insufficient food, difficulty with transportation and dissatisfaction with pregnancy, birth experience, baby's sleep pattern, partner relationship, and home. The large Tongan-Samoan prevalence difference remained when the effects of other risk factors were controlled statistically. The overall prevalence of PND among Pacific mothers is similar to rates from previous New Zealand general population surveys and the mean rate for studies in other parts of the world. Risk factors also are generally similar to those of previous studies. Focus on the overall PND rate, however, obscures substantial variation between Pacific ethnic groups. This and some of the other findings have important implications for public health policy and prevention practice.

Do Cultural Differences Make a Difference? Universal Prevention and Early Intervention Programs for Parents

Lea Crisante
Western Sydney Heath Service
Australia

This paper describes research on a number of initiatives aimed at developing culturally appropriate parenting programs through an evidence-based mental health program conducted in Western Sydney Area Health Service, which provides services to a very wide range of communities from culturally and linguistically diverse backgrounds. The Area Parenting Program has provided parent education courses to more than 3,000 parents based on the Positive Parenting Program (Triple P) developed by Sanders (2003). Courses have been conducted in English, Arabic, and Chinese and evaluated (Booth & Crisante, 2004; Crisante & Ng, 2003) through standardized measures such as the Strengths and Difficulties Questionnaire (Goodman, 2000). Other initiatives have included providing parenting courses to parents of refugee background using the TIPS program developed in New Zealand with Pacific Island communities and training bilingual community educators to provide parenting services. As a result of these activities, extensive quantitative and qualitative data have been collected regarding program impact and participants' experiences of doing parenting programs. The paper explores what evidence is useful and appropriate when working with culturally diverse communities in the context of the methodological difficulties associated with such research. It highlights some of the differences and similarities between parents of non-English speaking backgrounds who choose to attend a universal program conducted in English compared with those who choose to attend a course conducted by someone of their own cultural background. The paper argues for a range of strategies, varying in program type, location, format, and sponsorship as essential to good practice.

Deaf New Zealanders' Perception of Mental Illness and Mental Health Support Systems: Implications for Deaf Mental Health Promotion and Prevention

Geoff Bridgman
UNITEC Institute of Technology
Auckland, New Zealand

As part of the 2,000 national deaf epidemiological study, 119 deaf participants from five different areas of New Zealand answered some open-ended questions about what they thought mental illness was about, what its causes were, and how deaf people should be helped to avoid or recover from mental illness. Deaf people have a stripped-down understanding of mental illness that is frightening and stigmatizing. Some are unable to provide any description of mental illness or its causes. Causes of mental illness are seen overwhelmingly as environmental: lack of family support, societal discrimination, communication barriers, and poor support services for the deaf community. Only 20 percent refer to alcohol, drugs, abuse, or aggression as having a causal role in mental illness and only 5 percent to inherited causes. Ninety-one percent wanted prevention and recovery services to focus on environments that support good communication, signing, deaf culture, and/or use deaf staff. Turning to the kind of services wanted, *support* was named by nearly two thirds of the participants, particularly in relation to education and social networks. Only 23 percent saw medically oriented professionals as being the deliverers of support, with psychiatrists named only by 3 percent of the participants; in contrast, 54 percent looked for counselors to play a key role, emphasizing the importance of genuine dialogue that enables deaf people to make healthy choices. Finally, some participants were concerned that a one-size-fits-all model should not be applied to health promotion, prevention, and recovery services. Clear differences in socioeconomic factors and perception of meaning and needs were seen between Maori and non-Maori, men and women, and those with prior history of use of some form of mental health support services. Deaf health promotion and prevention requires different strategies and models of funding to enable the deaf community to overcome entrenched and overlooked disadvantage because of the small size of the deaf community and the need for cultural services, health promotion, and prevention services.

3.3 International Exchange and Cultural Variation: Miscellaneous

Rapua Te Hinengaro Tangata Toa (Seek the Mind of a Warrior)

Tui Taurua
Hapai Te Hauora Tapui Ltd.
Auckland, New Zealand

Program Aims:
- Participants will identify three models of Maori mental health (for example, Te Whare Tapa Wha, Maori Ora, Mauri Ora).
- Participants will identify one's own Whakapapa and its significance in relation to their spiritual destiny and life journey.
- Participants will learn what the word Tautoko (support) means from a Maori perspective and how this impacts on the well-being of Tangata Whaiora.
- Participants will learn to identify personal destructive patterns.
- Participants will gain a full understanding of being reconnected with what is important to Maori, for example, Tupuna (ancestors), Maunga (mountain), Awa (river), Moana (sea), Urupa (cemetery), Kai (food), Tangihanga (grief and bereavement), Karakia (acknowledgement of Io Matua Kore Spiritual beings), Kapa Haka (Maori cultural group), Whakawhanaungatanga (relationships), Marae (main gathering place for Maori), Te Reo (Maori language), Wairua (inner strength).

Learning Milestones:
- Participants have learned to practically implement three models of Maori mental health (Te Whare Tapa Wha, Maori Ora, Mauri Ora).
- Participants have researched their genealogical backgrounds (Whakapapa) by seeking advice from Kaumatua, Kuia, and Marae base.
- Participants have identified their main support structures and applied a Maori perspective that has impacted on their daily lives.
- Participants have learned preventive measures of care and incorporated a Maori perspective.
- Participants have learned the meaning of recovery and hope (Whakawhanaungatanga) from a Maori perspective.
- Participants have identified their inner tools required to walk their own paths' journeys.
- Participants have gained a renewed feeling of confidence, self-worth, self-respect, self-esteem, and inner strength.

Pacific Voice in Suicide Prevention

Pefi Kingi
Niu Developments Inc. and
Sarah Lee Te Huki
SPINZ
New Zealand

"Given support and direction, indigenous peoples will act and, indeed, want to act to reduce suicide in their communities and that external interventions cannot work with indigenous communities, that interventions must come from out of the hearts, minds and will of the communities most affected." Keri Te Aho-Lawson

As a nonclinical information service set up to support communities to reduce suicide among young people, SPINZ (Suicide Prevention Information New Zealand) has a responsibility to ensure that specific cultural groups can access information appropriate to their needs. SPINZ acknowledges the need for a mechanism by which Pacific communities could identify information needs in regard to suicide prevention. This workshop describes the process by which a formalized and mandated mechanism can be put in place to ensure that Pacific people have an ongoing role in advising and supporting the collection, management, and dissemination of suicide prevention information. This process was undertaken by Niu Developments in partnership with SPINZ.

Dual Stigma of Indigenous Peoples

Mark Lawrence
Te Whare Maiangiangi, Acute Psychiatric Inpatient Unit
Tauranga, New Zealand

Poor access to health services for indigenous peoples is well documented in the literature for all Pacific peoples and continues to be problematic. Stigma plays a significant role at all levels and impacts on the journey of those who navigate the health care systems. Using the process of literature reviews, narrative projects, and consultation with Maori and anti-stigma organizations and initiatives, we explore the concept of stigma and explain why it arises and some innovative approaches to minimize stigma. The current theories of stigma are adapted to include Te Ao Maori (Maori world view) as a complimentary paradigm for further exploration and discussion.

Antipodean Gothic: Political Economy of Madness in Antipodean Film

Dean Manley
University of New Zealand
Auckland, New Zealand

*New Zealand and Australia: "A Great Place to Grow Mad, Twisted and Bitter"/*The Politics of Madness: Representations of Madness in Antipodean Film

New Zealand and Australian film is riddled with atmospheres of dread, anxiety, and madness in what has been termed Antipodean Gothic. Representations of alienation, anomie, psychological distress, dislocation, and precariousness of existence add to stigma and discrimination of mental illness. This paper investigates the sources of Gothicism in settler culture and the affect this anxiety of existence has on the self-perceptions and esteem of those represented. Where the antipodes is depicted as a site of fate worse than death—purgatory—in images of doom and punishment, film becomes a marker of this nihilistic ideology, and antipodean film especially. Using various texts I investigate Antipodean Gothic and the role of madness in this sensibility and representation, and the role of this representation in antipodean identity. Investigating Antipodean Gothic film helps counteract stigma and unpack the cultural loading of horror and terror inherent within these texts. An archeology of images for loading of imperialistic guilt and sins of the father uses the idea of orientalism of mental illness (in a Saidian sense of othering) through the framework of Foucault's history of madness in the Age of Reason as point of departure for the investigation of these films. I look at "An Angel at My Table," "The Piano," "Heavenly Creatures," and "Lord of the Rings" along with "Picnic at Hanging Rock" and "Mad Max" to illustrate these points. I explore the ramifications of Antipodean Gothic on self-perceptions of individuals affected by mental illness and ask how representations of madness are specifically antipodean. I explore how imperialism has colluded with occult fears of divine affliction and heroic suffering regarding mental illness, making the antipodes the geographical equivalent of madness in colonialist thought. Unpacking representations will help provide an understanding of the horror and dread associated with mental illness by demythologizing Gothic madness, returning it to the everyday and the commonplace within the power of everyone to address. This is a critical dissection of the anatomy of madness from an antipodean perspective in pursuit of research into the popular culture art form of film—becoming influential in Aotearoa New Zealand and Australia to deconstruct mythologies of madness in aid of destigmatization.

3.4 Program, Practice, and Theory

Equine Facilitated Mental Health

K. Johnson
Riding for the Disabled Association Australia
Ballina, NSW, Australia

The Equine Facilitated Mental Health Association (EFMHA) is a globally recognized organization that promotes health by bringing people and equines together in mutually beneficial ways. Part of the mission of EFMHA is to:

- Promote professionally facilitated equine experiences designed to enhance psychosocial development growth and education
- Educate others to work with the horse in the treatment of people with emotional, behavioral, social, mental, physical and/or spiritual needs
- Provide a foundation to see Equine Facilitated Psychotherapy (EFP) in the future

EFP is experiential psychotherapy that includes equines. It may include a number of mutually respectful equine activities such as handling, grooming, lunging, riding, driving, and vaulting. EFP is facilitated by a licensed, credentialed mental health professional working with an appropriately credentialed equine professional. EFP may be facilitated by a mental health professional who is dually credentialed as an equine professional. This presentation looks at the development and growth of EFMHA in the United States, specific programs in the United States, my personal journey and involvement in the world of equus and working with horses in this field, and ways horses can assist in the development of issues such as trust, leadership, communication, and self-responsibility.

Background: I am qualified with the Australian National Coaching Accreditation Scheme specializing in coaching horse riding to children and adults with a disability at the Riding for the Disabled Association (NSW) Ballina and District Centre in New South Wales, Australia. I have always been interested in and believed in the power of the horse to have a positive and beneficial effect on people's sense of well-being and harmony. To pursue my learning I traveled to the U.S. in 2000 on a Winston Churchill Fellowship to study Equine Facilitated Mental Health programs. I returned there in 2001 for more theoretical and practical study. In 2003 I attended the annual conference of the North American Riding for the Handicapped Association, which focused on this work with people with mental health challenges. During my first visit I attended an Adventures in Awareness workshop and now base my program on this experience. Basically an Adventures in Awareness experience encourages participants to learn principles of responsibility, relationships, and communication. The program at Ballina and District RDA Centre offered to students at risk and/or adults with mental health challenges encompasses acquisition of horse-riding skills but also focuses on unmounted equine activities promoting issues such as relationship, trust, personal space, boundaries, leadership, and communication.

Nga Manu Kaha: Changing Attitudes by Sharing Stories

John Tovey
Te Ropu Pokai Taaniwhaniwha
Porirua, New Zealand

Nga Manu Kaha are a small team of Maori who have personally experienced mental illness. As part of New Zealand's Whakaitia Te Whakawhiu i Te Tangata (Like Minds Like Mine) campaign to reduce stigma and discrimination, they have put together a training opportunity that targets *groups* of people working in the Maori community. What they offer is simple in concept: an opportunity for the trainees and trainers to each share their stories and experience in a process that promotes whakawhanaungatanga (getting to know each other and making relationships) and draws on the usual ingredients of Maori hui: Karakia, Waiata, Mihimihi, Korero, and the sharing of Kai. Nga Manu Kaha see this process as a way of forging lasting relationships and memories that will impact on the understanding and attitudes of the community workers and be carried by them out to the wider Maori community. Nga Manu Kaha envisage using the presentation time allocated to run a shortened version of a real training experience, which could be watched by observers free to come and go quietly. A key ingredient of the experience is that it is an encounter of *groups* rather than training provided to assembled *individuals*. For this reason it is essential to identify in advance a small group of workers willing to take part as trainees.

"The Perspectives of Psychiatry": Toward a Theory of Preventing Mental Illness and Promoting Mental Health

Stephen C. Petrica
University of Maryland
Baltimore, Maryland, United States

Since the demise of the psychoanalytic hegemony that held sway over mental health through much of the twentieth century, psychiatry has lacked a cohesive theory of pathogenesis. Similar constellations of symptoms (or clinical syndromes) can have divergent causes, and the DSM's symptom-based diagnostic system eschews a theoretical foundation. Consequently, there is a void as well in contemporary theories of prevention and promotion in mental health. Rather than a unitary theory of mental illness (such as the Freudian notion that all mental illness arises out of intrapsychic conflict), McHugh and Slavney, in their work on "The Perspectives of Psychiatry," describe four different (but not mutually exclusive) understandings of mental illness in its various forms. The disease perspective follows the logic of an abnormality in bodily functioning, the result of pathological process, which in turn may have been initiated by an identifiable etiologic agent. The dimensions perspective follows the logic of gradation and locates one's vulnerability to mental problems as arising from one's position in the distribution of intellectual and temperamental traits within the general population. The behaviors perspective describes the mental problems that can arise from motivated behaviors that become maladaptive. The life-story perspective follows the logic of narrative and meaning to understand the subjective distress that individuals may experience as a result of certain life events. Intended to illuminate the clinical tasks of diagnostic formulation and treatment planning, the pathogenetic processes explicated by the perspectives also provide a theoretical framework for conceiving and designing upstream interventions to prevent the development of mental illness and, indeed, to promote mental health. The theoretical basis thus provided for prevention and promotion also provides grounding for testable hypotheses, thus contributing to the establishment of evidence-based practice. This paper introduces the perspectives of psychiatry and develops their implications for promoting mental health and preventing mental disorders.

3.5 Media and Mental Health Promotion

Mental Health Promotion: What's the Evidence for a Statewide Campaign?

Gillian Church
Mental Health Association NSW Inc.
Australia

The Mental Health Association NSW (MHA) is a leading mental health promotion nongovernmental association in New South Wales (NSW), Australia. During the latter part of 2003, the MHA's Mental Health Promotion Advisory Committee and the NSW Network for Promotion and Prevention in Mental Health discussed the possibility of conducting a statewide campaign in NSW. However, in true mental health promotion style, we asked the questions, "Are such campaigns actually effective, and, if so, what is the evidence?" The Centre for Mental Health authorized the expenditure of a limited amount of funds to employ a consultant to carry out the necessary research to find the answers to these and other related questions. Research on whether or not a NSW-wide campaign could be effective and efficient in achieving mental health promotion outcomes is considered. Researchers discuss:

1. Major mental health promotion campaigns, Australian and international. For example, what campaigns have been run, how were they evaluated, what conclusions were reached? What are the characteristics of effective and ineffective campaigns?

2. Major health promotion campaigns, with similar research questions asked, as well as noting what lessons could be learned and applied to a mental health promotion campaign

3. Contextual issues in NSW that may influence the effectiveness of a campaign. The Area Health Service structure, with seventeen geographically based areas, is unique.

4. Recommendations on how to proceed. They identify the strengths and weaknesses of large state-level campaigns and discuss the pros and cons of conducting such campaigns in NSW.

Mental Health and the Media: An Australian Approach

Jaelea Skehan
Hunter Institute of Mental Health
New South Wales, Australia

The media is a major source of information for the community and plays an important role in influencing social attitudes towards and perceptions of suicide, mental illness, and mental health. The Australian Government Department of Health and Ageing has funded the National Mindframe Initiative to work collaboratively with the Australian media to promote responsible and accurate reporting of suicide and mental illness. Through accurate and sensitive reporting, the media can play an important role in improving attitudes to mental illness, promoting help-seeking behavior, and in reducing the occurrence of copycat suicide. Sensationalist reporting, however, can promote stigma in the community by presenting people with mental illness in ways that are inaccurate and may place vulnerable members of the community at a greater risk of self-harm. The Mindframe strategy has successfully established the National Media and Mental Health Group as a way of bringing media and mental health representatives together to discuss appropriate ways to address this issue in Australia. The Mindframe Media and Mental Health Project is just one component of the National Initiative. It aims to work collaboratively with the working media to understand better the issues involved in reporting on suicide, mental illness, and mental health, and to promote a more accurate, sensitive, and balanced portrayal of the issues through direct and indirect training strategies. This paper highlights the key strategies of the Mindframe Media and Mental Health Project, including how the project has broadened its original focus to include culturally diverse population groups, consumer and carer organizations, the judicial system, and the mental health sector. The project's success to date and ongoing challenges are discussed in the context of the broader national approaches to suicide prevention and the promotion and prevention of mental health problems in Australia.

From Research to Effective Practice

The Pacific Art focus is on tapa printing; consumers gain skills, knowledge, and understanding of this traditional process. It is hoped that clients eventually will be able to exhibit their creations and perhaps gain financial rewards. The Exercise Group is an energetic session designed to improve physical health through enjoyment and fun. A trained instructor runs this session. There is a shared lunch prepared by staff and consumers that focuses on how to budget and prepare healthy and tasty food economically.

Proposed Outcome: The poster focuses on ways in which this unique group has strengthened decision-making skills and confidence of consumers.

Role of Information in Mental Health Promotion

Jo Beck
Mental Health Foundation of New Zealand
Auckland, New Zealand

Information has an important role in promoting mental health. It can:
- Empower people by enabling them to make informed choices about their treatment and lifestyle
- Increase understanding of mental health and mental illness needs, issues, and treatments
- Facilitate networks in mental health that can lead to sharing of resources and knowledge
- Reduce discrimination against people with mental illnesses by banishing myths and stereotypes
- Promote familiarity with current research in the field, which paves the way to evidence-based practice
- Increase help-seeking behavior from people who experience mental illness or their families
- Encourage safer and more balanced media coverage of mental health and mental illness
- Inform policy making, either at the organizational or governmental level

This session examines the role of information in mental health promotion and depicts the continuous flow of information from collection (research, consumer experiences, analysis, presentation of papers) to management (indexing, filing, classifying, abstracting) to dissemination (resource development, program development, and website) and back to collection (evaluation, feedback). Each process is examined in more detail and the relationship among them shown.

Green Prescriptions: The New Zealand "Feel Good" Factor

Diana O'Neill
SPARC (Sport and Recreation NZ)
Wellington, New Zealand

A dose of physical activity works wonders for many of the population health objectives listed in New Zealand's Ministry of Health Primary Health Care Strategy. A Green Prescription (GRx) is written advice for a patient to be more active as part of their health management. Over two thirds of general practitioners and an increasing number of practice nurses have issued GRx since the initiative went nationwide six years ago. The Green Prescription model is a proven and cost-effective way of reaching at-risk populations, including mental health consumers, and increasing their activity levels. In November 2003 44 percent of general practitioners surveyed stated that they issued GRx for relief of stress and anxiety in their patients and over one quarter of patients surveyed in May the same year said they felt calmer and more relaxed since being more active. SPARC (Sport and Recreation NZ) is now working closely with the Mental Health Foundation of NZ to ensure that the link between physical activity and mental health is strengthened. This presentation outlines the nature of the partnership between the two organizations and provides an update of mental health benefits to Green Prescription patients.

Public Perceptions of the SARS Outbreak in Taiwan

Shu-Yu Lyu
School of Public Health
Taipei Medical University
Taiwan

Background. The first probable case of severe acute respiratory syndrome (SARS) in Taiwan was found on March 14, 2003. The World Health Organization added Taiwan to the travel alert list on May 21 and lifted Taiwan from the list of SARS-affected areas on July 5, 2003. The cumulative number of SARS probable cases reached 665 in August 2003 and became the third SARS epidemic impact area in the world.

Objectives. To describe public perceptions regarding severity of and susceptibility to SARS, and to explore people's fears regarding the SARS outbreak.

Methods. Two telephone surveys were conducted using nationwide representative samples aged 18 or above. Data were collected using a computer-assisted telephone interview (CATI) system. The first survey (N=1,081) was conducted from May 15 to May 17, and the second survey (N=1,275) was conducted from June 1 to June 4, 2003. The maximum deviation of sampling error at the 95 percent confidence level for both surveys was less than ± 3 percent.

Results. Roughly 89.9 percent in the first survey and 76.2 percent in the second survey perceived SARS as a severe disease. Regarding personal susceptibility to SARS, 5.2 percent of subjects in the first survey believed that they would "very likely" and 19.3 percent of the subjects in the second survey believed that they would "likely" contract SARS. The personal susceptibility measure of "very likely" versus "likely" to contract SARS decreased to 1.4 percent and 15.6 percent, respectively, in the second survey. Approximately 29.5 percent in the first survey and 38.3 percent in the second survey believed that more than 80.0 percent of the SARS patients would survive. It was noted that 22.0 percent in the first survey and 7.1 percent in the second survey believed that fewer than half of the SARS patients would survive. Furthermore, 60.0 percent and 51.7 percent reported fear of the SARS epidemic in the first and second surveys, respectively. The impact of the SARS epidemic on the subjects' daily lives decreased from 67.3 percent to 56.3 percent.

Conclusions. The confidence of SARS survival rate increased over time, yet more than half the subjects reported fear of the SARS epidemic in both surveys. Mental health education in this regard needs to be strengthened.

Effectively Reducing Stigma and Increasing Mental Health Literacy: Role of Shared Personal Experience

Steve Druitt
Mental Illness Education ACT
CURTIN ACT
Australia

The impact of mental health consumers and carers telling their story of illness, treatment, and recovery has now been shown to be significant in increasing community mental health literacy and reducing stigma towards people with a mental illness. Mental Illness Education ACT is a community organization that provides support and education to consumer and carer presenters to tell their story and important factual information to schools and other community groups, with the main aim of reducing stigma. This program was evaluated in 2001 through the Centre for Applied Psychology at University of Canberra, Australia, with impressive results. At the time of writing this abstract, a report has been submitted for publication to the *International Journal of Mental Health Promotion*. The appeal of storytelling is universal, and we can all relate to the personal experience of others. Hearing someone who is well tell their story also directly challenges pre-conceived ideas about mental illness. Anecdotally, presenters also report that telling their story helps integrate their experience and gain self-confidence. In this workshop, a presenter from the program tells his or her story and talks about the experience of working in the program. A summary of the evaluation findings is presented.

Coping Strategies for Auditory Hallucinations in Schizophrenic Patients

Kazuya Norikane
Kagawa Prefectural College of Health Sciences
Japan

Auditory hallucinations are a general symptom experienced by more than 80 percent of individuals with schizophrenia. Corson et al. (1988) reported that auditory hallucination is difficult to improve despite pharmacotherapy in 25-50 percent of patients with schizophrenia. This study investigated characteristics and coping strategies for auditory hallucination experience in patients with schizophrenia, and examined the effects of these coping strategies on auditory hallucination.

Subjects: Thirty patients with schizophrenia who experienced auditory hallucinations (19 male, 11 female)

Methods: Semi-structured interview including inquiry about coping strategies and emotional reactions to auditory hallucination was carried out. Transcribed interviews were reviewed, coded, and analyzed using content analysis. Coping strategies were classified into two kinds, emotion-focused form of coping and problem-focused form of coping, based on Lazarus's stress-coping theory with respect to coping with auditory hallucination.

Results:
1. One hundred forty nine coping strategies were extracted. Of those coping strategies, 119 cases (79.9 percent) used an emotion-focused form, and 30 cases (20.1 percent) used a problem-focused form.

2. Emotion-focused forms of coping were classified into the following five categories: improve activity, check activity, have relations with auditory hallucination, have no relations with auditory hallucination, and obtain well-balanced mind through a faith. Furthermore, those five categories were classified into fifteen sub-categories.
3. Problem-focused forms of coping were classified into the following four categories: using effective coping methods, request advice from others, obtain accurate knowledge about auditory hallucination, and check whether auditory hallucination is real. Furthermore, those four categories were classified into eleven sub-categories.

Conclusions: It was shown that patients with schizophrenia who experienced auditory hallucination often used emotion-focused forms of coping, such as distract own mind from auditory hallucination, endure auditory hallucination, etc.

Developing a Psychosocial Health Assessment Questionnaire for the Singapore Working Population: Worklife Health Score

Siok Lin Gan
Ministry of Manpower
Singapore

Aim: To describe an assessment tool being developed to measure job stressors and strains, including aspects of work-life balance for the Singapore working population. The purpose of the tool is to enable managements to assess the stress level within their organizations and make informed decisions on interventions to reduce workplace stress levels.

Method: Experts in occupational medicine, organizational behavior, organizational psychology, and psychiatry collaborated to develop the tool, called the Worklife Health Score. This involved the development of a framework and the identification of constructs for the questionnaire. Constructs were developed or adapted from established inventories such as the Job Diagnostic Survey, General Health Questionnaire, and Work Environment Scale. Focus group discussions involving management and workers provided input on the optimum length, scope, and coverage of the questionnaire. The questions were phrased to take into consideration differences in language and culture in view of Singapore's cosmopolitan workforce, making it understandable to workers with the lowest level of education so as to capture respondent's actual experiences, perceptions, and opinions. The tool, composed of self-administered individual and organization questionnaires, has been field tested in 20 companies in the service (such as retail, hotels, transportation, education, healthcare) and manufacturing industries, involving about 1,200 respondents.

Result: Preliminary analysis indicates that the tool is relevant for both manufacturing and service industry groups, with the reliability coefficient Cronbach alpha, for the variables studied, ranging from 0.6 to 0.91.

Developing Policy into Effective Practice: Integrating Mental Health PPEI as Part of Mental Health Reform–The South Australian Experience

Adrian Booth
Health Promotion SA
Department of Human Services
Adelaide, Australia

Australia has been seen internationally as leading the way in the development of mental health promotion, illness prevention and early intervention (PPEI). This leadership has recently been continued with the release of the Australian National Mental Health Plan 2003-2008 that will assist in the ongoing implementation of mental health PPEI at both policy and organizational levels. In response, South Australia has developed its Mental Health PPEI Action Plan 2004-2010 that will assist in guiding mental health PPEI policy and practice within a broader mental health reform agenda. The Action Plan has been developed within an international context that is still challenged by what constitutes effective practice; evidence-based programs and the development of clear, measurable workforce practice guidelines for the mental health and related workforce. This paper provides an overview of how South Australia is developing and implementing mental health PPEI, using examples that demonstrate creativity, innovation and collaboration that form essential ingredients to any mental health PPEI approach. In addition the paper will describe how South Australia is continuing to form effective partnerships with diverse stakeholders from public health, mental health, consumers and carers and nongovernmental sectors. A number of challenges exist that include ensuring that our Action Plan is relevant to specific population groups that include Aboriginal, multicultural and rural and remote communities and that our mental health and related workforce has the necessary skills, knowledge and capacity to understand and assist in implementing mental health PPEI as part of everyday practice. South Australia is currently engaged in health reform that has added strategic benefits for the development of mental health PPEI policy and practice, particularly in relation to population health, effective and sustainable partnerships, and promotion and prevention. There has been no better time in South Australia to develop mental health PPEI structures and capacity. South Australia is confident that through our existing partnerships with, for example, Auseinet and other Government departments, such as Education and Justice, that the SA Mental Health PPEI Action Plan 2004-2010 will be an important first step in providing clear, innovative ways forward for all South Australians to assist in improving their mental health and well-being.

4.4 Miscellaneous Symposia

Body, Mind, and Spirit Are Keys to Mental Health

Hung Wen Lin, Chueh Chang, Kai Wang, Feng Jung Yeh, and Hung Chang
Taiwan Cancer Friends New Life Association/National Taiwan University
Taiwan

In the first section of the session, evidence-based research results and self-discourse by cancer patients are reported. In the second section, the "universal love hands" and the "spinal exercise" workshop are introduced. Cancer should not only be viewed as a physical illness but also as a reflection of an individual's life. Cancer should be defined as:

1. The reflection of congestion and distortion of mental power that results in physical illness. For this reason, we start to work with the mental part rather than the physical part. Few people realize the relationship between health and mentality.

2. It means a quest for quality of life and a motivation for change. The emergence of cancer signifies that the majority of the population do not meet their innate needs. The modern quality of life is greatly improved, but with the improvement of material standards of living, mental powers have become distorted. Human beings no longer can evade this issue.

3. It is a turning point in life. One must learn how to transform the suppressed emotions into a powerful motivation for improving quality of life. Unselfish love and care have created many miracles, such as rebirth from dying, optimism from serious depression; and recovery from the ordeal of surgery, chemotherapy, and radiation therapy. The people who came to the New Life Center have not only greatly improved their health, but also changed their life attitude positively. Thousands of people who struggled with death got help here in the past four years, which in turn helped thousands of families find light under the shadow of death.

The New Life Center was founded on a vision of love and combines traditional Chinese Chi-Gung, physical fitness, creative dancing, singing, art appreciation, group care, counseling, and a series of physical-mind-soul courses for the patients. The purpose is to encourage all our dear friends to have a positive and optimistic attitude toward life. Through unselfish love and care, they are led out of a state of fear and depression, advancing the process of recovery to a normal, healthy life.

Planning for the New Global Consortium for the Advancement of Promotion and Prevention in Mental Health

Clemens M. H. Hosman, PhD
Eva Jané-Llopis, PhD
Prevention Research Centre
Radboud University Nijmegen and Maastricht University
The Netherlands

This workshop considers the global effectiveness project of the International Union for Health Promotion and Education (IUHPE) and IUHPE's European databases; the promotion and prevention projects of the World Health Organization; NREPP (National Registry of Evidence-based Programs and Practices) of the U.S. Substance Abuse and Mental Health Services Administration (SAMHSA); and the European database of the European Platform for Mental Health Promotion and Mental Disorder Prevention.

Issues in developing global collaboration are examined, with particular attention to the role of cultural factors in programs, and problems in transferring programs from one country to another. The importance of linking international databases also is examined. The design of databases, quality assessment of projects to be included, and questions of compatibility among databases are discussed. To see examples of how material is organized, visit the IUHPE database at www.HP-Source.net, the SAMHSA database at www.modelprograms.samhsa.gov, and the database of Implementing Mental Health Promotion Action at www.imhpa.net.

Australian Developments in Promotion, Prevention, and Early Intervention (PPEI) for Mental Health

Auseinet: A National Initiative to Support the Implementation of PPEI and Suicide Prevention Initiatives: *Jennie Parham, Auseinet*
MindMatters: A National Mental Health Promotion Initiative in Schools: *Jo Mason*
PPEI and General Practice: *Leanne Wells*
Mindframe National Media Initiative: Working with the Media and Mental Health: *Trevor Hazell, Hunter Institute of Mental Health*

The symposium's presenters give an overview of major nationwide mental health initiatives in Australia and discuss their impact.

Peer Support in the Prevention of Relapse and the Promotion of Recovery

Celia Brown, Bill Compton
Larry Fricks, Shery Mead
United States

The report of the U.S. President's New Freedom Commission on Mental Health expresses a vision for a future when everyone with a mental illness will recover. To accomplish that vision the Commission recommends the use of consumers as providers to serve as a resource in the recovery of people with psychiatric diagnoses. Consumer-directed services and supports are emerging as evidence-based programs impacting consumers across the life span. This workshop presents a variety of consumer-directed initiatives that are preventing relapse and promoting self-directed recovery among individuals diagnosed with mental illnesses. Celia Brown discusses peer support as a relapse prevention tool and its importance in healing. She emphasizes the importance of shared experience in battling isolation and moving toward recovery. Larry Fricks provides information on Georgia's highly effective peer specialist training and certification program now being replicated in several other states, and the importance of Medicaid as a revenue stream for peer support services and peers teaching skills for self-directed recovery. His presentation offers insight into the values of consumer-operated services and the infrastructure necessary to achieve accountability and quality outcomes within a state mental health system. Bill Compton presents information on a successful consumer-run program known as Project Return: The Next Step. This program is composed of 115 consumer-run mutual support groups, or clubs, operating in homes, churches, and other community locations; two discovery centers, consumer-run facilities focusing on skill development, education, and employment; and a consumer-run wellness center employing nontraditional psychiatrists and nurse practitioners who focus on the needs of the whole person. The program also runs a warmline, available to respond to consumers who need to reach out for support and encouragement. Shery Mead discusses the value of peer-run crisis respite programs and trauma-informed peer services. Within the crisis respite programs, peers provide supports to individuals experiencing crises that could lead to relapse. Through peer support relapse is often averted and individuals enabled to resume their lives and return to their homes without the disruption of an inpatient hospitalization. Peers with special training in understanding the effects of trauma are effective in helping people process traumatic events in their lives, to prevent over-pathologizing the effects of the trauma.

5.1   Development of Training and Expertise: School Age

Overview of Family Support for Deployed Soldiers of the U.S. Army 25th Infantry Division

Michael E. Faran
U.S. Army
United States

The U.S. Army's 25th Infantry Division has deployed for a projected 13-month tour in two waves involving over 10,000 soldiers: the first half left in January to Iraq and the second half left in March/April to Afghanistan (total of about 18 months deployed). Approximately 25,000 family members, including about 800 pregnant mothers remained behind, most of whom have stayed within the state of Hawaii. Military children and their families face several unique challenges in Hawaii: isolated by several thousand miles from relatives, a culturally divergent community, and a very high cost of living. A multidisciplinary system coordinating various agencies developed at Schofield Barracks to provide a wide range of support to children and adults that has been unique to the Army. This presentation will provide an overview of ongoing efforts to care for military families during the deployments. It will include brief descriptions of the school-based mental health program (Hui e Malama), support to the Family Readiness Groups, the extensive outreach of Army Community Services and the coordinated behavioral health support at Schofield and TAMC.

Objectives:
1. Describe the support networks in place at Schofield Barracks to support families
2. Discuss the development and evolution of a school-based mental health program on a military installation
3. Identify key stakeholders in the Army and local community involved in family services
4. Discuss development of a grassroots community-based support network

Laughter and Fun for Results-Driven Mental Health Services in an Urban Middle School

Jennie Jennings
Dallas Independent School District
Dallas, Texas, United States

The U.S. public school system has increased federal and state mandates ("No Child Left Behind") to improve academic performance for all students. In Dallas, Texas, a school board member requested that the district's nationally recognized school-based health centers provide school-wide mental health services at one middle school (seventh and eight grades, 814 students, 86 percent African-American, 13 percent Hispanic, 83 percent below poverty level). The primary objective of these school-wide prevention and early intervention services is for "left behind" students to experience school success (improved state and national test scores, improved attendance/behavior/grades). The school-based health center's mental health team members joined with school staff, and immediately began programming that is fun, interactive, creative and healing. The results of this program in one of Dallas's most challenging middle schools demonstrates the overwhelming success of a systemic model of prevention and early

Population Mental Health Promotion: A 21st-Century International Paradigm for Policy, Practice, Research, and Training in Mental Health: How to Do It.

John Raeburn
University of Auckland
New Zealand

This presentation takes the principles of population mental health promotion, which consist of a combination of the demonstrably effective strengths-based approaches increasingly being found in the mental health literature, and the ecological approach of the Ottawa Charter for Health Promotion, which can be summed up as the new public health and blends them into an overall population, community and personal individual intervention approach called Resourcefulness + Resourcing. A planning model called the PEOPLE System is used for the planning, implementation and evaluation of any such projects. Here, the emphasis is on community control and empowerment, and on maximum participation by people in the context of their everyday lives. The essentially positive and truly human approach used here takes mental health endeavors out of the realm of illness and stigmatization into positive and constructive undertakings which people are proud to be part of, and which are seen as beneficial not just to themselves, but to their families, communities, and societies.

5.4   beyondblue: the national depression initiative

Nicole Highet
Leonie Young
Gabrielle Graff
Victoria, Australia

- The response of beyondblue: the national depression initiative to depression
- Postnatal depression: beyondblue's response
- Depression in older Australians: key beyondblue initiatives

5.5 Program, Practice, and Theory: Symposium

Evidence - Practice - Evidence: It's Not Rocket Science: Promoting Mental Health in Aotearoa New Zealand

Tim McCreanor
Massey University
Auckland, New Zealand
Dr. Airini
Auckland College of Education
Auckland, New Zealand
David Wharemate
Kids First Counties Manukau District Health Board
New Zealand
Nic Mason
Mental Health Foundation
Auckland, New Zealand

Bridging the gap between rigorous and useful evidence and effective practice is challenging, especially as the big picture of politics, history, culture, biology, spirituality, relationships, economics, and environmental factors significantly influence people's experiences of mental health and well-being. This presentation explores the embodiment of mental health promotion principles and practice in four different areas of work:
- Training of frontline workers
- Organizational and strategic development and delivery
- Community action
- Evaluation

Rigorous and diverse evidence bases underpin this workshop, including:
- Identification and adherence to indigenous protocols, practices and beliefs
- Client/consumer focus and input
- Quantitative research
- Development of shared principles
- "Big picture" influences and evidence

5.6 Developing Mental Health Promotion Policy in Primary Health Care

Organizing Services to Deliver Evidence-Based Mental Health Promotion and Prevention: The Roles, Performance, and Capacities of Community-Based Primary Care Services

Penny Mitchell
University of Melbourne
Australia

Despite an increasing body of research evidence demonstrating the effectiveness of particular types of interventions in enhancing protective factors for mental health and reducing risk factors for mental disorders, there has been slow progress in the adoption of these interventions.

Research capable of informing practice needs to direct more attention to better understanding the factors that affect adoption and delivery of evidence-based mental health promotion and prevention programs. Effective implementation of evidence-based mental health promotion and primary prevention programs is a highly complex task that requires collaboration between a wide range of professionals and community members. Leadership and management of this work requires more than knowledge about the efficacy of particular types of interventions. Leaders and managers need to be able to describe the range of roles to be performed; identify the workforces that are best placed to perform these roles; understand the current performance and capacities of these workforces; design strategies to build capacity; and create mechanisms to coordinate the activities of the various workforces. A sophisticated understanding of the organizational and inter-organizational requirements of delivering mental health promotion and prevention programs is needed to do this.

This paper presents and discusses results from research that is being conducted into the mental health roles, performance and capacities of community-based (non-medical) primary care services in Victoria, Australia. It will include findings from a series of focus groups with stakeholders working in key networking roles throughout Victoria, as well as data from a structured survey of primary care agencies within four networks located in both metropolitan and regional/rural areas. Findings to date indicate that community-based (non-medical) primary care services currently deliver a wide variety of social and psychosocial interventions that are highly relevant to mental health promotion and primary prevention, and that agencies in this sector have important strengths that can enable them to make a much more significant contribution with appropriate capacity-building support. Key strengths include widespread commitment to a social model of health and close connection to communities, an outreach approach to high risk population groups, and the ability to deliver mental health interventions in normalized, unstigmatized environments. Primary care agencies are beginning to organize themselves to plan and build capacity for mental health promotion initiatives through the development of networks. Major systemic barriers to further progress exist in the form of structural problems in the way that services are currently funded and managed.

Primary Health and Mental Health Promotion; Using a Public Health Approach to Address Mental Health in a Primary Care Setting

Sue Turner
Mental Health Foundation of New Zealand
Auckland, New Zealand

This paper explores ways in which a mental health promotion approach can be used to enhance the capacity of primary health organizations to improve and promote the mental health of their enrolled populations. Primary health organizations in Aotearoa are being asked to address the mental health needs of their enrolled populations in a more comprehensive way than they have in the past. The Mental Health Foundation has been involved with planning a pilot mental health promotion project which can be used by primary health organizations. The Mental Health Foundation believes that a mental health promotion approach can support primary health organizations to meet the diverse mental health needs of the people who use their services. The pilot looks at the establishment of mental health promotion activities based on the researched needs of enrolled populations and with their full involvement.

Building Mental Health Prevention and Promotion Strategies in Primary Care in New Zealand

Kristan Johnson
Elizabet Powell
Ministry of Health
Wellington, New Zealand

There is good New Zealand and international evidence showing a high prevalence of mental health problems presenting in primary health care service. Early intervention is fundamental in preventing or limiting the impact of mental illness. The New Zealand Primary Health Care Strategy (2001) with its population health focus is an excellent platform to begin to address the needs of people with mental health problems, particularly those with mild to moderately severe mental illness. Primary health organizations (PHOs) are the cornerstones of the strategy's implementation. To assist in recovery 59 PHOs (covering 2.5 million New Zealanders) have been asked to consider activities to reduce the incidence and impact of mental health problems on their enrolled populations, specifically education, prevention and early intervention activities. The presentation outlines the process undertaken to support PHOs, involving development of a PHO Service Development Toolkit for Mental Health in Primary Care and funding regimes that target areas of high deprivation, Maori and Pacific communities. Mental Health prevention and promotion strategies are key to addressing the needs of these groups. This presentation outlines a number of innovative programs that have been supported within PHOs and outlines a future way forward.

Promotion, Prevention, and Early Intervention for Mental Health in General Practice in Australia

Anne O'Hanlon
Auseinet (Australian Network for PPEI for Mental Health)
Adelaide, Australia

There has been significant government investment in primary mental health care in the last five years in Australia, along with recognition of general practice as an important setting for mental health promotion, prevention and early intervention (PPEI) activities. The Australian Network for Promotion, Prevention, and Early Intervention for Mental Health (Auseinet) and the Australian Divisions of General Practice (ADGP) worked in partnership to identify mental health PPEI activities conducted by the Divisions of General Practice and general practitioners, as well as barriers to adopting this approach to mental health care. A survey of the Divisions of General Practice and focus groups with general practitioners were conducted in mid-2003. Seventy-one (59 percent) Divisions of General Practice responded to the survey. Over 80 percent of them are involved in at least some type of mental health PPEI activity, mostly via education programs for general practitioners and, to a lesser extent, community and school liaison. Most work with allied health professionals, between half and three quarters of whom are involved in PPEI activities. GPs in the focus groups thought that all GPs should be aware of mental health issues and at least be able to detect and refer appropriately. They identified barriers to PPEI, including a lack of tailored, evidence-based resources to direct work in PPEI, the

- Maintaining the status quo
- Retaining familiar patterns
- Cementing identity
- Developing uniqueness

Individuals with low self-esteem use these strategies less frequently and are resistant to change—holding on to whatever they can. Their self is less well defined; they retain familiar patterns of self-knowledge; and they are responsive to external cues, have simpler self-concepts (fewer eggs in their baskets), and consequently can be more protective, defensive, and conservative. (For a more complete discussion see Fox ([1997].)

Multiple Dimensions of Self

As I indicated earlier, the self is multidimensional, and exercise is more likely to change some aspects of the self than others. For some years we have studied the physical self, which is made up of subdomains such as perceived attractiveness, sport competence, physical health and fitness, and physical strength. The Physical Self-Perception Profile can be used to assess the effect of exercise, and several studies have indicated that exercise can positively impact the way individuals see themselves physically. We now are involved with projects investigating exercise and physical self-perceptions in individuals with depression, alcohol abuse, arthritis, and schizophrenia, and in older adults, obese individuals, wheelchair athletes, and youngsters with congenital heart problems.

What we are not sure about is how exercise changes different aspects of the self. The mechanisms still are unclear, and we are interested in returning to five self-esteem needs consistently identified in the literature. These are:

- Competence
- Autonomy and control
- Significance and importance
- Love and regard
- Affiliation

The following processes have been identified as potential candidates for exercise in particular to improve self-esteem:

- Increased competence
- Increased sense of autonomy
- Greater sense of self-determination and control
- Increasing the perceived importance of elements of high competence
- Decreasing perceived importance of elements of low competence
- Improved social attractiveness and confidence
- Greater social support
- Greater social approval
- Stronger physical identity

Exercise Recommendations for Promoting Self-Esteem

Currently no generic recommendations exist for exercise for mental health, and, therefore no specific guidelines exist for the promotion of self-esteem. However, the previous discussion highlights issues that face the professional exercise facilitator in interactions with clients or patients. These are important in terms of improvement of self-perceptions and also adoption and adherence to physical activity programs.

1. A diverse view of activity could be considered that includes resistance exercise, aerobic exercise, expressive activity such as dance, adventurous activities, rambling and nature walking, and cycling. These can be chosen to suit individual experience and needs.
2. Consideration could be given to beliefs about how activity may affect feelings about self. For example, the following illustrate beliefs expressed by overweight women that can act as barriers to engagement.

   I don't exercise because . . .

   - it is too exhausting and painful for me
   - it does not help me lose weight
   - it will make me look *muscly*
   - it will make me want to eat more
   - I am not the sporty type
   - I always get left behind
   - I am too embarrassed

3. Similarly, consideration could be given to experience that is associated with feeling more positive about self through exercise, such as sense of achievement, improved body image and health, and pride in success.
4. Consideration could be given to emphasizing personal improvement and achievement of tasks, rather than comparisons against norms or against others.
5. Consideration could be given to finding ways of helping people develop autonomy and self-determination in exercise by handing over responsibility for successes.
6. Consideration could be given to emphasizing the social interaction and social support aspects of physical activity.

References

Biddle, S. J. H., Fox, K. R., & Boutcher, S. H. (2000). *Physical activity and psychological well-being*. London: Routledge.

Carless, D., & Fox, K. R. (2003). The physical self. In T. Everett, M. Donaghy, & S. Fever (Eds.), *Interventions for mental health: An evidence-based approach. Physiotherapists and occupational therapists* (pp. 69-81). Oxford: Butterworth-Heinemann.

Department of Health. (2004). *At least five a week: Evidence on the impact of physical activity and its relationship to health. A report from the chief medical officer*. London: Department of Health.

Fox, K. R. (1997). The physical self and processes in self-esteem development. In K. R. Fox (Ed.), *The physical self: From motivation to well-being* (pp. 111-140). Champaign, IL: Human Kinetics.

Fox, K. R. (2000). Self-esteem, self-perceptions and exercise. *International Journal of Sport Psychology, 31,* 228-240.

Conclusion

Hope is essential to recovery. Hope is not possible without real opportunity. This means changing the external world, not merely encouraging changes in the individual. Anti-discrimination work can support the external changes that can increase opportunities for people with mental health problems. Taking an approach to anti-discrimination work that learns from the physical disability movement, changes power balances, and uses evidence-based messages and methods could, over time, generate more possibility for hope. Employment opportunities in our cultures are particularly important in enabling people to contribute and find value and meaning in their lives.

INDEX OF PRESENTERS

GPO U.S. GOVERNMENT PRINTING OFFICE: 2006–320-312/30401

SOCIAL SCIENCE LIBRARY

Oxford University Library Services
Manor Road
Oxford OX1 3UQ
Tel: (2)71093 (enquiries and renewals)
http://www.ssl.ox.ac.uk

This is a NORMAL LOAN item.

We will email you a reminder before this item is due.

Please see http://www.ssl.ox.ac.uk/lending.html
for details on

- loan policies; these are also displayed on the notice boards and in our library guide.

- how to check when your books are due back.

- how to renew your books, including information on the maximum number of renewals. Items may be renewed if not reserved by another reader. Items must be renewed before the library closes on the due date.

- level of fines; fines are charged on overdue books.

Please note that this item may be recalled during Term.